MW01124231

Secret History Of The Court Of James The First

James I.

ABOUT TO TAKE ASSAY OF THE DEER.

See Page 196.

SECRET HISTORY

OF

THE COURT

OF

James the First

CONTAINING,

I. OSBORNE'S TRADITIONAL MEMOIRS.

II. SIR ANTHONY WELDON'S COURT AND CHARACTER
OF KING JAMES.

III. AULICUS COQUINARIÆ.

IV. SIR EDWARD PEYTON'S DIVINE CATASTROPHE OF
THE HOUSE OF STUARTS.

WITH

NOTES AND INTRODUCTORY REMARKS.

IN TWO VOLUMES.

VOL. II.

EDINBURGH:

Printed by James Ballantyne and Co.

FOR JOHN BALLANTYNE AND CO., EDINBURGH; AND
LONGMAN, HURST, REES, ORME, AND BROWN,
LONDON.

1811,

4496+16
8º 1810,65

CONTENTS

OF

VOLUME SECOND.

Head of James the First to face the Title.

iv

THE
CHARACTER
OF
KING JAMES,
BY
SIR ANTHONY WELLDON.

———

THIS kings character is much easier to
take than his picture, for he could never
be brought to sit for the taking of that,
which is the reason of so few good peeces ,
of him ;[1] but his character was obvious to
every eye.

He was of a middle stature, more corpulent through his cloathes then in his
body, yet fat enough, his cloathes ever
being made large and easie, the doublets
quilted for steletto proofe, his breeches in
great pleits and full stuffed; hee was na-

[1] See the frontispiece and subsequent note.

turally of a timorous disposition, which was
the reason of his quilted doublets; his eyes
large, ever rowling after any stranger that
came in his presence, insomuch, as many
for shame have left the roome, as being out
of countenance; his beard was very thin:
his tongue too large for his mouth, which
ever made him speak full in the mouth,
and made him drink very uncomely, as if
eating his drink, which came out into the
cup of each side of his mouth; his skin
was as soft as taffeta sarsnet, which felt so,
because hee never washt his hands, onely
rubb'd his fingers ends slightly with the
wet end of a napkin; his legs were very
weake, having had (as was thought) some
foul play in his youth, or rather before he
was born,* that he was not able to stand at
seven years of age, that weaknesse made
him ever leaning on other mens shoulders;
his walke was ever circular, his fingers ever
in that walke fidling about his cod-piece;

* Probably alluding to the murder of Rizzio in his
mother's presence during her pregnancy.

he was very temperate in his exercises and
in his dyet, and not intemperate in his
drinking; however, in his old age, Buckinghams joviall suppers, when he had any
turne to doe with him, made him sometimes overtaken, which he would the very
next day remember and repent with tears;
it is true he drank very often, which was
rather out of a custom than any delight,
and his drinks were of that kind for strength,
as frontiniack, canary, high country wine,
tent wine, and Scottish ale, that, had he not
had a very strong brain, might have daily
been overtaken, although he seldom drank
at any one time above four spoonfulls,
many times not above one or two;[1] he was

[1] " This year, 1614, as it was the meridian of the
king's glory in England, so was it of his pleasures. The
king was excessively addicted to hunting and drinking, not ordinary French and Spanish wines, but strong
Greek wines; and though he would divide his hunting from drinking these wines, yet he would compound
his hunting with these wines, and to that purpose he
was attended with a special officer, who was as much
as he could be, always at hand to fill the king's cup in
his hunting when he called for it. I have heard my

very constant in all things, (his favourites excepted,) in which he loved change, yet never cast down any (he once raised) from the height of greatnesse, though from their wonted nearnesse and privacy ; unlesse by their own default, by opposing his change, as in Somersets case : yet had he not been in that foul poysoning business, and so cast down himself, I do verily beleeve not him neither, for all his other favourites he left great in honour, great in fortune ; and did much love Montgomery, and trusted him more at the very last gaspe then at the first minute of his favouriteship : In his dyet,

father say, that being hunting with the king, after the king had drank of the wine, he also drank of it; and though he was young, and of an healthful disposition, it so disordered his head, that it spoiled his pleasure, and disordered him for three days after. Whether it were drinking these wines, or from some other cause, the king became so lazy and unwieldy, that he was treist on horseback, and as he was set so he would ride, without posing himself on his saddle ; nay, when his hat was set on his head, he would not take the pains to alter it, but it sate as it was put on."—ROGER COKE's *Detection of the Court and State of England during the four last Reigns.* Lond. 1697, p. 70.

apparrell, and journeys, he was very constant; in his apparrell so constant, as by his good will he would never change his cloathes untill worn out to very ragges; his fashion never, insomuch, as one bringing to him a hat of a Spanish block, he cast it from him, swearing he neither loved them nor their fashions. Another time, bringing him roses on his shooes, he asked, If they would make him a ruffe-footed dove? one yard of six penny ribbond served that turn; his diet and journies was so constant, that the best observing courtier of our time was wont to say, were he asleep seven yeares, and then awakened, he would tell where the king every day had been, and every dish he had had at his table.

He was not very uxorious, though he had a very brave queen that never crossed his designes, nor intermeddled with state affaires, but ever complyed with him (even against the nature of any, but of a milde spirit) in the change of favourites; for he was ever best when furthest from his queene,

and that was thought to be the first grounds
of his often removes, which afterwards proved habituall.   He was unfortunate in the
marriage of his´ daughter, and so was all
Christendome besides ; but sure the daughter was more unfortunate in a father then
he in a daughter ; he naturally loved not
the sight of a souldier, nor of any valiant
man ; and it was an observation that Sir
Robert Mansell was the only valiant man
he ever loved, and him he loved so intire-
ly, that for all Buckinghams greatnesse with
the king, and his hatred of Sir Robert
Mansell, yet could not that alienate the
kings affections from him ; insomuch, as
when by the instigation of Cottington, (then
embassadour in Spaine,) by Buckinghams
procurement, the Spanish embassadour
came with a great complaint against Sir
Robert Mansell, then at Argiers, to sup-
presse the pirats, that he did support them ;
having never a friend there (though many)
that durst speake in his defence, the king
himselfe defended him in these words :

" My Lord Embassadour, I cannot beleeve
this, for I made choyce my selfe of him,
out of these reasons; I know him to be va-
lient, honest, and nobly descended as most
in my kingdome, and will never beleeve a
man thus qualified will do so base an act."
He naturally loved honest men, that were
not over-active, yet never loved any man
heartily untill he had bound him unto him
by giving him some suite, which he thought
bound the others love to him again ; but
that argued a poore disposition in him, to
beleeve that any thing but a noble minde,
seasoned with vertue, could make any firme
love or union, for mercinary mindes are
carried away with a greater prize, but noble
mindes, alienated with nothing but publick
disgraces.

He was very witty, and had as many
ready witty jests as any man living, at which
he would not smile himselfe, but deliver
them in a grave and serious manner. He
was very liberall of what he had not in his
owne gripe, and would rather part with

100. *li.* hee never had in his keeping then
one twenty shillings peece within his owne
custody ; he spent much, and had much
use of his subjects purses, which bred some
clashings with them in parliament, yet
would alwayes come off, and end with a
sweet and plausible close ; and truly his
bounty was not discommendable, for his
raising favourites was the worst ; reward-
ing old servants, and relieving his native
countrymen, was infinitely more to be commended in him then condemned. His sending embassadours were no lesse chargeable
then dishonourable and unprofitable to him
and his whole kingdome ; for he was ever
abused in all negotiations, yet he had rather spend 100000. *li.* on embassies, to keep
or procure peace with dishonour, then
10000 *li.* on an army that would have forced peace with honour. He loved good
lawes, and had many made in his time,
and in his last parliament, for the good of
his subjects, and suppressing promoters,
and progging fellowes, gave way to that

nullum tempus, &c. to be confined to 60 yeares, which was more beneficiall to the subjects, in respect of their quiets, then all the parliaments had given him during his whole reign. By his frequenting sermons he appeared religious ; yet his Tuesday sermons (if you will beleeve his owne countrymen, that lived in those times when they were erected, and well understood the cause of erecting them) were dedicated for a strange peece of devotion.

He would make a great deale too bold with God in his passion, both in cursing and swearing, and one straine higher verging on blasphemie ; but would in his better temper say, " He hoped God would not impute them as sins, and lay them to his charge, seeing they proceeded from passion." He had need of great assurance, rather then hopes, that would make daily so bold with God.

He was very crafty and cunning in petty things, as the circumventing any great man, the change of a favourite, &c. insomuch, as

a very wise man was wont to say, he beleeved him the wisest foole in Christendome, meaning him wise in small things,
but a foole in weighty affaires.

He ever desired to prefer meane men in
great places, that when he turned them out
again, they should have no friend to bandy
with them : And besides, they were so hated by being raised from a meane estate, to
overtop all men, that every one held it a
pretty recreation to have them often turned out : There were living in this kings
time, at one instant, two treasurers, three
secretaries, two lord keepers, two admiralls,
three lord chief justices, yet but one in play,
therefore this king had a pretty faculty in
putting out and in. By this you may perceive in what his wisdome consisted, but in
great and weighty affaires ever at his wits
end.

He had a trick to cousen himselfe with
bargains under hand, by taking 1000. *li.* or
10000. *li.* as a bribe, when his counsell was
treating with his customers to raise them

to so much more yearly. This went into his
privy purse, wherein hee thought hee had
over-reached the lords, but cousened himselfe ; but would as easily breake the bargaine upon the next offer, saying, he was
mistaken and deceived, and therefore no
reason he should keep the bargaine : this
was often the case with the farmers of the
customes. He was infinitely inclined to
peace, but more out of feare then conscience, and this was the greatest blemish
this king had through all his reign, otherwise might have been ranked with the very
best of our kings ; yet sometimes would hee
shew pretty flashes of valour which might
easily be discerned to be forced, not naturall ; and being forced, could have wished
rather it would have recoiled backe into
himselfe, then carried to that king it had
concerned, least he might have been put to
the tryall to maintaine his seeming valour.

In a word, he was (take him altogether
and not in peeces) such a king, I wish this

kingdome have never any worse, on the condition, not any better; for he lived in peace, dyed in peace, and left all his kingdomes in a peaceable condition, with his owne motto :

Beati pacifici.

EXPLANATION

OF

THE FRONTISPIECE.

To illustrate this description of James's person, a striking, but unfavourable likeness of that monarch was prefixed to the second edition of Welldon's book, with this motto: MARS. PUER. ALECTO. VIRGO. VULPES. LEO. NULLUS, of which we have given a *fac simile* as frontispiece to the present volume. The motto subjoined was, according to the sapient Lilly, the line in which a prophetic monk of Italy answered an ambassador of Henry VII., who consulted him to know how long the crown acquired by his master in the battle of Bosworth should continue in the family.

The response appearing to the ambassador altogether enigmatical, the prophet was prevailed upon to exhibit in elucidation the following scene of phantasmagoria:

" The monk commanded the ambassadour, at a se-
lected time, to attend him, with some other English
gentlemen besides himselfe, and then he doubted not
but that he should fully content him.

" The time came, and the ambassadour and his friend
waiting for some great matter in a very large spacious
roome, to which they were purposely invited, in comes
the holy monke, and seating himselfe by them, commanding them without feare or affright, to observe
what they could, and to commit it to posterity, assuring
them of no hurt, but protesting they should see now the
former words fully explicated.

" Immediately there entered, and appeared in the
roome, a lusty stout young gentleman, strong, and of a
great proportion, with very furious majesticall looks; a
large strong sword by his side, and walking to the upper part of the chamber, there instantly appeared a
crowne, laid upon a faire table; to which crowne this
gallant with much jollity approached, and put it upon
his head, then walking up and down the chamber with
much strutting and bravery; but at last, as it were, unwillingly, he repaired to the place where he first tooke
up the crowne, and there gently laid it downe with
some obeysance, and vanished out of sight.

" He was no sooner out of sight, but there entred a
young youth, full of modesty, and looking carefully with
his eyes on the beholders, went directly to that part of
the roome where the crowne lay, with some difficulty

put it on his head, then traversing the roome with some labour and paines a little while, he discharged his head of its heavy burthen, and assigned the crowne to its proper seat, and then his apparition vanished.

" After whom, a lady all in mourning attire, of sad countenance, and much gravity, with a booke in her hande, entred the chamber; who, walking demurely to the upper end of the roome, put on the crowne upon her head, and then marched some few turnes up and downe, with much sadnesse or discontented looks, then repaired where the former apparitions left the crowne, and there also she disposed of it, instantly vanishing.

. " The next in order that appeared, was a young lady clothed in stately apparell, cheerfull and lively, who presently ascended to the upper part of the chamber, and there with much cheerfullnesse put the crowne upon her head, and afterwards, for a pretty space of time, with much majesty and state, passed up and downe the roome, and then gently left the crowne in the place she received it, vanishing instantly out of sight.

" After which, there immediately advanced in the room another apparition, in form of a huntsman, with a horne by his side, in rich green apparell, who, without ceremony, quickly espied the crowne, and put it upon his head, and then, with much carelesnesse, walked many times up and downe the chamber; but at last repaired to the same place where the rest had disposed of the crowne, and there he quietly left it.

" Which he had no .sooner done, and vanished out
of sight, but a fierce young man, active and nimble,
entred into the chamber, and made great haste to the
upper part of the roome where the crowne lay, which
he, as it were, snatched up and put on his head, and then
made many nimble turnings from one end of the roome
to the other; but when it was expected that he should
in gentle wise lay down the crown, as al the rest had
done, behold, both he and the crowne vanished out of
sight, and appeared no more, to the great wonder of the
ambassador and the English gentlemen there present:
more than these ayery apparitions, and the former hex-
ameter verse could never be procured from the Italian
monke, onely he oft times averred afterwards in conference with the ambassadour, that he had neither in
the words or apparitions expressed lesse than truth, and
that time would best explain his sense and meaning.

" Many hundreds of this kingdome, I well know,
have heard the words many yeares since, but whether
in full measure, as by me reported, I know not: But I
have twenty yeares since heard the Roman priests much
speak of it, and doe believe, that the foreknowledge
hereof was a strong inducement to goe on with that
activenesse in this kings raigne against protestantisme,
as for some years they have done."—LILLY's *Collection
of Ancient and Modern Prophesies.* London, 1645. 4,
p. 2, 3, 4.

This story appears to have been very popular, and is

alluded to by Osborne, who mentions the vision of a Green King, said to be aver'd from Italy.[1] And the cavaliers, instead of insisting that the prophecy was confuted by the restoration, endeavoured to give it a different turn, owing to his reigning for a year before his coronation, as if during that space he had been, as it were, a king and no king.

[1] See vol. i. p. 200.

THE

COURT OF KING CHARLES;

CONTINUED
UNTO THE BEGINNING OF THESE UNHAPPY TIMES,
WITH SOME OBSERVATIONS UPON HIM INSTEAD
OF A CHARACTER.

COLLECTED AND PERFECTED

BY

SIR A[NTHONY] W[ELLDON.]

Published by Authority.

1651.

COURT OF KING CHARLES.

Now having brought this peaceable king to rest in all peace, the 27th of March, his son, by the sound of the trumpet, was proclaimed king, by the name of Charles the First.

His fathers reign began with a great plague, and we have seen what this reign was; his sons, with a greater plague, and the greatest that was ever in these parts, we shall see what his reign will be, and the effects of this plague have also hung as a fatal commet over this kingdome, in some parts, and over London in more particular, ever since : and we earnestly pray we may not fall into the hands of men, but rather, ever with that divinely inspired royall prophet David, that we fall into the hand of the Lord, for his mercies are great.

This king was not crowned with that solemnity all other kings had formerly been, by riding through the city in all state, although the same triumphes were provided for them, as sumptuous as for any other; this some have taken as an ill omen. Its further reported, which I will not believe, that he tooke not the usual oath all our kings are bound unto at their coronation, and its to be read in Covells book; if so, sure its a worse omen.

One more observation is of this king, which I remember not to have happened in any other kingdome, I am confident never in this ; that with him did also rise his fathers favourite, and in much more glory and luster then in his fathers time, as if he were no lesse an inheritor of his sons favors than the sonne of the fathers crowne; and this, as it happened, was the worst omen of all; for whereas in the fathers time there was some kind of moderation, by reason he was weary of the insolency of his favorite; in the sons time, he reigned like an impetuous storme, bearing downe all before him that stood in his way, and would not yield to him or comply with him. This shewed no heroical or kingly spirit, for the king ever to endure him, that had put such scornes and insolent affronts on him in his fathers time.

This king (as the father did set in peace) did rise like a Mars, as if he would say, *Arma virumque cano;* and to that end, to make himselfe more formidable to Spaine and France, he called a parliament, wherein never subjects expressed more hearty affection to a sovereigne; and, in truth, were more loving than wise, for as if for an income to welcome him, they gave him two intire subsidies, and in so doing, they brake the very foundation and priviledges of par-

liament, which never was wont to give subsidies, but as a thankful gratuity for enact-
ing good lawes, therefore it is but Gods justice to repay them with Italian lawes, to have
their priviledges broken, seeing they first
chalked out the way; the king, in requital of
this great love of theirs, did instantly dissolve
the parliament, which hath bred such ill
blood in the veins of the subjects to their
sovereign, and in the sovereign to the subject, that it is like to produce an epidemi-
call infection.

But the occasion taken to dissolve it was
worst of all; for Buckingham, by his insolent behaviour, had not onely lost that
love his hatred to Spaine had procured
him, but was now growne into such an hatred, that they fell on him for the death of
his old master, which had been of long
time before but whispered; but now the
examinations bred such confessions, that it
looked with an ugly deformed poysonous
countenance, and nothing but the dissolution of that parliament could have saved his

dissolution, and that with a brand of shame
and infamy, as well as of ingratitude.

I remember I heard a noble gentleman,
an old parliament man of that committee
for examinations, say, at first he derided the
very thought of it ; but after the first dayes
examination it proved so foule, as that he
both hated and scorned the name and memory of Buckingham ; and though man
would not punish it, God would, which
proved an unhappy prediction.

This dissolving the parliament was ill
relished by the people, and that which to
them did seeme the cause worse, and to
make the case yet fouler, and that it must
needs be the evident cause, Buckinghams
counsels were so stupid, and himselfe so insolent, that he did thinke it a glory to disgrace all those that followed that businesse
in that parliament, or that seemed inquisi-
tive thereafter, and caused many old servants of the kings he formerly favoured very
much, to be banished from court, never to
return more, nor did they ever ; as Clare,

Crofts, Sir Fra. Stewart, &c., nay, Dr Cragg, his physitian, who, from his very childhood, had the generall repute of a very honest man ; for, expressing himselfe like an honest man in the kings presence, was instantly dismissed, never could recover his place or favour more.

Now also is Williams, Lord Keeper, turned out of his place, and Coventry, the kings atturney, who, had Buckingham lived, had as soon followed in the same steps.

Then goes Buckingham into France, on a stately embassie for that lady the king had seen and set an affection on in his passage to Spaine, which was obtained with small intreaty.

Now doth Buckingham soare so high both in his masters favours, and in the pride of his own heart, as he alters all great officers, makes war against Spaine and France, the quarrel only his, voiced to be on strange grounds, the success accordingly ; navies, armies, and nothing but war appears, as if we intended in shew to conquer all that opposed. Lord Wambleton the generall, from whom as little could be expected as he performed, carrying a powerful army to Cales, after an infinite expence, and drinking much Spanish wines, and beating out the heads of what they could not drinke, (as if they intended to overthrow that yeares trade of Spanish wine,) returned as like a valiant commander, as he ever was reputed; whereas, had he brought home those wasted wines, it may be they would have defrayed the charge of that expedition.

After the returne of that wise pageantisme, Denbigh is sent into France to aide Rochell, who managed it better than his great kinsman Buckingham, who would afterwards needs goe to doe great exploits, for he brought his ships and men safe againe, the other left his men in powdering tubs, as if he meant to have kept them sweet

---

Alluding to the misadventure of the Duke of Buckingham at the Isle of Rhé, where, in endeavouring to re-embark, the rear of his army was cut off in a piece óf ground broken by salt-pits.

against his next coming thither. In short, this unhappy voyage lost all the honour our glorious ancestors had ever gotten over that nation, there being so many brave gentlemen wilfully lost, as if that voyage had been on purpose plotted to disable our nation, by taking away so many gallant brave young spirits; so many of our colours lost, as trophies of their victory, and of our shame, hung up in Nostredame church, that the brave Talbot and Salisbury, with many other our valiant ancestors, will rise up in judgement against him for that every way inglorious act. Nay, to how low an ebbe of honour was this our poore despicable kingdome brought, that (even in Queene Elizabeths time, the glory of the world,) a great nobleman being taken prisoner, was freely released, with this farewell given with him, that they desired but two English mastieffes for his ransome!

But the king, by that unnecessary and dishonourable war, was driven to that exigency for want of money, that he was for-

ced to pawne his rich cupboard of plate to
Amsterdam, ' and to send Cottington into
Spaine, in a manner to beg a peace, which
having obtained, it was thought so great a
service of him, that it raised him to all his
honour and fortunes.

Yet all the while Rochell, in sharpe dis-
tresse, was left unreleeved, although otherwise intended, or but pretended rather.
For the courting betwixt the duke and the
governour of the Isle of Ree, in sending
compliments and presents to each other,
shewed rather an intimate dearnesse, then
any hostility to be meant between them.
And sure I am, the successe made it ap-
parent, that their purpose was no better
then to carry so many goodly gentlemen to

---

* The favourite Buckingham himself went to the
Hague to accomplish this sale of the crown jewe's, under pretence of engaging the united states in a joint
effort for recovery of the palatinate. A curious list of
the articles pledged or sold upon this occasion may
be found in the notes on the Duke's life, in the Biographia Britannica.

the slaughter-house and powdering-tub, as
even now I instanced.

Yet was the king so content to be abused, as publickly at his dinner, he delivered
it for a miracle, that having such ill successe, there were so few men lost, for that
as many came home as went forth, as appeared at the chequer-roll, within five hundred. At which a gentleman, (whose faithfull valour prompting him to speake a truth
in season, though theirs did not them to
fight,) standing at the back of the kings
chair, said, " Yea, sir, as you hear that hear
very little of truth ; but if you please to inquire of such as can and dare informe you
truly, you shall find many thousands fewer
came home then went forth." For which
relation this honest tell-troth was commanded presently from his court attendance,
which doom he never could get reverst,
wherein you may behold the power of
Buckingham with the king, whose word
stood for a law.

4

Which power of his grew now so exorbitant, he aspires to get higher titles both in honour and place, as, Prince of Tipperary, (a place so called in Ireland,) and Lord High Constable of England, (an office aimed at by that monster and Machivillain, Leicester, in Queen Elizabeths time; but he therein was crossed and contradicted by the then Lord Chancellour Hatton,) now affected by Buckingham, who herein wrote after Leicesters ambitious example, but he crossed too (by president) with Coventry, now Lord Keeper, and no question but upon those just grounds his predecessor did. For you must understand, this office hath an authority annexed unto it, to call any subject in question for his life, by trying, condemning, and executing him, in despight of the king himselfe. Nay, some have made no bones on't to affirme, that (for misgovernment) the king himselfe is not exempted from that officers power; politickly, therefore, did the aforementioned

Hatton, (who well understood the validity
of such a power, when Leicesters commission was in dispute,) to tel the queen that
his own hand should never strike off his
own head ; which word was enough to her
who was hereat so wise as also in all other
matters of state-concernment, wherein, as
she were hinted to a fore-sight of any prejudice, she knew how to prevent it. And
thus that ended in his time.

But Buckinghams ambition would not
be so bounded ; for, upon the opposing it
by Coventry, he peremptorily thus accost-
ed him, saying, " Who made you, Coventry, Lord Keeper?" he replyed, " the king;"
Buckingham sur-replyed, " Its false, 'twas
I did make you, and you shall know that
I, who made you, can and will unmake
you." Coventry thus answered him : " Did
I conceive I held my place by your favour,
I would presently unmake my selfe, by rendering the seale to his majesty." Then
Buckingham, in a scorn and fury flung

from him, saying, " You shall not keep it long." And surely, had not Felton prevented him, he had made good his word.

And before that hapned, Weston was, by his power, and for his ends, made treasurer, it should seem, upon some assurance from him, that he would find ways whereout to raise monys into the treasury, (he judging him to be one, that out of his own necessitous condition would adventure oh any desperate projection to raise himself, but yet withall to fill the chequer coffers,) who was no sooner warmed in his office, but hee began to shew his inbred base disposition to his rayser Buckingham, as formerly he had don to Cranfield, who was indeed his preserver from perishing in a prison, whence he redeemed him, making him a free partaker, first of his bounteous table, then raising him shortly after to be Chancellour of the Exchequer ; who, at length, for requitall, supplanted him. But for all this Buckingham feared not, his high spirit in himselfe and vast power with the king were so predominant and unmoveable : He now, therefore, used at his owne pleasure to come to the counsell-table, (he being then honoured as the oracle from whom they gaped for all answers,) but ever made them wait his comming, and were so tutored to their duteous observance of him, that at his approach, or returning thence, they ever must rise, as if he had been the king himselfe. So that you may see to what a pretty passe those great men by their poor spirits had brought themselves.

But on a time there issued this amongst other passages of insolencies from Buckingham, who comming into the councell, without any other court-preface, sayes to the treasurer Weston, " My lord, the king must have 60,000*l.* provided against to-morrow morning." The lords startled at the mention of such a sum, (the whole exchequer not having seen within its keeping scarce 1000*l.* in many yeares,) and could not imagine how, unlesse by the philosophers stone, such a sum was possible to be gotten, but

yet all looking on Weston, (to whom it was
in this case proper to make answer,) who
bethought himselfe what to say, (the rest
every one, the while, gazing at each other,
another while againe all at Weston, as a
man of great wisdome, for so was hee accounted (of a plebeian.) At length, up he
stands, and thus he answers Buckingham:
" My lord, the exchequer is in a deep consumption." Whereat Buckingham interrupts
him, saying, " How, sir! You came in to
cure that consumption, and to restore it to
its usefull plenitude. I remember you promised (like a mountebanke) when you were
to be invested by the king, you would do
so, therefore, sir, see you the money be provided, otherwise you shall hear further of
it." With that high strain he rose up and
departed.

Now are all ways indeavoured to get
mony from the subjects, which was not to
be gotten by fair means, the king having
tryed all the shifts which any former prince
(out of the parliamentary way) had ever

12

don, and had great sums brought in, such as none of his predecessors ever had ; of which, one was the royall subsidy, every man lending as much as the summe in the subsidy towards which he was assessed : as if (for example) assessed at 40. *li*. besides so much payd, he lent also 40. *li*. and so from the least to the greatest proportions assessed.

Yet all this would not serve him, but that quickly vanished, then all other fair means proving (as was thought for their profusenesse) too scant and slow, force then must be the last remedy ; the king must keep standing garrisons to awe his good subjects, and they consisting too of strangers, not of natives. To that end, one Dalbier (that had been generall of Count Mansfields horse) is dealt with for the raising of 1000

---

[1] This appears to be the same person who acted as Commissary General of the horse under the Earl of Essex, and who afterwards was slain at the rising at Kingston, where the Earl of Holland, his patron, was made prisoner.

or 2000 German horse, the most whereof
to bee quartered betwixt Gravesend and
London ;[1] for advancing of which service,
Sir William Balfore (as great a servant and
confident he is now of this parliament)[2]
was sent to Hamborough with 30000l. to
buy and to bring over those horse with their
impressed riders and furniture, but many
of them ready to be imbarked, it should
seeme they were told by the way, by some

[1] Nothing could be more rash and ill-concerted than
this project of entertaining foreign mercenaries to support the intended commission of trail-baston. Charles
had no money to pay a strong force of these strangers,
and a few could but serve to render him odious to his
subjects.

[2] Sir William Balfour, a Scotchman, whom the king
had made Lieutenant-Governor of the Tower of London, " to the great and general scandal," says Lord
Clarendon, " and offence of the English nation," began
notwithstanding to take part with the parliament, which
he particularly evinced in the rigour he exercised in the
captivity of the Earl of Stafford while under his charge.
He was dismissed by the king, who incautiously placed
in the office Colonel Lunsford, a man peculiarly odious
to the citizens. The parliament remonstrated upon Balfour's removal, and he afterwards enjoyed their trust,
and held considerable command in their armies.

well-affected to England, that the king had
not mony to continue them in pay ; and
plunder they could not there, for they
should be so invironed with sea, that there
was no flying, but they must expect to have
all their throats cut, if they took any thing
from any man : Upon which, those rascals,
out of feare, not conscience, refused to come
over. However, Balfore so wel lickt his
fingers in that employment, as that he therewith laid the foundation of his future fortunes ; yet, if this parliament consider well
this action of his, there is no reason he
should be so deare unto them : For, of any
thing yet toucht upon against any man by
this parliament, I dare affirme this (of his)
to be the greatest peece of villany, and to
be the nearest way to render us all slaves,
and to make us have neither propriety in
our estates, wives, nor children. And yet
was this Balfore a principall undertaker
and actor in this pernicious designe, and
(perhaps for that very cause) the greatest
creature of Buckinghams that ever was.

In this intervall their shifts not avayling them, (to see therefore if by this faire means their ends might be obtained,) another parliament was summoned, wherein, after some expostulations on both sides, there proved no better a good speed and successe then a meere frustration of all hopes on both hands; which, for the kings part, hee apprehended with so great aversnesse, that, as 'twas said, he made a vow never to call more parliaments.

Forreigne forces, and fraudulent and faire devices home-spun, failing all; now must projects in all their variegated inventions bee set on foot; to which sage (or rather rufull) purpose, one Noy, a very famous lawyer as ever this kingdome bred, and (formerly) a great patriot, and the only searcher of presidents for the parliaments; by which he grew so cunning, as he understood all the shifts which former kings had used to get monies with.

This man the king sends for, tels him he

will make him his attorney Noy,[1] (like a true cynick as he was,) for that time went away, not returning to the king so much as the civility of a thankes ; nor indeed was it worth his thankes, I am sure he was not worthy of ours. For, after the court solicitings had bewitched him to become the kings, he grew the most hatefull man that ever lived. And its to me a wonder that this parliament of wonders doth not enact a law, that his very name should never more be in this kingdome, he having been as great a deluge to this realme, as the flood was to the whole world : for he swept away all our priviledges, and in truth hath been the cause of all these miseries this kingdome

[1] Sir William Noy, Attorney-General to Charles I., and deviser of the odious tax of ship-money, has left a character more estimable for talent than probity. He was a most acute and laborious lawyer, as was quaintly expressed in an anagram on his name, *I moyle in law*. But in temper he was rough, bearish, and morose, and devoid even of the shadow of patriotism. He died 9th August, 1634, flying, as it were, to the tomb, from the approaching hour of popular vengeance.

hath since been ingulphed; whether you consider our religion, (he being a great papist, if not an atheist,) and the protector of all papists, and the raiser of them up unto that boldnesse they were now growne unto, who formerly had some moderation; or, if you consider our states and liberties, they were impoverished and enthralled by multitudes of projects and illegall wayes: this monster was the sole author of all.

But first, now because there must be some great man (as a captaine projector) to lead some on, and hearten others to follow, Sir George Goring leads up the march and dance with the monopolie of tobacco, and licensing of tavernes, setting some up, where, and as many as he pleased, and this done by a seale appendicular to an office erected by him for that purpose, as if authorised by a law; besides all this, hee hath pensions out of the pretermitted customs: insomuch, as I have heard it most credibly reported, that his revenue was 9000*l.* per annum, all of these kindes; and for this

peece of good service he was made a lord
and privy councellour, to countenance his
traine of projectors the better.

Then did Weston enhance the customes,
and laid new and heavyer impositions on
all things exported or imported; with such
unconscionable rates upon tobacco, that
millions of pounds of it lay rotting in the
custome-house, (the merchants refusing to
pay the custome,) besides losse of all other
charges for the tobacco it selfe. In short,
there was not any thing (almost) that any
man did eate, drinke, or weare, or had in
his house from forraine parts, or scarce any
domesticke commodities exempted, but he
paid, as it were, an excise for it; yea, at
last, even cards and dice escaped not, but
they were monopolized by a great councellour, the Lord Cottington : yea, (to keep
their hands in use,) they got patents for the
very rags, marrow-bones, guts, and such
like excrements, as were thought of no use
but be cast on the dunghils ; and he was
held the bravest common-wealths man that

could bring in the most money, (yet, the
kings private purse, or publick treasury, little or nothing bettered, but) to impoverish
and vex the subject, and to no other end ;
for which he was ordinarily rewarded with
honour.

This good service (the quite contrary
way) did Weston and Noy doe for the king;
and, I beleeve you shall see God reward
them and their posterity ; for the one, like
a Jonas gourd sprang up suddenly from a
beggerly estate to much honour and great
fortunes, will shortly wither ; the other, his
son and heire, was killed in France, presently after his death;[1] and when both are dead,
let their names and memory rot, and be
extinct from the face of the earth.

Now doth Buckingham provide for ano-

---

[1] This was probably Noy's eldest son, to whom, after
some bequests to the rest of his family, he left his fortune under this remarkable form: " Reliqua meorum
omnia primogenito meo Edwardo dissipandado, et lego
nec melius unquam speravi ego." The manner of this
unfortunate young man's death seems to confirm his father's opinion of his profligacy.

ther forraigne enterprise, but carried so
close, I could never learne what it was;
nor did any wise men much inquire after
it, assuring themselves that such counsells
could produce no better effects than those
former. In the beginning, yea, even at the
very entrance thereunto, he did so stinke
- in the nostrils of God and man, that God
made one Felton his instrument to take
such a monster (as he was indeed) from his
longer domineering amongst men, by a blow
as fearefull as strange; after which he had
not time to say, Lord have mercy on him;
a just judgement on him that forsooke God,
to seeke to the devill by witches and sor-
cerers in his life; one whereof was Doctor
Lamb, (who was his great defensitive preserver as he thought him,) whose fate it was
to be brained by a shoe-makers last when
he least look'd for it;' the other was stabb'd

---

* The pretended astrologers, with whom the country
swarmed at this period, often wrought themselves into
the confidence of the great, and suggested by their prophecies schemes of ambition, which they sometimes

the next morning after that night he had
caused a fellow to be hanged, (not suffer-

doubtless aided by their villainy in realizing. We have
seen the share which Forman, a knave of this stamp,
had in the favour of Somerset and his lady. Buckingham was less attached to these impostors, but a person
high in his favour was the celebrated Dr Lamb.

" Dr Lamb, a man of an infamous conversation, (having been arraigned for a witch, and found guilty of it
at Worcester, and arraigned for a rape, and found
guilty of it at the king's bench bar at Westminster,
yet escaped the stroke of justice for both by his favour
in court,) was much employed by the mother and son,
which generally the people took notice of, and were so
incensed against Lamb, that, finding him in the streets
of London, in the year 1628, they rose against him,
and with stones and staves, knocked out his brains.

" And, besides Lamb, there was one Butler, an Irish-
man, (which vaunted himself to be of the house of Or-
mond,) who was a kind of mountebank, which the duke
and his mother much confided in. This Butler was
first an apprentice to a cutler in London, and before his
time expired, quitted his master, having a cunning head,
and went to the Bermudaes, where he lived some time
as a servant in the island ; and walking by the sea-side
with another of his companions, they found a great
mass of ambergreece that the seas bounty had cast up
to them, which they willingly concealed, meaning to
make their best markets of it. Butler being a subtle
snap, wrought so with his companion with promises of
a share, that he got the possession of it; and in the next

ing him to have that nights respite) after
his sentence and offence (what ere it was)

Dutch ship that arrived at the Bermudaes, he shipped
himself and his commodities for Amsterdam, where,
having sold his bargain at a good rate, and made his
credit with his fellow-venturer cheap enough, engrossing all to himself, he came into England, lived in a
gallant and noble equipage, kept a great and free table
at his lodgings in the Strand, which were furnished
suitable to his mind, and had his coach with six horses,
and many footmen attending on him, with as much
state and grandeur as if his greatness had been real.
But though his means lasted not to support this long,
yet it brought him into great acquaintance; and being
pragmatical in tongue, and having an active pate, he
fell to some distillations, and other odd extracting practices, which kept him afloat; and some men thought he
had gotten the long dreamed-after philosopher's stone;
but the best receipe which he had to maintain his greatness, after his amber-money fum'd and vapour'd away,
was suspected to come from his friends at Whitehall:
and the story of his death, if it be true, is one great evidence of some secret machination betwixt the duke and
him, that the duke was willing to be rid of him. For
mischief being an engrosser, is unsure and unsatisfied
when their wares are to be vended in many shops.
Therefore, he was recommended upon some plausible
occasion by the duke's means (as fame delivered it) to
some jesuites beyond the seas, where he was entertained
with a great deal of specious ceremony and respect,
in one of their colleges or cloysters; and at night they

to repent him of his sins, with this vow, he would neither eate nor drinke untill he see him dye; God, in requitall of his merci-lesse cruelty, would neither suffer him to eate nor drinke before he dyed by that dis-

attending him to his chamber with much civility, the chamber being hanged with tapistry, and tapers burning in stretched out arms upon the walls; and when they gave him the good-night, they told him they would send one who should direct him to his lodging; and they were no sooner out of this room of death, but the floor that hung upon great hinges on one side was let fall by artificial engines, and the poor vermine Butler dropped into a precipice, where he was never more heard of. That there are such secret inquisition-conveyances, of a horrid nature, is obvious; and such close contrivances may fly up and down upon the wings of rumour; but it is impossible to find out the bottom of such black pit-fals, but with as much danger as those that find the bitter effects of them. And this was reported to be the end of Butler."—WILSON, *ut supra*, p. 791.

The death of Lamb is more minutely narrated by Rushworth and Whitelocke. The poor wretch, upwards of eighty years of age, was driven from street to street under the opprobrious epithets of devil, witch, the duke's conjurer, &c. by at least five hundred people, and for the space of three hours, until they had literally pelted him to death. The city was most deservedly fined for this cruel outrage, not a single peace officer having interfered in his behalf.

mall stroake of a poore tenpenny knife, of
the said Feltons setting home. Thus neare
alike in time and manner were these two
hellish agents catastrophees. And now is
set this great sun, or rather portendous
comet, from whose influences all the officers and ministers had by reflexion their
life and heat.

After his death, the very name of a favourite dyed with him, none singly engrossing
the kings care and favour; but a regular motion was set to all officers, as appertained
to their severall places; as to the arch-bishop
the management and chief superintendency
of the church; to the Lord Treasurer the
Exchequer and the Customs; to the Lords
keepers of the Great and Privie Seales,
what belonged to equity; to the Judges
what belonged to law : so that, one would
have thought, all things now went so just
and equall, and in their proper channell,
as none but might expect now from that
new and better government halcyon dayes.

But it far'd farre otherwise (God being

angry at the nations sins the generall juggling of the state was one, and a great one;)
all those procedures being but in appearance righteous, nothing really so : but, like
the apples of Sodome, faire in shew, rotten
and corrupt within. For now, instead of
the late (but one) favourite, every great
officer and lord of the councell proved a
very tyrant; and it appeared that not their
vertues, but the former favourites power
only did restraine them from being so; for
that falling (together with himselfe, as you
have heard) and they left to their owne
arbetrary power, you would verily have beleeved that hell had been broke loose :
And to make good that metaphor, one of
the Councell being told by a gentleman
that the country was much troubled at a
certaine great grievance, replyed, Doth that
trouble them ? by God, there are seaven
worse devills to be shortly let out amongst
them. And in sober sadnesse, they all
might truly have undergone the name of
legion, for they were all many devills;

and like true devills, tooke pleasure in tormenting. So that hereby may be perceived the kingdome in generall had no benefit, (though some particular men, as Weston Treasurer, Coventry Lord Keeper, and all such as paid his beggerly kindred pensions, which now were ceased) by this mans death, whose purpose 'twas to have turned out of place both Coventry and Weston, before his last intended voyage. But now did Weston begin to be more cruell in pride and tyranny than Buckingham had been before him, and had not the archbishop (Laud) ballanced him, he would have been more insufferable. He cheated the king in the sale of timber and of land, and in the letting of his customs, the archbishop notwithstanding truly informing the king thereof. Weston was so mad at the thoughts of it, he would often say to his friends in private, That little priest would monopolize the kings eare, for he was ever whispering to the king.

And now begin the Councel Table, the

Star-Chamber, and High Commission to be
scourges and tortures to the commonwealth,
by imprisonments and mutilations of members; and were made, some of them, by
finings, the greatest incomes to the Exchequer; and in truth did now put down the
common laws deciding of *meum* and *tuum*.
And if any, desiring to appeal from them,
refused to stand there to their censures,
they were committed untill they would submit thereunto. If men sent unto by them
for money, refused it, they would imprison
them till they would give or lend; and if any
were summoned thither they had a mind to
quarrell with, in whom they could not find
a fault, they would make one by saying,
The gentleman laughs at us, or the gentleman saith thus and thus; it may be that he
had not in his thought, and yet there should
not want a false witnesse; for some lords
that sat with their backs towards them, or
so farre off that they could not heare, yet
would testifie either the words or actions;
or for want of this, a clerk of the councell

should bee called to witnesse, who, for his
profit, must swear what any lord said : If
they hit not upon that trick, then sometimes they would contrive to put a gentleman into passion by calling him some dis-
graceful name, or by scoffing at him ; so
that, indeed, the councell-table was grown
more like a pasquil then a grave senate.
But if the spirit of the man were such, that
he could not take those indignities without
some regret, it was well for him if he escaped
with imprisonment, and not called *Ore tenas*
to the Star-Chamber, and fined, (as many
were) to his undoing, for to that point were
now the fines of that court risen.

As for the High Commission court, that
was a very (Spanish-like) inquisition, in
which all pollings and tyrannizings over our
estates and consciences were practised, as
were in the other over our estates and
bodyes.

Then were the judges so much their servants, or rather slaves, that what ere they
illegally put in execution, they found law
to maintaine.

But that which is a wonder above all wonders is, that Coventry, who formerly had gained the opinion of a just and honest man, was a principall in all these miscarrages, yet dyed he unquestioned ; when, had his actions been scanned by a parliament (in that they were not, you may see what opinion is which in the multitude blindeth the understanding) he had been found as foul a man as ever lived.

Finch, a fellow of an excellent tongue, but not of one dram of law, made, for all that, Cheife Justice of the Common-Pleas, the onely court most learned in the law ; yet he brought all the learned judges, except two only, Hutton and Crook, to be of his illegall opinion for ship mony. This surely must be a punishment from God on them and us for our sins, otherwise it had been impossible so many grave judges should have been over-ruled by such a slight and trivial fellow.

Now also all officers in all places took what fees they pleased, as if in a jubilee

Amongst the rest those of the Star-Chamber, the Councell Table, and the High Commission were very grandees: Yea, the very messengers to them were countenanced in their abuse and insultings over the gentry, when in their clutches: and to such a strange passe were disorders come unto, that every lacquey of those great lords might give a check-mate to any gentleman, yea, to any country nobleman, that was not in the court favour.

And to fill full the measure of the times abounding iniquity, the court-chaplines, and others else where, with the reverend bishops themselves did preach away our liberties and proprieties, yet kept they divinity enough for their own interests: for, they concluded, all was either God or the kings, their part belonged to God, in which the king had no propriety: Our part belonged wholly to the king, in which we had propriety no longer, when the king were disposed to call for them; so that, betwixt the law and the

gospel, we were ejected out of lands, liberties, and lives at pleasure.

And now is Gods time come to visite
with his justice; and behold it: For the
pit they digged for others they themselves
are fallen into, for all their honours, lands,
and liberties are a gasping (and the judges
are but in very little better case) for the
parliament will doe that to them by the law
which they would have done to us by wrest-
ing the gospel.

But what needed all that joy for the
death of Buckingham, sith the times succeeding him have been so infinitely beyond
him in all oppression, as they are like to
bring all manner of miseries both upon king
and people? So that in truth his hydra's
head being struck downe, an hundred more
instead thereof appeared, which never durst
in his life time: And as he got much by
suites, so did Weston, much, by cheating,
(yet all came out of the subjects purses;)
and Coventry (that so generally a reputed
honest man) got such an estate by bribery

and injustice, that he is said to have left a
family worth a million; which may commend his wisdome, but in no wise his honesty.

And now also dies Weston, after he had
first brought in (as you may remember I
told you, himselfe was by Cranfield) Sir
Thomas Wentworth, after Earl of Strafford,
the active manager of the state, and sole
governor of the king.

This Strafford, without doubt, was the
ablest minister that this kingdome had since
Salisburies time; and, to speak uprightly,
there was not any but himselfe worthy of
that name amongst all the kings councell;
yet I am confident, by the weaknesse of
that boord, his abilities in state affaires
were judged more than they were; and besides, that very word of statesman was now
grown a stranger to our nation. Nor was
he, as Salisbury, or our ancient heroes, a
generall statesman, nor was it possible he
should be, he not having that breeding himselfe; nor kept he any upon his charge in

forraigne parts for intelligence; nor had he such a tutour as the other had of his father, who was the most absolute statesman in the world, whose very papers (which were left to this Salisbury, and served as so many rich presidents and instructors to him) were able, if wanting in abilities of his own, to make him an able statesman. But I held Strafford's abilities to be more on this side then beyond the seas; yet might he challenge the title of a good patriot: And so indeed he was, before he turned a courtier; after that he converted his studies and endeavours to make the king an absolute arbitrary monarch, by screwing up the regall prerogative to so high a strain as hath made it crack, and by raising his revenues so high that he made them fal; in which also his owne interest was concerned, for he did neither serve God nor the king for naught. Nor would Straffords abilities have been so transparent had any such concurrents as Buckhurst, Walsingham, or Hatton been now living, or such an one as the Earl of

Essex, who was Salisburies antagonist. But this man had onely the archbishop (whose proper element too was but the church) and they drew both in one line. And here I shall give you one note of Strafford's failing in his master-piece, that he was no such absolute wise man (that could not find the just medium of the peoples temper) but by striving to make the king all, and on a sudden, he made the king lesse and himselfe lesse then nothing. And had he beene wise, he could not but find the kings spirit was not to undergoe, nor to goe through with great actions, but would faile under them and crush the owners: which he to his lamentable experience hath found and felt too true. Besides, I much doubt Straffords owne spirit, that, seeing his wisdom was too short to protect him, his spirit was so low to faile him, that hee did not, like Sampson, pull down the house upon others heads, but fall like a tame foole, himselfe alone, caught in a gin, and lay still without any fluttering; when, surely, some others of the cabinet councell were as deep as himselfe in any designe.

You have here now seene a greate subject, yea, the greatest that ever our eyes beheld, that was no favourite, and greater in his fortunes then many favourites.

. You have also seen a king, the greatest that our nation ever had, both in prerogative, power, and revenues, and the most absolute over his subjects ; the one fallen below the earth, the other so low upon earth, that I wish I could but see him in the same state his peaceable father left him, who kept his prerogative to the height, without cracking it, because he had able ministers and councellors left, who were of Queen Elizabeths stocke ; but this kings ministers straine all so high, that the very ligaments and nerves of sovereignty are quite broken in sunder ; I wish them well sothered again.

But because, if I write further, I must tune to a much lower key, I will here end with my prayers, That God would give the king a wise councell and an understanding heart, to bee able to give himselfe councell, what will be best for himselfe, his posterity, and the people committed to his charge; and that he may discern such as councell him for their own private ends and interest, not for his honour and safety.

And here do I draw a curtaine betwixt the time past, and that to come in this kings reign, desiring it may never be remembred to posterity.

OBSERVATIONS

(INSTEAD OF A CHARACTER)

UPON

THIS KING FROM HIS CHILDHOOD.

IT being improper to write the character of
kings before their deaths, (I wish this were
not much nearer the period of his happinesse than his death,) give me, therefore,
leave to present into your view some remarkable observations of this unfortunate
king.

In his very infancy, he was so subject to
that wilfull humour, still possessing him,
that if any thing crossed him, he could

hardly be stilled; which then they were
forced to give way unto, by reason of that
extreame weaknesse which disabled him,
(as the like did his father) untill the 7th
yeare of his age, to goe, or scarce to stand
alone; crawling, when of himselfe he would
be in motion, upon all four, in a most unseemly manner: For the recovery whereof
he was beholding to the skill of one master
Stutavile, an excellent artist for strengthen-
ing limbs and straitning crooked bodies; -
but, for the rectifying his wayward disposition, to the tender care of the lady Carey,
afterward Countesse of Monmouth. [1]

[1] Sir Robert Carey, in his Memoirs, gives the following account of the state of Charles's health, (then Duke
of York,) while he was under his lady's charge. "The
duke was past four years old when he was first delivered to my wife; he was not able to go, nor scant
stand alone, he was so weak in his joints, and especially
his ankles, insomuch, as many feared they were out of
joint; yet God so blessed him both with health and
strength, that he proved daily stronger and stronger.
Many a battle my wife had with the king, but she still
prevailed. The king was desirous that the spring under his tongue should be cut, for he was so long beginning to speak, as he thought he would never have

This humour of his principally he tooke
from his mother, who notwithstanding was
a gallant lady ; nor was he free from it by
the fathers side, though his timorous nature
gave it an allay.   His mother (who loved
him so dearly, that she said, she loved him
as she did her soul, yet) was wont to say,
that she must with griefe of heart confesse,
he was a foole and wilfull, which would
hereafter endanger him the losse of his
crowne.

A sad censure, yet it should seeme pro-
pheticall.   But it were a lesson fit for all
parents learning, rather to leave their children to Gods providence, than to pry into
his office of fore knowledge.

spoke.   Then he would have him put in iron boots to
strengthen his sinews and joints ; but my wife protested
so much against them both, as she got the victory, and
the king was fain to yield.   My wife had the charge of
him from a little past four till he was almost eleven
years old, in all which time, he daily grew more and
more in health and strength, both of body and mind,
to the amazement of many that knew his weakness
when she first took charge of him."—*Edit.* 1808, p.
140.

He ever exprest an ill nature, by taking delight to doe ill offices to his fathers servants as well as to his owne; witnesse that instance concerning Master Murrey his tutor, and Doctor Hackwell placed about him, to instruct him in the principles of religion, who (rightly) judging it co-incident to that his employment, did therefore (upon the treaty for the Spanish match) deliver him a small treatise in manuscript, therein intimating his advice and judgement to informe his conscience aright, against coupling himselfe with a papist, saying to him, " Sir, I beseech you make use of this, by reading it your selfe, but if you shew it to your father, I shall be undone for my good will." The prince returned him many thankes, and assured him it should never goe farther then the cabinet of his owne breast; but withall, he asked him, To whom he had shewed it? Hackwell replyed, " The Arch-bishop (Abbot) hath read it," who, returning him it, said to him, " Well done thou good and faithfull

servant." Besides him, he told the prince,
he had only shewed it to Mr Murrey the
tutor, who belike, being better acquainted
with his masters perfidious disposition then
the other, did then disswade him from de-
livering it to the prince; " For," saith he,
" He will betray you." And it so fell out,
for within lesse then two houres after his
said engagement to the doctor, he presents
it to his father; upon which, he, or any
through whose hands and cognizance it had
passed before, were all under a disgrace,
and banished the court, (only Murrey was
afterwards provost of Eaton.) Here was an
embleme of his breach of oathes and pro-
testations in future, and of his untrustinesse,
which in a subject would have been called
treachery.

Such a one too he shewed himselfe in the
businesse of Rochell ; which, after his faire
promises, and deep imprecations for their
reliefe and assistance, wherein they put
some confidence, was meerly betrayed by
him; insomuch, that when the Rochel agents

found themselves abused through their whole
yeares attendance, they left this bitter jeere
upon him, that now they could rightly call
England the land of promise.

He seldome loved any but to serve his
turne, and would himselfe serve a turne to
doe any mischiefe, as was to be seene by
his saying amen to every full point of Buckinghams accusation in the face of the parliament against Bristol for his miscarriage
in Spaine; when it appeared by Bristols
defence in publick, before the face of that
same parliament, that there was not scarce
one syllable had any truth in it; who also
freely put himself upon the test, that if
there were any truth in that combined accusation against him, hee would yeeld himselfe guilty of it all.

He was of a very poore spirit, which may
be conceived (amongst other things) by his
making Buckingham his privado, after he
came to the crown, otherwise would he never have forgotten those unsufferable insolencies offered him being prince; what they

were you have already heard. His predecessor Henry the Fifth, (and so his brother Henry,) would have instructed him otherwise; for although (its true) noble mindes should forget injuries, so as not to revenge them, yet so, as not to countenance the doers of them, especially to take them into so much nearenesse and dearnesse as he did him after those two proud affronts, which argued in him, as I said before, a poore and ignoble spirit.

He had all his kingdomes left in peace and tranquility by his father, which he soone after made a shift to distemper by a foolish warre upon France and Spaine, and by a more foolish conduct of either ignorant, unexperienced, or cowardly commanders. And in truth, if you will give credit to *Vox Populi,* ' (the book so called, written by one Scot,) they were suitable to the grounds of such quarrels, being no fairer than the satisfying the beastly appetite of his favourite,

' Reprinted in Somers' Tracts, vol. iv.

who must be reveng'd (forsooth) upon those states. In which I admire Gods justice, that he who unjustly made war upon unwarrantable grounds, should have warre thus brought home unto him ; so that now God hath given him the same measure he hath met to others, even full, pressed down, and running over.

I wish I may have a time to give him a rairer character when he is dead, then are my observations in his life ; but I may rather wish then hope, in that course he yet continues,

CERTAINE OBSERVATIONS

BEFORE

QUEENE ELIZABETH'S DEATH.

I CANNOT but admire Gods providence in bringing peace, when nothing was thought of but war; and now bringing a cruell warre, when nothing could be expected but peace: Peace with all forraigne estates, peace at home. Not long before the death of Queene Elizabeth all the discourse was in a secret whispering on whom the succession would fall; some said, the Lady Arabella, some the King of Scotland, and reason given *pro* and *con* on both sides; they who were for her, saying, the Lady

Arabella was a native, and a maid, and
that this kingdome never flourished more
then under a maidens reigne : Others for
the Scot, said, that the King of Scots was
more neare to the crowne by descent; farther off, say others, as being a stranger, and
that nation ever in hostility against us.
Nor did the king himselfe beleeve he should
have come in with a sheathed sword, which
appeared by that letter he produced of the
Earle of Northumberlands, that if he made
any doubt hereof, he would bring him forty
thousand catholicks should conduct him
into England.   But the queene dyed, the
king comes in peaceably, even to the admiration of all forraigne princes, and to
the gnashing of their teeth ; but the reason
was, they had lived in obedience under a
just sovereigne, who was wont ever to say,
when any great man had opprest a poore
gentleman that petitioned her for redresse
against such oppression, when all the great
lords and officers would hold together to
support the oppressor, and trample upon

the oppressed : " My lords, (quoth she,) content you, 1 am queene of the valleys as well as of the hills, and I must not suffer the hills to over-top, nor yet to over-shade the valleys."

A worthy saying, which if it had been imitated by her successors, these our miseries had never happened ; but I say (and this is it I now drive at) her justice made her subjects to beleeve there could be no injustice in monarchy ; and that was it did facilitate the kings peaceable entrance. In that tranquility did the kingdome continue all his dayes, and about fifteen yeares of his sons reign : when behold, there was nothing but jollity in the court, as if saying to themselves, Who dares molest us ? the king having now a plentifull issue ; for, let me tell you, the kings issue made him and his courtiers the more to trample on the country gentry. But behold, when nothing but peace, peace, sudden destruction came on them and us unawares ; and God sends such a war as no man could dreame of.

Now the corollary of all is this, the high injustice of church and state was the cause of this warre.   And O, may not the continuing of that in any other government prove the continuance of this war! there being a farre greater appearance of the continuance thereof then ever there was of the beginning:

But Gods will be done.

A

PERFECT DESCRIPTION, &c.

————

To Welldon's Memoirs, Court and Character of
James I., &c. it seems proper to subjoin the Character
of Scotland by the same author. It was written during
a visit of James to his native and original kingdom, in
1617, and contains a severe and satirical account of
the poverty and fanatical manners of the Scottish nation at that period. The piece having been found
wrapped up in one of the records of the Board of Green
Cloth, was traced to Sir Anthony Welldon, and led to
his dismissal from court. See vol. i. page 301.

The satire seems to have crept to the press like the
Court and Character of James I., after the writer was
no more. That it is the libel of Welldon mentioned
by Wood, appears as well by internal evidence as from
the period at which it was written. It seems to have
been compiled in the shape of a letter from Edinburgh.

A

PERFECT DESCRIPTION

OF THE

PEOPLE AND COUNTRY OF SCOTLAND.

LONDON, PRINTED FOR J. S. 1659.
12. 21 PAGES.

———————

First for the country, I must confess, it is too good for those that possess it, and too bad for others to be at the charge to conquer it. The aire might be wholesome, but for the stinking people that inhabit it. The ground might be fruitful, had they wit to manure it.

Their beasts be generally small, women only excepted, of which sort there are none greater in the whole world. There is great store of fowl too, as foul houses, foul sheets, foul linen, foul dishes and pots, foul trenchers and napkins; with which sort, we have bin forced to say, as the children did with their foul in the wilderness. They have good store of fish too, and good for those that can eat it raw; but if it come once into their hands, it is worse than if it were three days old. For their butter and cheese I will not meddle withall at this time, nor no man else at any time that loves his life.

They have great store of deer, but they are so far from the place where I have been, that I had rather believe then go to disprove it. I confesse, all the deer I met withall was dear lodgings, dear horsemeat, and dear tobacco and English beer.

As for fruit, for their grandsire Adams sake, they never planted any; and for other trees, had Christ been betrayed in this countrey, (as doubtlesse he should had he come as a stranger,) Judas had sooner found the grace of repentance, then a tree to hang himself on.

They have many hills, wherein they say is much treasure, but they shew none of it.

Nature hath only discovered to them some mines of coal, to shew to what end he created them.

I see little grasse, but in their pottage. The thistle is not given them of nought, for it is the fairest flower in their garden. The word hay is heathen Greek unto them; neither man nor beast knows what it is.

Corn is reasonable plenty at this time, for since they heard of the kings comming, it hath been as unlawfull for the common people to eate wheate, as it was in the old time for any but the priests to eat shewbread. They prayed much for his comming, and long fasted for his welfare; but in the more plainer sense, that he might fare the better, all his followers were welcome but his guard; for those, they say, are like Pharaoh's lean kine, and threaten death wheresoever they come. They could perswade the footmen that oaten cakes would make them long-winded; and the children of the chappel they have brought to eat of them for the maintenance of their voices.

They say our cooks are too sawcy, and
for grooms and coachmen, they wish them
to give to their horses no worse then they
eat themselves; they commend the brave
minds of the pentioners, and the gentlemen of the Bed-Chamber, which choose rather to go to taverns, then to be always eating of the kings provision ; they likewise do
commend the yeomen of the buttery and
cellar, for their readiness and silence, in
that they will hear twenty knocks before
they will answer one.' They perswade the
trumpeters that fasting is good for men of
that quality; for emptiness, they say, causes
wind, and wind causes a trumpet to sound
well.

The bringing of heralds, they say, was a
needless charge, they all know their pede-
grees well enough, and the harbingers might
have been spared, so hence they brought
so many beds with them ; and of two evils,

' The allusion seems to refer, though obscurely, to the
knock on the dresser, by which the cooks announced
that dinner was ready to be served. '

since the least should be chosen, they wish the beds might remain with them, and poor harbengers keep their places, and do their office as they return. His majesty's hangings they desire might likewise be left as reliques, to put them in mind of his majesty; and they promise to dispense with the wooden images, but for those graven images in his new beautified chappell, they threaten to pull down soon after his departure, and to make them a burnt-offering to appease the indignation they imagined conceived against them in the brest of the Almighty, for suffering such idolatry to enter into their kingdom. The organ, I think, will find mercy, because (as they say) there is some affinity between them and the bag-pipes.

The skipper that brought the singing men with their papistical vestments, complains that he hath been much troubled with a strange singing in his head ever since they came aboard his ship. For remedy whereof, the parson of the parish hath perswaded him to sell that prophane ves-

sel, and to distribute the money among the
faithfull brethren. *

* We learn from graver authority, that the episcopal
vestments, music, and decorations, introduced by James
into the chapel at Holyrood palace, during his visit in
1617, were regarded with great horror by his Scottish
lieges. " The Scots," says one of their own historians,
" are in all acts of religious devotion, simple, rude, and
naked of ceremonial. The king, accustomed to the use of
the organ and church ritual, commanded them to be
used in his chapel of Holy-Rood, and in the moment of
joy, occasioned by the general expectation of his arrival,
did that by exertion of authority, which he could not
have done otherwise consistently with the customs and
religious establishment of his native country. This was
ill endured by the common people of Edinburgh, who
considered it as staining and polluting the house of religion by the dregs of popery. The more prudent indeed
judged it but reasonable that the king should enjoy his
own form of worship in his own chapel; but then followed a rumour, that the religious vestments and altars
were to be forcibly introduced into all the churches,
and the purity of religion, so long establised in Scotland, for ever defiled. And it required the utmost ef-
forts of the magistrates to restrain the inflamed passions
of the common people."—*Translated from Johnston's
Historia Rerum Britannicarum, ad annum,* 1617.

It is impossible to read this passage and some of those
in the satires, without being astonished that Charles I.,
aware of the strong prejudices of the Scottish nation
against the English form of worship, should have ever

For his majesties entertainment, I must needs ingenuously confess, he was received into the parish of Edinburg (for a city I cannot call it) with great shouts of joy, but no shew of charge for pageants; they hold them idolatrous things, and not fit to be used in so reformed a place.* From the castle they gave him some pieces of ordnance, which surely he gave them since he was King of England, and at the entrance of the town they presented him with a golden bason, which was carried before him on mens shoulders to his palace, I think, from whence it came. His majesty was conveyed by the younkers of the town, which were some 100 halberds, (dearly shall

attempted to impose the Book of Common Prayer upon them

* They gave James entertainments which were probably more to his taste: For James Hay, the town clerk, made him a long and adulatory harangue; the professors of the university held a public disputation for his pastime; and the citizens presented to him 10,000 marks Scottish money, in double golden angels in a gilt silver bason.

they rue it, in regard of the charge,) to the
cross, and so to the High Church, where the
only bell they had stood on tip-toe to behold his sweet face ; where I must intreat
you to spare him, for an hour I lost him.

In the mean time, to report the speeches
of the people concerning his never-exam-
pled entertainment, were to make this discourse too tedious unto you, as the sermon
was to those that were constrained to endure it. After the preachment, he was con-
ducted by the same halberds unto his palace, of which I forbeare to speak, because
it was a place sanctified by his divine majesty, onely I wish it had been better wall-
ed for my friends sake that waited on him.

Now I will begin briefly to speak of the
people, according to their degrees and qualities ; for the lords spiritual, they may well
be termed so indeed ; for they are neither
fish nor flesh, but what it shall please their
earthly god, the king, to make them. Obedience is better then sacrifice, and therefore
they make a mock at martyrdom, saying,

that Christ was to dy for them, and not they for him. They will rather subscribe then surrender, and rather dispence with small things then trouble themselves with great disputation ; they will rather acknowledge the king to be their head then want wherewith to pamper their bodies. '

They have taken great pains and trouble to compass their bishopricks, and they will not leave them for a trifle ; for the deacons, whose defect will not lift them up to dignities, all their study is to disgrace them that have gotten the least degree above them ; and because they cannot bishop, they proclaim they never heard of any. The scriptures, say they, speak of deacons and elders, but not a word of bishops. Their discourses are full of detraction ; their

' James had, with infinite difficulty, after long intriguing, and by never letting slip a favourable opportunity, established in Scotland the order of bishops, who, conscious that they were detested by the inferior clergy and the common people, clung for support to the king, who had raised them to their tottering dignity.   -

sermons nothing but railing; and their con-
clusions nothing but heresies and treasons.
For the religion they have, I confess they
have it above reach, and, God willing, I will
never reach for it.

They christen without the cross, marry
without the ring, receive the sacrament
without repentance, and bury without divine service ; they keep no holy days,
nor acknowledge any saint but S. Andrew,
who, they say, got that honour by present-
ing Christ with an oaten cake after his forty
days fast. They say likewise, that he that
translated the Bible was the son of a mault-
ster, because it speaks of a miracle done
by barley loaves, whereas they swear they
were oaten cakes, and that no other bread
of that quantity could have sufficed so many
thousands.

They use no prayer at all, for they say it
is needless; God knows their minds without pratling, and what he doth, he loves to
do it freely. Their sabbaths exercise is a
preaching in the forenoon, and a persecu-

ting in the afternoon ; they go to church in the forenoon to hear the law, and to the crags and mountains in the afternoon to louse themselves.

They hold their noses if you talk of bear-beating, and stop their ears if you speak of a play. Fornication they hold but a pastime, wherein mans ability is approved, and a womans fertility discovered. At adultery they shake their heads ; theft they rail at ; murder they wink at ; and blasphemy they laugh at ; they think it impossible to lose the way to heaven, if they can but leave Rome behind them.

To be opposite to the pope, is to be presently with God : to conclude, I am perswaded, that if God and his angels, at the last day, should come down in their whitest garments, they would run away, and cry, The children of the chappel are come again to torment us, let us fly from the abomination of these boys, and hide ourselves in the mountains.

For the lords temporal and spiritual, temporizing gentlemen, if I were to speak of any, I could not speak much of them; only I must let you know, they are not Scottishmen, for as soon as they fall from the breast of the beast their mother, their careful sire posts them away to France, where, as they pass, the sea sucks from them that which they have suckt from their rude dams; there they gather new flesh, new blood, new manner, and there they learn to put on their cloaths, and then return into their countrys to wear them out; there they learn to stand, to speak, and to discourse, and congee, to court women, and to complement with men.

They spared of no cost to honor the king, *In the original forme.* nor *form or* complimental curtesie to welcome their countrymen; their followers are their fellows; their wives their slaves; their horses their masters, and their swords their judges; by reason whereof, they have but few laborers, and those not very rich. Their parliaments hold but three days, their statutes three lines, and their suits are determined, in a manner, in three words, or very few more, &c.

The wonders of their kingdom are these, the Lord Chancellor he is believed; the Master of the Rolls well spoken of; and the whole counsel, who are the judges for all causes, are free from suspicion of corruption. The country, although it be mountainous, affords no monsters, but women, of which the greatest sort (as countesses and ladies) are kept like lions in iron grates; the merchants wives are also prisoners, but not in so strong a hold; they have wooden cages like our boar franks, through which sometimes peeping to catch the air, we are almost choaked with the sight of them. The greatest madness amongst the men is jealousie; in that they fear what no man that hath but two sences will take from them.

The ladies are of opinion, that Susanna could not be chast, because she bathed so often. Pride is a thing bred in their bones; and their flesh naturally abhors cleanliness.

Their breath commonly stinks of pottage;
their linen of p—; their hands of pigs t—;
their body of sweat, and their splay-feet never offend in socks. To be chained in marriage with one of them, were to be tied to
a dead carkasse, and cast into a stinking
ditch. Formosity and a dainty face are
things they dream not of.

The oyntments they most frequently use
amongst them are brimstone and butter for
the scab, and oyl of bays, and stavesacre.
I protest, I had rather be the meanest servant of the two of my pupils chamber-
maid, than to be the master-minion to the
fayrest countess I have yet discovered The
sin of curiosity of oyntments is but newly
crept into the kingdom, and I do not think
will long continue.

To draw you down by degrees from the
citizens wives to the country gentlewomen,
and convey you to common dames in Sea-
coal lane, that converse with rags and marrow bones, are things of minerall race;
every whore in Houndsditch is an Helena;

and the greasie bawds in Turnbal-street are Greekish dames in comparrison of these; and therefore to conclude. The men, of old did no more wonder, that the great Messias should be born in so poor a town as Bethlem, in Judea, then I do wonder that so brave a prince as King James should be born in so stinking a town as Edenburg, in lousy Scotland.

FINIS.

INTRODUCTION

AULICUS COQUINARIÆ.

————

The *Aulicus Coquinariæ* is a professed answer to the Court and Character of James I.
by Sir Anthony Welldon. It is obviously
the work of a zealous loyalist; the materials of which were chiefly compiled by Dr
Godfrey Goodman, Bishop of Gloucester.
This prelate suffered under the arbitrary
authority of the Primate Laud, by whom he
was committed to a pursuivant, and afterwards to the Gatehouse, for dissenting from
the canons imposed on the church in 1640.
In 1643, Bishop Goodman was plunder-

ed, and utterly ruined by the prevailing republican party, and ever afterwards lived
obscurely in the parish of St Margaret's, in
Westminster. He embraced the Roman catholic faith, and died in that persuasion,
19th January, 1655. Upon the publication
of Sir Anthony Welldon's Court of King
James, Goodman compiled an answer, entitled, "The Court of King James, by Sir
A. W. reviewed," which, as Wood informs us,
still exists in the Bodleian library, and begins thus: "Though I cannot say I was an
ear and eye-witness, but truly I have been
an observer of the times, and what I shall
relate of my own knowledge, God knows is
most true." And it concludes abruptly thus:
" Yet notwithstanding, I have given him
the name of a knight, because he hath pleased so to stile himself, and that I might not
offend him." The following extract from
Wood, relating to Bishop Goodman's Review, will shew that it was the source whence
the author of Aulicus Coquinariæ drew much
of his information.

" This manuscript book was made in answer to a published book, entitled, *The Court and Character of King James. Lond. 1650, Oct.* written and taken by Sir A. W.; which book being accounted a most notorious libel, especially by the loyalists and court-party, was also answered by this Bishop Goodman, much of whose manuscript above-mentioned is involved in an anonymous book, entitled, *Aulicus Coquinariæ ; or, a Vindication in Answer to a Pamphlet, entitled,* The Court and Character of *K. James,* &c. *Lond.* 1650. The author of the said *Court and Character* was one Sir Anth. Welldon, of Kent, whose parent took rise from Queen Elizabeth's kitchen, and left it a legacy for preferment of his issue. Sir Anthony went the same way, and by grace of the court got up to the Green Cloth; in which place, attending K. James into Scotland, he practised there to libel that nation. Which, at his return home, was wrapt up in a record of that board; and by the hand being known to be his, he was deservedly removed from his place, as unworthy to eat his bread, whose birth-right he had so vilely defamed. Yet, by favour of the king, with a piece of money in his purse, and a pension to boot, to preserve him loyal during his life, though, as a bad creditor, he took this course to repay him to the purpose. In his lifetime, he discovered part of this piece to his fellow-courtier, who earnestly dissuaded him not to publish so defective and false a scandal; which, as it seems, in conscience he so declined. I have also been credibly informed, that Sir A. Welldon did, at the beginning of the long-parliament, communicate the MS. of it to Lady Eliz. Sidley, (mother to Sir Will. and Sir Charles,) accounted a very sober and prudent woman; who, after perusal, did lay the vileness of it much to Sir Anthony's door, that he was resolved never to make it public, which perhaps is the reason why a certain au-

thor ' should say, that ' With some regret
of what he had maliciously written, did
intend it for the fire, and died repentant;
though since stolen to the press out of a
lady's closet.' And if this be true, our
exceptions may willingly fall upon the
practice of the publisher of the said libel, who, by his additions, may abuse us
with a false story, which he discovers to
the reader in five remarkable passages ;
and therefore, in some manner, gives us
occasion to spare our censure on Sir Anthony, who was dead some time before the
said libel was published. The second edition of it printed at Lond, in Oct. an. 1651,
is dedicated to the said noble Lady Eliz.
Sidley, and hath added to it, (1.) *The Court
of K. Charles, continued, unto the Beginning
of these Unhappy Times,* &c. (2.) *Observations (instead of Character) upon this King
from his Childhood.* (3.) *Certain Observa-*

* Will. Sanderson, in his poem on the Reign and
Death of K. James I., printed 1655, fol.

tions before Q. Elizabeth's Death. But these are not anima.'verted upon by *Aulicus Coq.* or B. Goodman, because they came out after they had written their respective answers. The said Bishop Goodman hath also written, *The two Mysteries of Christian Religion, the ineffable Trinity and wonderful Incarnation explicated,* &c. Lond. 1653. qu. dedicated by one epistle to Oliver Cromwell, L. Generall, and by another, to the master, fellows, scholars, and students of Trin. College, in Cambridge. Also, *An Account of his Sufferings,* which is only a little pamphlet, printed 1650."—WOOD's *Athenæ,* i. 729.

The Aulicus Coquinariæ itself, which derives its quaint title from Sir Anthony Welldon's being the son of Queen Elizabeth's clerk of the kitchen, is generally supposed to have been compiled from Goodman's materials by William Sanderson, author of the Histories of James I. and Charles I. This author was born in Lincolnshire, and originally secretary to Lord Holland, afterwards a sufferer in the royal cause, and upon the restoration, promoted to the honour of Knighthood, and the post of Gentleman of the Privy Chamber. He died 15th July, 1676, at the advanced age of ninety.

PREFACE.

THERE are some men so delight in sinne, who rather than be idle from doing evil, will take much pains to scandall the dead.

My fear to offend hath withheld my hand a convenient time, lest I should fall into the like error with him that published the pamphlet, entituled, The Court and Character of King James, and father's the brat upon Sir A. W. And if common fame mistake not the meaning, his parent took rise from Q. Elizabeths kitchin, and left it a legacy for preferment of his issue.

This man went the same way, and by grace of the court got up to the Green-cloth. In which place, attending King James

into Scotland, he practised there to libell
that nation, which at his return home was
found wrapt up in a record of that board,
and by the hand being known to be his,
he was deservedly removed out, as unworthy to eat of his bread, whose birth-right
he had so vilely defamed. Yet by favour
of the king, with a piece of money in his
purse, and a pension to boot, to preserve
him loyall during his life, though as a bad
creditor, he took this course to repay him
to the purpose.

And I have heard, that in his life, he discovered a part of this peece to his fellow
courtier, who earnestly diswaded him not
to publish so defective and false a scandall,
which as it seems in conscience he so declined.

And therefore my exception willingly
falls upon the practice of the publisher,
who by his additions may abuse us with
this false story, which he discovers to the
reader in five remarkable passages, and gives
me the occasion to spare my censure on

the deceased person: but to bestow my
unkindness (which necessarily intervenes
in this vindication) on him who yet lives,
to make out his bad act with a reply (if he
please) more pestilent, upon me.

AULICUS COQUINARIÆ,

OR THE

CHARACTER OF HIM

WHO SATYRIZ'D

KING JAMES AND HIS COURT.

———

QUEEN Elizabeth died, anno domini 1602, having bin long sick; and indeed desperate, which gave this state time enough to conclude for his reception the undoubted heir to these crownes, James, then King of Scotland; she hath been highly valued, since her death; the best of any former sovereigne over us. She was fitted for fortunes Darling, but with some imprisonment, the better to mould her for the rule and sovereignty of a kingdome, and for the custody of a scepter. She shewed her justice

Queen
Elizabeth.

and piety as a president to posterity. She
was a princesse learned, even then, when
letters had estimation and began them into
fashion ; which brought forth many' rare
and excellent men, both of the gowne, and
of the sword. Some say she had many favorites, but in truth she had none. They
were neer and dear to her, and to her affaires, as partners of her care, not minions
of phansey. And yet such as they were
she ever mastered by her own rules, not
they her by their own wills. And she want-
ed not many of them at need, or pleasure.
She was magnificent, (comparative with
other princes ;) which yet she disposed fru-
gally ; having alwaies much to do with
little money : for truly, those either wise or
gallant men were never cloied with her
bounty more then in her grace ; which,
with her mannage, passed for good pay-
ment.

The Irish affaires was to her maligne,
which drew her treasure almost dry ; the
only cause of distemper in the state, and

12

ended not but with her life. At which time
she left her cofers empty, and yet her enemies potent; and therefore it could be no Pamp. 34.
treason in them, that afterwards councelled
the peace, but rather in such who indeavoured then and after the re-establishing a
new war.

: Amongst her favourites of the sword,
none could boast more of her bounty and
grace then the Earl of Essex, whose in- Essex.
Pamp. 10.
grate disposition, blown beyond the com-
passe of his steere, by too much popularity
and pride, cosened him into that absolute
treason against his soveraigne, that, not with-
standing many forewarnings of his neerest
friends, and unwilling resentments of his
deerest mistresse; his open rebellion at last
brought him to publique tryall, condemned
and executed as the most ingrate that former times could produce. (Of which we shall
take occasion hereafter in some particular.)
Wherein Sir Robert Cecill acted no more
then a dutiful subject, councelour, and
judge ought to have done against him, and

such like of her time, evermore attempting
by assassination or poyson to take away her
life. As were also the like attempts, by
others in Scotland, (witnesse the fore-
warning of the Duke of Florence, by ex-
presse message of Sir Henry Wootton to
King James, a year before his comming to
these kingdomes) against her beloved and
undoubted heir; and in them to destroy
the protestant religion.

Gowrie's
conspi-
racie.

    The most remarkable was, that of Gow-
ries conspiracy in Scotland. And I never
read or heard (till our pamphlet) that Sir

Pamph. 8.

George Hewms his gravity and wisdome
ushered him into the secrets of the king
(therefore) and chiefly to make good that

The first
passage of
the preface
remark-
able.

story. For of that nation, both the wisest
and most honest, gave great credit thereto;
and the commemoration was advisedly settled by acts of their parliament; which
anathematize upon Gowries house and
name. And solemnized there and here, with
narratives in print, of each particular cir-

cumstance, and the ground and cause in-
viting that treason.

And truly, the anniversary feast-day in
August was usually solemnized to God's
glory by the most reverend preachers : witnesse those rare divine sermons of our Bishop Andrews and others, whose consciences
no doubt were not so large, to cozen God
Almighty with a fained tale. Indeed there
might have been more additionall truths
annexed to the relation, which I have heard,
to make it more apprehensive to our pamphleter; whose speculations, in this, as in
other histories of court and state, took information (belike) but in his office, below-
staires ; and which makes his faith drawe
downe the effects of those sermons for the   Pamp. 10.
father, as a cause of the sad events and
sufferings of the son, and us all, to this present.

The name of Ruthen in Scotland was not
notorious, until anno 1568, when Ruthen,
amongst others, confederates, in those divided times of trouble, laboured much for the

imprisoning Queene Mary, mother to King
James.[1] In 1582, his sonne William was
created Earle Gowry, in the time of that
king's minority, though the father bore
deadly hatred to the king's prosperity; and
in 1584, himselfe was in actuall rebellion,
in which he suffered at Dondee. His eldest
son John, then in travell in Italy, returns
home to inherit his lands and honours;
but not one jot changed in disposition,
from the traiterous wayes of his predecessors: For not long after he falls into this
conspiracy; which is not so ancient, but
that many then and now living can, and
myselfe, have often heard the repetition.

The house of Gowry were all of them
much addicted to chimistry.[2] And these

---

[1] The author is as inaccurate in his account of Scottish affairs as he whom he attempts to confute. William, fourth Lord Ruthven, could not be concerned in
imprisoning Queen Mary; for, having fled for his deep
participation in the murder of David Rizzio, he died at
Berwick, 1566-7,

[2] The first Earl of Gowrie, beheaded in 1584, is said,
by Spottiswood, to have been too curious in inquiring

more to the practise; often publishing (as such professors usually do) more rare experiments then ever could be performed; wherein the king (a general scholar) had little faith. But to infuse more credit to the practise, Alexander Ruthen, the second brother, takes this occasion; and withall conspires with Gowry to assassinate the king; and taking opportunity in his hunting, not far from his house, St Johnstone, invites the king to be an eye-witnesse of his productions. In their way, Sir Thomas Erskin (after Lord Kelly) overtakes them and others, demanding of the Duke of Lenox, then present, why Alexander had ingrossed the king's eare, to carry him from his sports? Peace, man, said the duke, wee's all be turned into gold. Not far they rid,

at wizards about the events of futurity. And his son, slain in the course of the memorable conspiracy, was also supposed to be addicted to mystical studies and natural magic. William and Patrick Ruthvens, his brothers, were celebrated for their knowledge of chemistry, which was then believed connected with occult science; and the latter practised as a physician.

but that the Earle Gowry made good by protestation his brother's story ; and thus was the king brought to guest. Neere the end of dinner, at his fruit, and the lords and waiters gone to eate, Alexander begs of the king, at this opportunity, to withdraw, and to be partaker of his production; to the view of that which yet he could not believe.

And up he leades the king, into by-lodgings, locking each door behind them, till they came into a back-roome; where, no sooner entered, but that Alexander claps on his bonnet, and with sterne countenance faces the king; and saies: Now, sir, you must know, I had a father whose bloud calls for revenge, shed for your sake. The king amazed, deales gently with his fury, excuses the guilt of his death, by his then infancy, advising him not to lay violent hands on the sacred person of his anointed soveraigne, especially in a cause of his innocency, pleading the laws of God and man; which so much wrought upon him,

that he said, Well, I will speak with my
brother ; and so put the king into a lobby
room next the chamber, where no sooner
entered, but that there appeared a fellow,
weaponed, ready for execution ; to whose
custody the king is committed till his return.

Alexander gone downe, the fellow trem-
bles with reverence, puts down his sword,
and craves pardon ; which gave the king
occasion to worke upon that passion, and
to aske him whether he resolved to murther
him ? Being assured to the contrary, the
king gets leave to open a window that
looked into a back court, when presently
Alexander returnes, and tells the king that
he must dy. But much affrighted, at the
fellowes countenance, with his sword offers
violence to the king, which the fellow
seemingly opposes ; and betweene them began a scuffle, which gave advantage to the
king to cry treason at the window, which
looked into a back court; where Sir Thomas
Erskin and one Herries were come in pur-

suite of the king, who was rumored to be
gone out the back way to his hunting.

At the cry of treason, and known to be
the king's voice, they both hastened up a
back staire, called the Turnepike, being
directed by a servant of the house, who saw
Alexander ascend that way ; and so for-
cing some doores, they found them above
panting with the fray ; and up comes also,
at heeles of them, John Ramsey (after Earle
of Holdernesse ;) by them Alexander was
soon dispatched.

Not long after came the Earle Gowry
(by his double key) the first way, with a
case of rapiers, his usuall weapons, and
ready drawn ; to whom Erskin said, as to
divert his purpose, What do you meane, my
lord ? the king is killed, (for the king was
shadowed, having cast himselfe upon a
bed from his sight; and his cloak was
thrown upon the body of Alexander, bleeding on the ground.) At which Gowry stops,
sincking the points of his weapons; when
suddenly Herries strickes at him with a

hunting fawlchion ; and Ramsey having his hawke on his fist, casts her off, and steps into Gowry, and stabs him to the heart ; and forthwith more company came up.

And the truth, very notorious then to every eye and eare-witnesse, not a few.

There remained but one younger sonne of that house, who, though a childe, was from that time imprisoned, by act of their parliament, and so continued afterwards here in the Tower of London until that king's death ; and the grace of the late King Charles restored him to liberty, with a small pension, which kept him like a gentleman to these times ; but now failing, he walks the streets, poore, but well experienced also in chimicall physick, and in other parts of learning.

Not long after this conspiracy, Herries dies well rewarded. John Ramsey hath the honor of knighthood, with an additional bearing to his cote of armes, a hand holding forth a dagger, reversed proper, piercing a bloudy heart, the point crowned emperiall, with this distick, *Hæc Dextra Vindex Principis et Patriæ*. Afterward he was created Lord Haddington and Earle of Holdernesse.

Pamp. 9.

And our pamphlet bestowes on him this character, a very good gentleman by nature, but (in this story) a lier by practise : for which all these favours were too little reward.

Sir Thomas Erskin was afterwards created Earl of Kelly, Knight of the Garter, captain of the king's guard, and groome of the stoole; and the fellow designed for the murtherer had a large pension confirmed by act of their parliament.

And all these men (but Herries) were living, with other witnesses at King James' journey, when he went from hence to visit Scotland ; and met together by direction at the same house, with ceremony ; and all of them, with a number of courtiers, ascended into the same roome, the bloud yet remaining, where the king related the story, and confirmed by them ; and afterwards

kneeling down, with tears of contrition for
his sinnes to God, and thankfulnesse for
this mercy, using many pious ejaculations,
embraced all these actors in the former tragedy ; when the poor fellow also kist the
king's hand.

These circumstances gave occasion then,
that this whole story was freshly revived, to
the common satisfaction of the whole countrey, and our English courtiers; and in
especiall, unto the very reverend bishop,
and nobly borne, James Mountegue, then
present ; to whom the king addressed himself, in this relation, and from whose mouth
I received these particulars at his return
into England.

And thus much we have by word of
mouth ; somewhat I shall add out of writings for more satisfaction.

This treason was attempted the 4th of
August, 1600; and though there followed
sundry suspitions and examination of several other persons supposed abbetters and
contrivers, yet it lay undiscovered, *tanquam à*

postliminio untill eight years after, by the circumspection principally of the Earle of Dunbar, a man of as great wisdome as those times and that kingdome could boast of, upon the person of one George Sprot, no-tary-publick, of Ayemouth, in Scotland. From some words, which at first he sparing-ly or unawares expressed, and also by some papers which were found in his house, whereof being examined, with a little adoe he confessed, and was condemned and exe-cuted at Edenburgh the 12th of August, 1608.

A relation I conceive not common, but in my hands to be produced, and written by that learned gentleman Sir William Hart, then Lord Justice of Scotland, and princi-pall in all the acts of judicature herein.

And first, George Sprot confesseth, That he knew perfectly that Robert Logane, late of Restalrig, was privy, and upon foreknow-ledge of John, late Earl of Gowrie's trea-sonable conspiracy: That he knew there were divers letters interchanged betwixt

12

them, anent their treasonable purpose, July
1600, which letters, James Bour, called
Laird Bour, servitor to Restalrig, (imployed betwixt them, and privy to all that ar-
rand,) had in keeping, and shewed the same
to Sprot in Fast-Castle. That Sprot was
present, when Bour, after five daies absence,
returned with answers by letter from Gowry,
and staid all night with Restalrig, at his
house Gunnesgreen, and rode the next
morne to Lothiane, where he staid six daies,
then to Fast-Castle, where he abode a short
space.

That he saw and heard Restalrig read
these letters, which Bour brought back
from Gowry, and all their conference there-
anent. And that Bour said, " Sir, if you
think to get commodity by this dealing,
lay your hand on your heart;" and that
Restalrig answered, " though he should lose
all in the world, yet he would passe through
with Gowry ; for that matter would as well
content him as the kingdome." To whom
Bour said, " You may do as you please,

sir, but it is not my councell that you should be so suddain in that other matter; but for the condition of Darlton, I would like very well of it." To this Restalrig answered, " Content yourself, I am not at my wits end."

That Sprot himself entered into conference with Bour, demanding what was to be done between the earle and the laird? Bour answered, " That he beleeved that the laird would get Darlton without gold or silver; but he feared it would be deerer to him."

That Sprot inquiring further how that should be done? Bour said, " They have another pie in hand then buying and selling of land; but prayed Sprot for God's sake, that he would let be, and not be troubled with the lairds business; for he feared that within few daies the laird would be landlesse and livelesse."

And Sprot being demanded afterwards, if all these confessions were true, as he would answer upon the salvation of his

soul, seeing his death was neer approaching ? Sprot said,

" That he had no desire to live, and had
care only of cleering his conscience in the
truth ; and that all the former points and
circumstances were true, with the depositions made by him the 5th of July last, and
the whole confession made by him since,
as he hoped to be saved, and which he
would seale with his bloud."

And further being demanded, Where was
now the letter of Restalrig to Gowry ? he
answered, " That he had this letter amongst
other of Restalrig's papers which Bour had
in keeping, and which Sprot copied out,
and that he left the principall letter in his
chest amongst his writings when he was taken and brought away, and that it is closed
and folded in a sheet of paper."

These depositions made by George Sprot,
the 10th of August, 1608, and others before, (being all included in this indictment
following, to which for brevity I shall remit the reader,) and written by James Prim-

rose, clerk of the king's councell, and subscribed George Sprot.

Present,

Earl of Dunbar, Earl Lothiane, Bishop of Rosse, Lord Schone, Lord Hallo-rodhouse, Lord Blantire, Sir William Hart, Lord Justice, Mr John Hall, Mr Patrick Galloway, Mr Peter Hewet, ministers of Edenburgh, and subscribed with all their hands.

The next day, 11th of August, Sprot was re-examined, and to him declared the assurance of his death, and was advised not to abuse his conscience to witnesse untruths, and upon the innocency of the dead or living. To which he deposeth, That being resolved to die, and as he wishes to be participant of heaven, upon the salvation or damnation of his soul, that all that he had deposed were true in every point and circumstance, and no untruth in them.

The next day; being the 12th of August, 1608, Sprot was presented in judgement

upon pannell, within the talboth of Edenburgh, before

Sir William Hart, Knight, Lord Justice
of Scotland, assisted with these persons, viz.

Alexander, Earle of Dunferling, Lord
Chancellour; George, Earle of Dunbar,
Lord Treasurer; John, Arch-bishop of Glas-
coe; David, Bishop of Rosse; Gawen, Bishop of Galloway; Andrew, Bishop of Bre-
chine; David, Earl of Crawford; Mark,
Earl of Lothaine; James, Lord Aberne-
thie of Saltonne; James, Lord of Balme-
rinoth Senitapie; Walter, Lord Blantire;
John, Lord Burley; Sir Richard Coburn,
Knight; Master John Preston, Collector
General; Sir John Skewe, Knight, Register.

And he was declared accused, and pursued by Sir Thomas Hamilton, Knight, advocate to the king, for his highnesse entries
of the crimes contained in his indictment,
whereof the tenure followes, viz. :

George Sprot, notary ih Ayemouth, you are indicted and accused, forasmuch as John, sometime Earle of Gowry, having most cruelly, detestably, and treasonably conspired, in the moneth of July, the year of God 1600, to murther our deere and most gracious soveraigne the king's most excellent majesty; and having imparted that divelish purpose to Robert Logaine of Restalrig, who allowed of the same, and most willingly and readily undertook to be partaker thereof. The same comming to your knowledge, at the times, and in the manner particularly after specified, you most unnaturally, maliciously, and treasonably concealed the same, and was art and part thereof in manner following: And first, In the said moneth of July, 1600, after you had perceived and known that divers letters and messages had past betwixt the said John, somtimes Earl of Gowry, and the said Robert Logane of Restalrig, you being in the house of Fast-Castle, you saw

and read a letter written by the said Restalrig, with his own hand, to the said Earl
of Gowry, viz.

My lord, &c. at the receipt of your letter I am so confuſed, that I can neither
utter my joy, nor find my selfe sufficiently able to requite your lordship with due
thanks; and perswade your lordship, in
that matter, I shall be as forward for your
honour as if it were my own cause; and I
think there is no Christian that would not
be content to revenge that Machiavilian
massacring of our deer friends; yea, how-
beit it should be to venture and hazard life,
lands, and all things else. My heart can
bind me to take part in that matter, as
your lordship shall find proof thereof; but
one thing would be done, namely, that your
lordship should be circumspect and earnest
with your brother, that he be not rash in
any speeches touching the purpose of Padua.

And a certain space after the execution
of the aforesaid treason, the said Robert Lo-

gane having desired the Laird of Bour to
deliver to him the said letter, or else to burn
it; and Bour having given to you all tickets
and letters which he then had, either concerning Restalrig or others, to see the same,
because he could not reade himself, you
abstracted the above-written letter, and retained the same in your own hands, and
divers times read it, containing further, to
wit,

My lord, you may easily understand,
that such a purpose as your lordship in-
tendeth can not be done rashly, but with
deliberation; and I think for my self, that
it were most meet to have the men your
lordship spake of ready in a bote or bark,
and addresse them as if they were taking
pastime on the sea in such faire summer-
time; and if your lordship could think
good, either your self to come to my house
Fast-castle by sea, or to send your brother,
I should have the house very quiet, and well
provided after your lordships advertisement;
and no others shall have accesse to haunt

the place, during your being here. And if your lordship doubt of safe landing, I shall provide all such necessaries as may serve for your arrival within a flight-shot of the house. And perswade your lordship, you shall be as sure and quiet here, while we have setled our plot, as if you were in your own chamber; for I trust, and am assured, we shall have word within few daies from them your lordship knowes of; for I have care to see what ships come home by. Your lordship knows I have kept the lord Bothwell quietly in this house in his greatest extremity, in spite of king and councell. I hope, if all things come to pass, (as I trust they shall,) to have both your lordship and his lordship at a good dinner ere I dy, *Hæc jocose.* To animate your lordship, I doubt not but all things will be well: and I am resolved thereof, your lordship shall not doubt of any thing on my part: peril of life, lands, honor and goods; yea, the hazard of hell shall not affray me from that; yea, though the scaffold were already set up. The sooner the matter were done, it were the better: for the king's buck-hunting will be shortly, and I hope it will prepare some daintier cheer for us to live the next year. I remember well, my lord, that merry sport which your lordship's brother told me of a nobleman at Padua: for I think that a *parasceve* to this purpose.

My lord, think nothing that I commit the secret hereof to this bearer; for I dare not onely venture my life, lands, honour, and all I have else on his credit, but I durst hazard my soule in his keeping, I am so perswaded of his fidelity. And I trow (as your lordship may ask him if it be true) he would go to hell-gates for me, and he is not beguiled of my part to him. And therefore I doubt not but this will perswade your lordship to give him trust in this matter as to my self. But I pray you direct him home again with all speed possible; and give him strait command, that he take not a wink sleep till he see me again after he comes from you. And as your lordship desireth in your letter to me, either rive or burn this letter, or send it back again with the bearer; for so is the fashion I grant.

RESTALRIG.

Which letter, writ every word with the said Robert Logane's own hand, was also so subscribed with this word, *Restalrig.*

And albeit by the contents of the aforesaid letter, you know perfectly the truth of the said most treasonable conspiracy, and the said Logane his foreknowledge, allowance and guilt thereof, like as you were assured of the same by his receiving divers letters sent by Gowry to him, and by his returning letters to Gowry for the same purpose, and by sundry conferences betwixt Logane and Bour, in your presence and hearing, concerning the said treason, as well in July preceding the attempt thereof, as at divers other times shortly thereafter; as likewise by Bour his revealing thereof to you, who was upon the knowledge and devise of the treason, and was imployed as

ordinary messenger by Logane to Gowry;
whereby your knowledge, concealing, and
guilt of the same was undeniable.

Yet, for further manifestation thereof,
about July 1602, the said Logane shewed
unto you, that Bour had told him, that he
had been somewhat rash, to let you see a
letter which came from Gowry to Logane,
who then urged you to tell what you understood by the same: to whom you answered,
that you took the meaning thereof to be,
that he had been upon the councell and
purpose of Gowrie's conspiracy: and that
he answered you, what e're he had done,
the worst was his own: but if you would
swear to him that you should never reveale
any thing of that matter to any person, it
should be the best sight that ever you saw:
and in token of further recompence, he gave
you twelve pounds of silver. Neverthelesse,
albeit you know perfectly the whole practise and progresse of all the said treason,
from the beginning to the end; as also by
your conference with Bour and Logane,

during all the daies of their lives, who lived till the year 1606, or therabouts: and so by the space of six years you concealed the same, and so you was and is art and part of the said treason, and of the concealing; and so you ought to suffer under the pain of high treason. To the token, that you have not only by your depositions subscribed by you, and solemnly made in presence of many of the lords of his majestie's privy councell, and the ministers of the borough of Edenburgh, of the dates of the 5. 15. and 16. daies of July last past, and 10. and 11. of August instant, confessed every head, point, and article of the indictment abovesaid, but also by divers other depositions subscribed by you; you have ratifyed the same, and sworn constantly to abide thereat, and to seal the same with your bloud. Which indictment being read openly, before Sprot was put to the knowledge of inquest, he confess'd the same and every point to be true; and therefore the indictment was put

to the inquest of the honest, famous, and discreet persons, that is to say,

William Trumball, of Ardre; William
Fisher, merchant and burgesse of Eden-
burgh; Rob. Short there; Ed. Johnstone,
merchant burgess there; Harb. Maxwel,
of Cavens; Ja. Tennent, of Linchouse;
Wil. Trumbill, burg. of Edenburgh; Geor.
Brown, in Gorgy Mill; Joh. Hucheson and
John Lewes, merch. burgh. of Edenburgh;
Ja. Somervill and Wil. Swinton, of the same;
John Crunison, of Dirlton; Th. Smith and
John Cowtis, burg. of Edenburgh.

Which persons of inquest, sworn and admitted, and reading over the same indictment again in his and their presence, the
said George Sprot confessed the same to be
true. Whereupon the said Sir Thomas Hamilton, his majesties advocate, asked act
and instrument; and therefore the inquest
removed to the Inquest-house, and elected
Harbert Maxwell to be their chancelour or
foreman: And after mature deliberation,

they all re-entred againe in court, where the
said foreman declared the said George Sprot
to be guilty, filed, and convict of art and
part of the said treason; for which cause
the said justice, by the mouth of the dem-
ster of court, by sentence and doom ordained the said George Sprot to be taken to the
Market-crosse of Edenburgh, and there to
be hanged upon a gibbet till he be dead,
and thereafter his head to be stricken off,
and his body to be quartered and demean-
ed as a traytor, and his head to be set upon
a prick of iron upon the highest part of the
talboth of Edenburgh, where the traytor
Gowrie and other conspiratours heads stand,
and his lands and goods forfeited and es-
cheat to our soveraign lord the king's use.

Extractum de Libre Actorum Adjornalis
S. D. N. Regis per me D. Johannem
Coburne de Ormeston Militem, Clericum
Institiarii ejusdem generalem. Sub meis
signo & subscriptione manualibus.

And so was George Sprot conveyed to a
private house, remaining at his meditations;

and afterwards conferred with the ministers, confessing all aforesaid with extreame humiliation and prayer. Afterwards, ganging up the ladder, with his hands loose and untyed, he was again put in mind of the truth of his confessions. He, for the greater assurance thereof, perform'd an act marvelous, promising, by God's assistance, to give them an evident token before the yielding up of his spirit; which was, when he had hung a very good while, he left up both his hands a good height, and clapped them together three severall times, to the wonder of thousand spectators, and so dyed.

For more confirmation of the afore narration, there was present George Abbot, then doctor in divinity, and Dean of Winchester, after Arch-Bishop of Canterbury, who was present both at his examination and execution, and hath made the same writing and observance even almost verbatim, as all the afore specified relation intends; which I can produce also.

And more, one ——, doctor of divinity,

present also, saies as much ; which no doubt
is sufficient satisfaction to all reasonable
men, that there was such a conspiracy, and
not fained.

And now we come to remember the Earl
of Essex ; the universal love of whose memory was but of such whom he formerly
caught by his affected popularity, or of
others, that followed his treasonable practises, which were grosse enough to be fore-
apprehended by every faithful subject,
especially, being prosecuted against the
person of that glorious sunne, his obliging
mistresse, whom a little before our pamphlet commemorates with much passion, till
now that he comes to treason ; a small fault
belike, and pardonable in Essex. For he
saith, that King James hated Sir Robert
Cecill ; it seems for but prosecuting,
amongst other councelours and peers, a
traytor's death. Intimating, no doubt, the
king's impatient desire to inherit these
crownes by any treason. But he spares no

Earle of
Essex his
treason.

Pamp. 10.

invectives against any of worth or honor that comes in his way.

Robert E. of Essex. This earle was eldest sonne to Walter Devoreux, (of a Norman family,) Viscount Hereford and Bowrchier, Lord Ferrers of Chartley; and by Queen Elizabeth created Earle of Essex and Ewe, anno 1572, and Knight of the Garter.

He was sent into Ireland Lord Marshall against the rebells; and, as if but sent of an errand, he presently falls sick, and dies at Dublin, 1576: His body brought over, and intomb'd at Carmarthen, in Wales.

This Robert succeeded his father's honours, and was looked upon in court by all with pity, through the sacrifice of his father; but by the queen with great affection, whome she advanced (his fortunes being lowe) with many gifts of grace and bounty; at his arraignement accounted to the Lord Treasurer Dorset to be 300,000 l. sterling, in pure gift for his only use, besides the fees of his offices, and the disposition of the treasure in his armies: Of all which he soon became a bold ingrosser both of fame and favour.

And first, in anno 1585, he receaves knighthood; in 1588, Knight of the Garter; in 1589 he had command in chief in an expedition into Portingal against Lisbone; in 1595, sworn councelour of state; 1596 he was sent with a navy to the isle Cadiz, in Spain, and presently after made Lord Marshall of England. In 1597 he commanded in another fleet, to the islands Sercera's; his contemporaries who stood in competition with him for fame, were, Sir Charles Blunt, afterwards Earle of Devonshire, and Generall Norris, his neer friends; and yet whom he envied, the last to his ruin; men of greater merit and truer value. And after the destruction of Norris, he takes upon him the expedition into Ireland, the place of exercise for the best of the militia.

Blunt, late E. of Dev.

And who durst oppose him? Though the queen had an eye of favour upon Blunt, often saying, that she presaged him the

3

man to end her cares in that kingdome.
And she was a true prophetesse, though
not in her time, but in her successor, King
James.

This Blunt was a gallant gentleman, and
learned, on whom she bestowed a jewell
for his behaviour at a tilting, which he
wore after, tackt with a scarlet riband, upon
his arme; and for no other cause Essex
must needs fight with him, and was runne
through the arme for his labour.[']

But Essex got imployments from them
all; offering the service evermore, at lesse
charge of men and money, then others his
competitors.

Deputy of Ireland and Generall. And over he goes, Deputy of Ireland,
and generall of all the forces there; with
commission strict enough to imbound his
popularity with the souldiery and his own
family, which followed him in troops, either
to devour or undo him.

No sooner landed, but ere he drew sword

['] See vol. I. p. 47, note.

on the enemy, he dubbs knighthood upon
seven gentlemen, volunteers; which honour
he had very lavishly bestowed at Cadiz, and
was therefore soundly chidden by the
queen.

And now restrained by his commission,
with much a-do, unlesse to men of known
merit, and those after battaile.

For this first act, the queene swore he
began his rant: Of which he had present
intelligence from his deerest friend and uncle, Sir Francis Knowls, a councelor of
state and controwler of her household, and
after Earl of Banbury; who spared not his
advise and councel at all times: And between them there passed intelligence with
every dispatch; whose letters and papers,
principall from Essex, and copies to him I
have seen; by which there appears, even
from the beginning of that imployment, a
very plaine and intentional resolution in
Essex to make himself master of his own
ambition, and by this way and meanes to
effect it; grounding all his discontents and

Sr Francis
Knowles
his cor-
respon-
dent.

dislikes, that the queens eare was open to
his enemies at court ; and therefore it behoved him to guard himself, which he resolved to do by help of his friends and fate ;
and, indeed, having fallen into remarkable
offences, together with the treaties with Tyrone the arch-rebell, without order from
England, and without acquainting his
councell of warre, with whose advise he was
limetted to act.

Treats
with Ty-
rone.

'Tis true he advanced against the enemy,
and soon accepts an invitation to a treaty,
accompanied with his councell of warre;
but comming to the brinck of a river, the
place assigned, he plunges his horse to the
middle stream alone, and there meets him
Tyrone on horseback, where their private
discourse gave sufficient caution to all that
looked on aloof-off, that Essex meant no
fair play for his mistresse. For which fact,
and no blow stroock in all this time, men
and money wasted, he was soundly blamed
by the councell at home, and no more letters from the queens own hand, which he
usually received afore.

In great choler, as to dispute or revenge, Returns home. and without leave from hence, he leaves his command to a lieutenant, and comes over with a hundred gentlemen, his best confidents; hastens to court, ere it was known to any but to his deer uncle, to whom he writes, " Dear uncle, receiving your last at my entring on ship-board, I return the accounts thereof at my landing; being resolved, with all speed, (and your silence,) to appear in the face of my enemies, not trusting afarre off to my own innocency, or to the queens favour, with whom they have got so much power," &c.

At sight of him, with amaze to the queen, she swore, God's death, my lord, what do you here? Your presence is most unwelcome without Tyrone's head in your portmantle. But he, falling more to a dispute then any excuse, she, in disdaine to be taught but what she pleased to do, bid him begone, his boots stunck.

And so was he presently commanded Is committed and censured. and committed to the Arch-bishop of Canterbury to Lambeth, where, not long after, he was convented before a committee of the councel, *ad correctionem,* not *ad destructionem.* The queen very gracious, hoping his offences might discerne favour, for according to his examinations then and the merit of his cause. I have seen his uncles papers, breviates, (who was one of his judges,) intended as his censure to condemnation, and so fitted for further tryall. But the day before they had other direction from the queen, saying, " He was young enough to mend and make amends for all.",

And so their censures shewed him his errors, and left him to her grace and mercy, only restraining him to his own house against Saint Clements, not without dayly letters from Knowles, with advice to be rid of his ranting followers, captaines, and swordmen of the town, flocking and incouraging him to a revenge on his enemies.

His rebellious designe.

It was not long that he could contain, saying, " He was engaged to go on ;" and

on a Sunday morning the councell sat,
(which was usuall, untill the late Arch-bishop Lawd, in honour of the morning sacrifice, altered that course to the afternoon,)
then the first flame brake out.

To him they sent their clerke of the councell, to know the reason from his lordship
of the meeting of so many weaponed men
at his house; but the messenger not returning, being kept prisoner, the chiefest councelours commanded by the queen came to
him; and no sooner entered Essex house,
but the gates were clapped too, all their
train kept out, the court-yard full of gal-
lants. Some cryed kill them, imprison
them, to the court, seise the queen, and
be our own carvers. Essex comes down
with all reverence, ushers them up, resolving to detain them prisoners, and pledges
for his successe.

Indeed, in this hurly burly of advice he
took the worst; for, leaving them in safety
with Sir Ferdinando Gorges, he, with the
Earle of Southampton in one boat, and

*Imprisons
the clerk
of the
councell,*

*and the
lords of
the coun-
cell.*

6

some others in other boats, took water at his garden staires, and landing neer the bridge, went on foot up the streets, with such stragling company as came in their way; to whom he protested, that the queen should have been murthered, and his and other good councellors lives in perill by enemies of the state, that forced a power from the queene to the imminent destruction of the kingdom. These speeches, with their swords drawne, took little effect with the people, who came running out of the churches, being sermon-time, without weapons or any offensable assistance, contrary to his expectation.

But on he goes to Sir Thomas Smith's, where he kept his shreevealty, neere Fan-church, his confiding friend, by whose countenance he hoped to worke with the multitude. He being absent at Paul's crosse sermon, Essex staid no longer then to shift his shirt, and so passed through Cheap-side. to Paul's west-end, where he found his first opposition by some forces got together by the Bishop of London and the trained band.

And after proclamation, that Essex and Southampton were traitors, and all those that followed their faction ; many dropping from the crowd, there was little defence by his party, though some were killed, and himselfe forsaken of the wisest. He retires back to Queenhithe, and so to Essex house by water; where, finding the birds flowen, the councellors released by their keeper, who, in hope of pardon, accompanied them to the queenes presence, discovering so much as he knew concerning his lord, who, finding himselfe too weake to withstand the force of a peece of cannon, mounted upon the church to batter his house, he and Southampton yeelded themselves prisoners to the Tower ; where, being arraigned and condemned, Southampton had repreeve, and after pardon ; but Essex, the reward of his merits, and executed in March, 1601, upon the inner hill in the Tower, to the regret of none either wise or honest; leaving behind him one only son, the last of his line.

Arraigned and executed.

Cecil.
Pamp. 10.William Cecill, illustrate from the family of Cecils, (who suffered persecution in the times of Henry Eighth, Edward Sixth, and Queen Mary,) he was knighted by Queen Elizabeth, so soone as she was settled in her crowne, then Secretary and Councellor of State, afterwards created Baron of Burligh, then made Lord Treasurer of England, and Knight of the Garter, and died Chancellor of the University of Cambridge, anno 1598, intombed at Westminster, leaving two sons : the elder, Thomas, was then Lord President of the North, and afterwards created Earle of Exeter by King James, and Privy Councellor of State. He died anno   , discreet and honourable, whom the world could never tax with any taint.

Sir Robert
Cecill.The other son, Robert, was the second, but a true inheriter of his fathers wisdome, and by him trained up to future perfections of a judicious statesman. After his knighthood, the first imployment from court, (for he was not at all bred out of it,) sent him

assistant with the Earle of Darby, embassadour to the French king. At his returne,
the queen took him second secretary with
Sir Fr. Walsingham ; after whose decease,
he continued principal, and so kept it to
his death, not relinquishing any preferment
for the addition of a greater ; a remarkable
note, which few men of the gowne can boast
of. His father lived to see him setled in
these preferments, and after Master of the
Wards and Liveries : these he held to the
queenes death, being in all her time used
amongst the men of weight, as having great
sufficiencies from his instruction who begat
him. Those offices here in public, with per-
petual correspondence by emissaries of his
own into Scotland, might no doubt make
him capable of reception with King James,
who was to be advised by him how to be
received here of his people. Without any
necessity then, to make use of Sir George
Hewmes or his initiation afterwards with
any juggling trickes, his merrits certainly Pamp. 12.
appeared to the king, who not onely not

diminished his former preferments, but often added to them even to the day of his death.

As first, Baron of Essenden, then Viscount Cranborne, after Earle of Salisbury, and Knight of the Garter; and lastly, Lord Treasurer of England.

He was a councellor of singular merit, a very great discoverer of the late queens enemies abroad, and of private assinations at home: For which she valued him, and the papists hated him, which they published by several manuscripts (which I have seen) and printed libels; and that most pestilent against his birth and honour, threatening to kill him, which himselfe answered wisely, learnedly, and religiously, extant in English and Latine, *Adversus Perduelles.*

Indeed it behoved the king to bestow upon him the waight of the treasurers staffe, the cofers then in some want, which the king was not likely soon to recover, but rather to increase in debt, having the addition of wife and children to boot. And being now come, with common opinion into the capacity, (by his additional crownes,) to reward his old servants, and to appear obliging unto new ones.

The world wondering at the worth of this great councellor, I know not upon what score our pamphleter should endeavour to scandal his memory.

Which he rancks into numbers of ill offices to his nation, as the burning of a whole cart-load of parliaments presidents, which no man can be so sottish as to beleeve that knowes the strict concerving of those records by sworne officers. *Pamp. 12.*

As for the baronets, it was the earnest suite of two hundred prime gentlemen of birth and estates to my knowledge, for I copied the list before ever it came to this lord. And as true it is, that this lord's reception thereto was in the same words which our pamphlet puts upon the king, that it would discontent the gentry, to which themselves replyed, " Nay, my lord, it will rather satisfie them in advance of *Baronets.*

dignity before others, who now come behind those meaner men, whom the king
was forced to knight for his own honour,
and some merits of theirs, having no other
reward or money to spare, and therein not
much to blame to oblige them that way.

Pamp. 13.

As for that supposed jugling which the
Duke of Bullion should discover, as it
was never known to wiser men, so we may
take it a devise of his, who in these, as in
other such like of his own, may truly merit
that character which he bestowes before
[on the good gentleman.]

Pamp. 9.

I desire pardon if I speake much and
truth in the memory of this noble lord, being somewhat concerned to speak my owne
knowledge.

I know that this Earle of Salesbury, de-
clining his health with continuall labour for
the good of this nation, both in the former
and in this his soveraign's service, and am
willing to give some light thereof to such
as are pleased to read these particulars, being an account of his concernments.

For first, he found the king's mannors and fairest possessions most unsurveyed and uncertain, rather by report then by measure, not more known then by ancient rents ; the estate granted rather by chance then upon knowledge. Salisbury his service to the state. Mannors, lands.

The custody-lands, (antiently termed crown-lands,) much charged upon the she-riffs, yearly discharged by annual pensions. A revenue which seemed decayed, by des-cent of times, and worne out of all remem-brance: these he evermore revived by com-missioners of asserts. Custody-lands.

The woods were more uncertain then the rest ; no man knew the copices, number of acres, growth, or value, nor of timber-trees, either number or worth. So as truly he might well find himself in a wood indeed : the trees wasted without controwle, because no record kept thereof ; these he caused to be numbred, marked, and valued, easily to be questioned when thereafter missing. Woods.

The copy-hold lands, where the arbitrary fines ceased by the discretion of the stew- Copy-holds.

ards, and did seldome yeeld the parsons part, and that also vanished in fees and charges. The state was then after like to raise of these natures the true values, and to receive equal benefit with the rest of the subjects, if the book had bin since observed, which he caused in print.

And for the copy-holders of inheritance, who by many records prove their fines certain, they did hereupon offer for their freedome 20, 30, 40, and 50 yeares purchase, where they could shew probable records without fine to free themselves. The wastes

Wastes and commons.

and commons were tender titles, full of murmering and commotion, which truly he never durst offer to inclose, nor to urge the tenants to become suitors themselves, with whom commissioners were to be appointed to compound for a part, and so he made a good president for the rest.

Casual fines.

The casual fines due to the king out of the private possessions, (as other lords have by their courts of leets, court barons, and such like,) and out of publique offences,

l

as the king was parent of the commonwealth ; unto whom belonged *et præmium
et pæna.* These being natures lèft for the
king's bounty, he commended them also
to commissioners for a better revenue to
be raised, being till his time utterly neglected and almost lost.

As for the extended lands, where the officers became indebted to the crown, and
made it an art to have their lands extended at easy rates, he caused the most of
these to be surveyed, commended the im-
provement to commissioners, and commanded the tenants to appear before them.

The improvements of the customes he
advanced from 86,000*l.* to 120,000*l.*, and
from that to 125,000*l.* by the year.

He bargained for the river-water to be
brought to London, and so to the driest
parts, which brought a great yearly value.

*River wa-
ter.*

He alwaies incouraged all industry of
manufactures : such inventions as the statutes admit and countenance, as home-ma-
king of allome, salt by the sunne, busses

*Manufac-
tures.*

for fishing, salt upon salt, by new fires and inventions, copper and coperas of iron, and of steele, that the subjects at home might be set on work, and the small treasure of the nation kept within.

Intelligence.

It concerned him as secretary to have intelligence from all parts of the world, and correspondence with all embassadours and forreigne states, not to be neglected at any hand, which he did at his own cost. So did all parts grow confident of such a councelour; and so he kept rules with the United Provinces, whose friendships he would say much concerned this state.

Ireland improved.

I may not forget his Christian care for poor Ireland; plantations there, and transplantations of the natives, to advance the customes there, and to abate the charges of the garrisons; and he did endeavour, and in manner did effect, an universall course of law and justice in the most barbarous and remote parts of that nation.

Wards and liveries.

And now concerning the court of wards and liveries. By constitution of this state

all the lands of this nation are holden by
two tenures, by soccage, or by knights service, by the plough to feed us, or by the
sword to defend us ; and who so died leaving an heir within age, unable to do this
service, his heir and lands fell both to the
protection of the soveraign ; and this in
antient time was promiscuously carryed in
the court of Chancery until the middle
time of Henry the Eighth, when this court
of wards was first erected.   Since which
time, the masters thereof, by favour of the
soveraign, did accustome (as a bounty of
state) to grant unto noble men, the king's
servants, and their owne followers, both the
marriage of the body and the lease of the
lands for a third peny of their true worth.

But in all humility, his lordship finding
the estate in a retrograde consumption, did
with all obedience present his patent at the
kings feet, and so the whole benefit became
the profit of the crown.

Thus he wrought in the mine of the state-
affaires, and wasted his carkasse with desire

to have done better service in these his offices of Treasurer, Secretary, and Master of
the Wards ; and yet these were sufficient
just and true merits, without friends, wit,
or wealth, to raise him so much in his master's esteem ; or without ill offices done by
him to this nation, as our pamphlet will
make us believe in many absurd particulars.

Pamp. ii.
1½.

And truly his studious labours in the
state brought him the sooner to sicknesse,
a consumption of the lungs, wherein he
wasted some years : and at last, by advise for cure at the Bath, he took leave of
the king, who came to visit him at Salisbury house, and, with tears at his parting,
protested to the lords attending, his great
losse of the wisest councelour and best servant that any prince in Christendome could
paralel : of whom one saies,

*Tu pater et patriæ princeps, prudentia cu-
jus extulit immensum reges, populosque Bri-
tannos.*

His time at the Bath was short, being

spent to extremity ere he came thither, and returning back by the way, he was taken out of his litter, and put himself in his coach, and died afterwards at St Margarets, in the house of that worthy gentleman Mr Daniel, in May 1612. My Lord Viscount Cramborne, now Earle of Salisbury, and the Lord Clifford, Sir Robert Manton, and many more gentlemen of quality then pre-sent whom I saw there. He was imbalmed, and after intombed at his princely mannor of Hartfield; a fairer corps then any brasen face that belies his disease. His death was extreame sadness to the king and to all his friends, and others of worth and honour. For in spite of the pamphleter, he will be valued, as he does confesse,

Pamp. 14.

Pamp. 14.

Never came a better.

The next we meet with is Henry, Earle of Northampton.

Henry Howard, Earle of Northampton.

The antient and illustrious family of the Howards were here more eminent then any

other that ushered the king to his additionall crownes.

This Henry Howard was brother unto
Thomas, Duke of Norfolke, who suffered
for his attempt of marriage with the Queen
of Scots whilst she was prisoner here in
England, which might be some motive to
induce the king to consider the advance of
that family, though they were indued with
large possessions from their ancestors.

The duke left two sons, Philip, Earl of
Arundell, and Thomas Howard, Earl of
Suffolk, afterwards Lord Treasurer.

Pamp. 15.   Henry Howard their uncle was more
wedded to his book then to the bed, for he
died a bacheler, and so had the lesse occasion to advance his fortune by court-flat-
tery or state-imployment; nor indeed was
he ever any suitor for either.

He was accounted both wise and learned, and therefore out of the kings great affection to letters, especially when they are
met in a noble person, he was advanced

in his creation of Baron of Marnhill and, *North* Earle of <u>Southampton</u>, then Privy Councelor, Lord Privy Seale, and Lord Warden of the Cinque. Ports, and Knight of the Garter. He had very plentifull for his single life, and to spare for his friends.

In his expence not over frugal, maintaining his port, the most remarkable (like the antient noble man) in his family and dependants, of any other lord then or since his time. He assisted his nephew the Earl of Suffolk, by his designing and large contribution to that excellent fabrick Awdley-end. He built the noble structure at Charing-Crosse, from the ground Northampton house, and presented it a new-years gift to the Lord Walden, Suffolkes eldest sonne, and now called Suffolk House; and yet left his other nephew the Earl of Arundell the rest of his estate, so to appear to the world his equal distribution to such even kindred. He was religious, and gave good testimony thereof in his life, built that handsome convent at Greenwich, and in-

dued it with revenue for ever, for maintenance of decaied gentlemen a sufficient number, and for women also considerable. He
died in anno 1613, full of years and honour-
Pamp. 16. able fame, though our pamphleter will not
know so much, and yet no doubt must
needs be intimate with his person; for he
tells us his thoughts, that he had assuredly
promised to himself the treasurers staff,
although we can produce this lords letters
and other testimonies, imploying all his
owne and his friends interest for that preferment upon his nephew Suffolke, and ex-
cusing himself of the burthen and weight
of that office, by his known infirmity of
stone, of the which he died.

**James
Hay, Earle
of Carlile.
Pamp. 18.**   Indeed it is no matter upon what score
that the king gave his affection to this favorite James Hay.

The Scots were never very eminent with
neighbour princes, what credit they had
came by the French to keep ballance with
England and them. The beginning might
then be hoped, when their union with these

crownes should afford the meanes to set them forth.

And it was prudentiall in the king to pick out one of his own to splendour that nation in our way of peace and courtship, especially when all was done at the master's cost. For Hay was poor, unlesse what he got by his first match with the Lord Dennis heir, for by his last he had nothing, the great spirit of Pearcy, Earle of Northumberland, disdaining the marriage, and refused to afford a groat to a beggerly Scot, as he called him.[*]

And now this lord (for so was he soon made Lord Hay, then Viscount Doncaster, and Earl of Carlile) did most vainly prodigallize what he often begged; and in truth he had it granted for no other purpose to put down the English courtier at that vanity; and which, both abroad and at home, was often paid for by the king's privy purse. As that feast at Essex house, and many his

His vaine expences.

Pamp. 19.

[*] See vol. i. p. 214, note.

masquerades at court, (for he medled not
with the tilt-staff, as being no sword-man,)
but in the other and such like, he never
escaped to act one part.

And these expences famed him with little credit, who ere he appears to our pamph-

Pamp. 21. leters judgement, who cries up the bounty
of his mind beyond the moon at least, who,
in truth, was never good to man or beast.

His em-
bassies to
Germany. His embassies were not so weighty when
he posted so long through Germany to find
out the emperor, who afforded him the wild-
goose-chase, as knowing his errand, before
he came at him ; which, in truth, was purposely so designed by the king, only to
spend time, and to amuse mens expecta-
tions (who were wild after a warre) to beget a treaty concerning the lost palatine.
The effects whereof (as the king wisely pro-
phesyed) would produce distemper through
all Christendome, if not destructive to his
son-in-law.

France. He went into France extraordinary; it
was to treate with that king in favour of

the Hugenots, the religion (as they account
it) being risen to a civill warre by management of the Duke d'Róhan, Count Sobeeze,
and others, to a dangerous consequence in
severall places almost over France ; which
to allay, that king had raised a great army,
resolving, with countenance of his own person, to give end thereto. But King James
being invited by several troublesome commissioners, their agents, to implore for their
cause, and take upon him their protection,
which he (a wise prince in that) declined ;
yet not to neglect them, and the rather to
satisfy some of our people of the like gang,
medled thus farre to mediate by embassy
of Hay, who, as in that of Germany, did
nothing with effect, but went up to Monta-
ban, and so came home again.

'Tis true he went into Spain with a mes-   Spaine.
sage to our prince, with no more matter
then others that came after to waite on him
in that courtship ; for there, as in other
kingdomes, his Scots vanity must also be
blazoned.

And for his last embassy in France about
our match with that daughter and our queen,
he came not into commission till the treaty
was confirmed and the marriage concluded,
by embassy only of the Earle of Holland,
and Carlile put in afterwards to dance out
the measures; his name being used in the
proxie for that ceremony, and at this time
the Earl of Holland had some colour for
his expence which he lavished without reason to the weakening of his unsettled fortunes, being forced to follow the other then
in all his fashions. And which infection,
by after-custome, became his disease also,
and almost, if not over-mastering, yet over-
shadowing his natural eminent parts, with
which his inside was habited, and perspicuous to such as knew him.

But I am not delighted to urge out this
story of the Earle of Carlile, as not willing
to speak ill of any, unlike our pamphlet
that spares none but him; for I should
know that vertue and vice are inherent in
man, and as it becomes us to tell truth

when we speak their vertue, yet with modesty and compassion to discover their vices, either being examples for the future, that to imitate, this to shun. And I cannot but with compunction remind, that the monstrous excesse of the belly and the back, by his first president, became then the mode of those times for great persons (the most part) to follow, and for the common people to this hour to practise.*

* There are several passages of Wilson's History which serve to illustrate the extravagant expence of the Earl of Carlisle in his embassies.

"But to returne to the Lord Hayes. Thus accouter'd and accomplish'd he went into France; and a day for audience being prefixed, all the argument and dispute betwixt him and his train, (which took up some time,) was, how they should go to the court. Coaches, like curtains, would eclipse their splendor; riding on horseback in boots would make them look like travellers, not courtiers; and not having all footcloths, it would be an unsuitable mixture: Those that brought rich trappings for their horses were willing to have them seen; so it was concluded for the footcloth, and those that have none (to their bitter cost) must furnish themselves. This preparation begot expectation; and that fill'd all the windows, balconies, and streets of Paris, as they passed, with a multitude of spectators. Six trumpeters and two marshals (in tawny velvet liveries, com-

And truly a wise and a good man ought
justly to have hated his condition in this

pleatly suited, laced all over with gold, richly and closely laid) led the way; the ambassador followed with a
great train of pages and footmen in the same rich livery encircling his horse, and the rest of his retinue
according to their qualities and degrees, in as much
bravery as they could devise or procure, follow'd in
couples, to the wonderment of the beholders. And some
said (how truly I cannot assert) the ambassadors horse
was shod with silver shoes, lightly tack'd on; and when
he came to a place where persons or beauties of eminency were, his very horse prancing and curveting in
humble reverence, flung his shoes away, which the
greedy understanders scrambled for; and he was contented to be gazed on and admired, till a farrier, or rather an argentier, in one of his rich liveries, among his
train of footmen, out of a tawny velvet bag took others,
and tack'd them on, which lasted till he came to the
next troop of grandees: And thus, with much ado, he
reached the Louvre."—WILSON, *apud*, Kennet, ii. 704.

Another embassy of the same nobleman upon the
hopeless errand of interceding for restoration of the
palatinate, was even more expensive than that to France,
as well as more fruitless.

" The king was modest, and almost ashamed to tell
the parliament how much money the Viscount Doncaster's journey cost; therefore he minces it into a small
proportion. But this we know, when he landed at Rotterdam, the first night and morning before he went to
the Hague, his expences of those two meales, in the inn
where he lay, came to above a thousand gilders, which

without suspition of malice or envy, as it is Pamp. 21.
said Northampton did, who yet, as may be

is a hundred pound sterling. And the innkeeper at the
Peacock at Dort (hoping he would make that his way
into Germany) made great provisions for him upon no
other order but a bare fancy; and the ambassador taking his way by Utrecht, the innkeeper of Dort follow'd
him, complaining that he was much prejudiced by his
baulking that town : for hearing of a great ambassador's
coming, and what he had expended at Rotterdam, I
made (saith he) preparations suitable, and now they
will lye on my hands. Which coming to Doncaster's
ear, he commanded his steward to give him thirty
pounds sterling, and never tasted of his cup. And we
have been assured by some of his train, that his very
carriages could not cost so little as threescore pounds
a-day; for he had with him a great many noblemens
sons, and other personages of quality, that the Germans
might admire the glory of the English, as well as the
French did in the last ambassage. And he was out so
long following the emperor in his progresses from city
to camp, and from camp to city, a poor humble solici-
tor, if not petitioner, that his expence could not amount
to less than fifty or threescore thousand pounds."—
Ibid, p. 730. Yet Wilson adds, that, setting aside these
vanities of grandeur, the Earl of Carlisle was a gentleman every way accomplished, unaffectedly courteous,
liberal, and insinuating. So that he was in every respect fit for the high charges which he supported with
such cost,

remembered, took leave of this life ere Hay was setled on horsback.

And that other mark of reproach also may without partiallity be taken off the score from that noble Northampton, who, on my conscience, (for I knew him well,) disdained the guilt in that frivolous story of Sir Robert Mansell. Nor is it material to credit the rest of that rant in his vice-admirall voyage.

Second
remarke.
Pamp. 30. The second remark of the preface falls upon the treason of Sir Walter Ralegh, which the pamphlet calls an arrant trick of state, and Cecil the *invenire facias* thereof.

Sir Walter
Ralegh. Sir Walter Ralegh was a gentleman of good alliance in the west of England, and very well descended. He began his improvements by the university and inns of court; the latter was alwaies the place of esteem with the queen, " Which", she said, " fitted youth for the future;" but he staid not there. And as his fate would have him of the sword first, so his destinie drew him on to have a mixt reputation with the gown; for he was often called to councell, but never sworn. He was twice in expeditions of land-service into Ireland under Generall Norris and Grey, a volunteer in either, as also in the Low Countries, and a voyage at sea, ere he was known at court.

And such waies as these were his introductions (the best hopes of his rising): some naturall parts he had, a good wit and judgement; but his best weapon was his tongue, which gave him repute to be learned then; but after he improved to a great value, in his future troubles; the best school to a wise man.

He had a quarrel with Grey in Ireland, which being referred to a councell of warre, it had like to cost him his life; but by reference came afterwards to repetition at home before the lords. Grey had the better cause, but Ralegh the advantage in pleading, who so took them, especially Lester, that the queen was told the tale, and

somewhat more of him. And no sooner he
came to be known to her, but she took him
to grace. In whom (as in other of the like
form) their alwaies meet oposites, enemies
of greater ranck, and they kept'him under,
sometimes in, sometimes out, which when
it fell out to be so, he would wisely decline
himselfe out of the court-rode: And then
you found him not but by fame; in voyages
to the West Indies, Guiana, New Plantations, Virginia, or in some expeditions
against the Spaniard; against whom, his
and other the like successe, of Drake, Can-
dish, Forlisher, Hawkins, with other island-
voyages, neer home, confirm'd Ralegh a
grand opposer of the generall peace which
King James brought in with him, and that
brought Ralegh to his ruin.

And for all these his good parts, he rose
to no more then Governor of Jersey, Lord
Warden of the Stanneries in the West, and
Captain of the Guard to the queen's person;
which last place brought him to esteem in
the court, but not in the state at all.

Yet busie he had been heretofore to speak his mind of the generall affaires; and therein he pleased his late mistresse; for then his inclination went with the humour of those times of war, but nów his councell came out of season; for at the entrance of the king, he was presented by Ralegh with a manuscript of his own, against the peace with Spain. It was alwaies his table-talk, to beget the more esteem, which took accordingly; and the way to make him the contrary, was the work of the Spanish faction; either to buy him out of that humour, or to abuse him into a worse condition, which was thus effected.

And indeed to mould this treason there was a medly of divers conditions; but the contrivers were two priests, Watson and Clarke, and Count Arembergh, Embassedor Extraordinary for the Arch-Duke, who brought in the Lord Cobham; and he his brother, George Brooke; and he, Parham; and these, the Lord Grey of Wilton. Then came in Sir Walter Ralegh, the wisest of

His treason,

12

them all, who dallied like the flie with the flame, till it consumed him. Willing he was (it seemes) to know it, and thought by his wit to over-reach the confederates, whom he knew well enough, though none but Cobham, for a good while, dealt with him; and with him Ralegh plaid fast and loose till himselfe was caught in the gin.

There was one Mathew de Lawrencie here at London, a merchant of Antwerpe, with whom Cobham held intelligence for many years before, and, for some reasons of state, connived at by the late queen and her councel. This man was the property whom Arenbergh made use of to Cobham, who now was much discontented.

These three made the first step to the contrivement; and it hath bin my jealousie that Lawrency betrayed it to this state; for I never could be assured how it was discovered, though I have bin often present with Sir Walter, in his imprisonment, when he privately discoursed hereof.

But being ripe, they were severally examined and restrained; first to their owne homes, not without watchful eyes on either of them, then to imprisonment, and, lastly, to their tryals at Winchester, whither the terme removed, out of this evermore pestilentiall city.

And on the 17 November, 1602, the day of arraignment for Ralegh, and the jury called to the bar; against whose persons he did not except, nor could, for they were the most able, sufficient, in Middlesex, (where the fact had its scene.) His arraignment.

I shall name them: Sir Ralphe Conisby, Sir Thomas Fowler, Sir Edward Peacock, Sir William Roe, Knights; Henry Godwin, Robert Wood, Thomas Walker, Thomas Whitley, Thomas Highgate, Robert Kempton, John Chalke, and Robert Bromley, Esquires.

The indictment was managed by the king's atturney, Sir Edward Cook, Serjeant Heal, and Serjeant Philips, and drawne from the 9th Jun. 1603. The accusation was double, against the king and the state.

The personal had two parts, first against his life.

Secondly, to disable his title to this crowne.

To the first was read Brookes confession, that his brother Cobham used these speeches, That it would never be well till the king and his cubs were taken away, and said, that he thought it proceeded from Ralegh. .

To this Ralegh answered, that Brookes was his enemy. It was replyed, but Cobham was ever your friend ; and it would seeme a strange malice in Brooks to ruin his brother to undo you.

To the second part there was produced a booke, (which I have read,) a defence of the Queens proceedings against Mary Queen of Scots, which Cobham confessed Ralegh had delivered to him, and he to Brookes, and Brookes to Gray, upon Cobhams discontent.

Ralegh acknowledged that it contained matter of scandal to the kings title ; and that he had leave of Sir Robert Cecill, after his fathers death, to search his study for cosmographicall manuscripts of the West Indies, and so lighted on this book.

Sir Robert Cecill, then present upon the bench, acknowledged this leafe; and said, He would then as really have trusted him as any man; though since, for some infirmities of Sir Walter, the bonds of affection were crackt; and yet, reserving his duty to the king, which may not be dispensed withall in this his masters service, he swore by God he loved him, and had a great conflict in himself, that so compleat a member was fallen from this state.

Sir Robert Cecils word.

And this passage needs no soothing, to excuse Cecill, either for the father or the son, for I have heard Sir Robert Cecill, when he was Salisbury, say publickly at his own table, that he had intercepted and kept all the considerable libells against the late queen and this king. But though justifiable in them, as councelours of state, yet it was a crime in Ralegh, who never was any. And this book, as I remember, was of one Bragg, or Stagg, a Jesuite ; but Sir Walter excused it, that there was nothing acted thereby to the kings prejudice, for the book was burnt.

But to insist hereupon, Cobham had confessed, that Ralegh had agreed that Cobham should treate with Aremburgh for 600 thousand crownes, to the intent to advance the title of the Lady Arabella to this crown. That Cobham, under pretence of travelling, should prosecute this designe in the Lowe-Countries, France, and Spaine, and to carry three letters from her to the Arch-Duke, Duke of Savoy, and to the King of Spaine, and to promise toleration of religion, and her marriage to be disposed of by them. That at his returne he should meete Ralegh at Jersey, the place of his command, and there agree to dispose the money to discontents ; and Ralegh should have seven thousand crownes from Arenberge for himselfe.

And further confessed, that Ralegh had instigated him to all these treasons.

And that Ralegh should say, that he thought the best way to trouble England, was to cause division in Scotland.

To this, onely of Scotland, he answered and confessed the words, and that he had so thought these twenty years. It seems by the sequell since he was not mistaken.

Lawrencie confessed that he and Cobham and Ralegh being together, he delivered a letter to Cobham from Arembergh; and presently Ralegh went with Cobham in private to conferre thereof.

To all these confessions Ralegh craved that Cobham might appeare, to accuse him face to face.

I may not omit one passage acted heretofore, which comes in here properly to be considered. When the confederates had suffered under some examinations, and were restrained to their several houses, and Ralegh knew well that Lawrency was then suspected, but not examined, then did Ralegh discover, in a letter to Sir Robert Cecil, where Cobham was with Lawrency,

and that then was the time to apprehend
Lawrency, and so to intercept their intelligence ere. matters were ripe.

What Ralegh's design was herein I must
confesse my conceipt is very blunt; but
this use was made of it to Raleghs ruine;
for after that Cobham had denied much of
the former stuffe upon his first examinations, this letter was shewed him, under
Ralegh's hand, and upon mature and often
deliberation, to be assured that it was his
hand, then Cobham, in an extasie, calling
Ralegh villain, traitor, delivered his positive
accusation of Ralegh as aforesaid; and
added, that Ralegh, after his first examinations before the lords, had writ to Cobham,
that although he had bin examined of many
things, yet that he had cleered Cobham of
all, when (as the lords protested) he had not
at all been examined concerning Cobham.
And thereby this was inferred (by the councell) to confirm Cobham to deny all when
he should be examined: Sir Walter said,
that Cobham had not signed his accusa-

tion, and that he was at the worst but *singularis testis.* To which my Lord Chief Justice gave it for law, that it was not necessary to signe, nor to have more then one witnesse. After much pleading herein, and Ralegh alledging law and scripture for not admitting a single witnesse to condemn one, yet the court was satisfyed therein, by the judges, to the contrary.

Ralegh said, then prove it by one witnesse face to face, and I will confesse my self guilty: but the judges were of opinion that it was not to be permitted by law: yet Ralegh insisted hereupon, with many stories, which took up much time: then being asked, if he would be concluded thereby if Cobham would now justify his accusation under his hand? To this it may be observed, that Ralegh made no answer at all, but consented that the jury should go together.

Then was produced Cobham's letter to the lords, writ but the day before, in effect thus:

That Sir Walter had writ a letter to him wrapt in an apple, and cast in at his window ten daies since, in the Tower, to intreat him for God's sake to write to him, under his own hand, that he had wronged him in his accusations, and advised him to be constant in denialls, rather then to appeale to the king. And now (writes Cobham) it is no time to dissemble, and therefore protested before God and his angells, that all and every part of his accusation of Sir Walter Ralegh was substantially true: and added, that Ralegh had dealt with him, since the king's coming, to procure him a pension from Spain, for intelligence, &c.

Then Ralegh, rayling against Cobham, confessed this letter was in an apple, to which Cobham returned an answer, which Ralegh produced, and desired that it might be read: but the atturney opposed Sir Robert Cecil's consent thereto: to whom Cecil replied; Sir, you are more peremptory then honest; come you hither to direct us? and so read it. Which in effect was a confes-

sion that he had wronged Sir Walter, and
that he was innocent. This bore date ten
days before. And here Ralegh confessed,
that Cobham had offered to him a pension
from Spain, to the effect before confessed,
and that he had concealed it, as loth to
ruine Cobham.

Then the jury went out, and returned in
halfe an houre, with their verdict, Guilty.
So was sentence, as in case of treason. And
he was returned to the Tower of London,
and there lay upon reprieve twelve yeares,
and three years after was executed, in October, 1618.

And because this second remarke in the
pamphleter and this prefacer stickes in their
stomacks, with which they indeavour to
choke the readers, I have therefore bin the
more prolix, that thereby the whole world
may judge, with the jury, of his guilt or
innocency.

*Observa-
tions upon
this tryall.*

Pamp. 35.

Ralegh's rise of preferment was occasioned upon a contest with the Lord Grey, in
the queenes time, which they were to plead

face to face, where indeed, but not in truth, Sir Walter had the better by the tongue, telling his tale to advantage, which tooke the queene, who tooke him from that instant into favour, as before remembered. Belike he expected the same providence at this time, when so oft he desired to plead
Pamp. 35. face to face, with Cobham.

How could Wade, the lieutenant of the Tower (as is surmized) tamper with Cobham, to write his name to a blanck, to which Wade framed the accusation against Ralegh; when it appears Cobham never signed at all to his examinations; which, therefore, was so much insisted upon at his tryall, for his advantage.

But in truth, besides the confession of Cobham, the fatal evidence was Cobham's own voluntary last letter of accusation, or confession over night, writ every whit with his own hand.

The king commanded (as the court was assured at the triall) that upon any examination, there should none be rackt, which made Captaine Kemish (who was the instrument of messages and letters betweene Ralegh and Cobham) often to protest, in my hearing, that in truth he was threatened with the rack, which was shewed to him, but had he tasted thereof, he said, that he should have bin inforced to tell an odd tale, meaning of discovery.

Sir Walter was admitted a chair, pen, inck, and paper for his memory ; and truly he rather tryed the court and jury with impertinences.

And thus was Sir Walter Ralegh reprieved to the Tower, and many years of imprisonment in that liberty, till his future merits and fame of learning begat many to pitty his sufferings ; so that at last, by meanes of the French embassadour, with others of our own lords, he had freedome to repair for his health to his house at Saint James ; and after a yeare or two, he procured a commission to make a vóyage to Gueana, in the West Indies, for the return of gold ore or mine ; but was expressly limited

Repreeved.

not to trench upon the Spaniard to the breach of peace.

His landing was at St Thomas, a town of the Spaniards, upon the opening of the great river Orenoque, in America, where he killed many of them, and there lost his eldest son Walter under the walls. Then sends he Captain Kemish, his old servant, (upon whose confidence it appears this voyage was resolved) up this river, to the foot of a mountain, where heretofore, and also during Ralegh's imprisonment, he had been sent, and returned with wonderfull remarks of a rich mine, or rather Madre-del-Ore; but now comes from thence, and all the account came to no more, but that the mountain was fled away, he could not find it.

Upon this the whole fleet, four or five saile, mutiny, forces him home againe as a prisoner; in the return, Kemish kills himself in his own cabin, and so no tales could be told.

Ralegh's ships were first cast upon the

south of Ireland; then they land in the west of England, where warrants were ready to apprehend him prisoner to the Tower. In the west, he is discovered to deal with a French master of a ship to steal away into France. Then in his journey to London, he combines with a French mounte-banck, who assisted him with ingredients, (which he desired,) that would, without danger of life, bring him to breake forth into blanes, purposely done by this meanes to get longer time to work opportunities to save his life, which he knew he had so deeply forfeited.

Then being delivered into the hands of Sir John Stukely, Lieutenant of the Tower, he deales with him for a sum of money, part in hand being paid, to join with him in escape both of them into France; Stuke-ly yields to all, and accompanies him by water in the way to Gravesend, where (by designe of Stukelie's treachery in that, and so it prospered with him, being hanged af-terwards for clipping of gold) they were

seized and brought back to the Tower.
From whence, very speedily, Ralegh was
commanded to the King's-Bench bar, at
Westminster, before the Lord Chief Justice
Montegue, where the records of his former
sentence only were read, and he demanded
why execution should not be done?

Sir Walter acknowledged that sentence,
and the king's mercy for his life thus long;
and that he hoped, seeing he had bin imployed by commission, with power of life
and death over the king's liege people, it
did make void that former sentence.

He was told to the contrary, and that his
time of execution was the next morning;
and so the Sheriff of Middlesex took him
into custody to the Gate-house, and to execution the next day, in the old Palace-yard,
at Westminster; where he had the favor of
the ax, " Which," he said, (smilingly touching it,) " was a sharp medicine, but a true
physitian to cure all diseases;" and so it
proved to him at this very time in his ague
fit.

At his death, himselfe endeavoured to cleere some points, which it seemes our pamphleter knew not of, otherwise he would have done it for him.

To have had often plots with France, which he denied, but confessed that he had bin solicited thence, and endeavoured to escape thither at twice. That the French agent came oft to him with commission from that king to him; but he returned the commission.

That he should speake disloyally of the king: His accuser, he said, was a base runagate Frenchman, and perfideous, whom he trusted, being sworne to secrecie, which he betrayed; much he said in these particulars, which he did not deny, but traversed.

So then there were other businesse of charge, to which he was liable to a new tryall; but the prudence of the king would not hazard further proceedings, having a sufficient upon the old score. And now for that additional tale of the pamphleter concerning Sir Walter's recovery of Queen

Pamp. 38.

Anne, for which he begged the boone, viz.
for the examination of the Lord Cobham
by four earles and two councelors.

I never heard nor read thereof before,
nor can beleeve it ; for this I know, by severall relations of those great ladies of her
bedchamber, and of her chirurgians and
physitians now living, that she was never
cured of her disease, but by death, that
ends all maladies.

It followes in the pamphlet, that after
he hath ranted his stories of Mansell and
Monson, and of the peace, ratifyed and
sworne, he makes Cecill the chief ringleader
of the king by the nose.

But to say truth, the king was alwaies
brought up to his ease, though the fore-
part of his raigne in Scotland proved troublesome enough to his councell ; and therefore now he was to follow his affaires in
peace, and his own inclination in a sport-
full life. The rather, he being much subject to unwildines or weakness in his limbs,
and which, because of his extream disaffec-

tion to physick, he was advised to the best
aire, most agreeable to the nature of Scotland, fresh, and bleak ; and for that end he
chose Roystan and Newmarket.

Without that scandalous intimation of
leaving his queen, without any love or liking.

We are forced to fall upon one Lake, Sir Tho.
whom we find to be that learned gentle- Pamp. 54.
man Sir Thomas Lake, apted in his youth
with rudiments of the book, to attend Sir
Francis Walsingham (that subtile Secretary
of State to Queen Elizabeth) as amanuensis
to him ; and after good experience of his
desarts, he was recommended to the queen,
and read to her French and Latine. In
which tongues, she would say, that he sur-
passed her secretaries, and was so imployed
to her death ; for he was reading to her
when the Countesse of Warwick told him
that the queen was departed.

But not long before, she received him merit
Clarke of her Signet ; and he was chosen
by this state in that place to attend the

king from Barwick. And so sufficient he
was, that the king made use of his present
service in some French affaires after he
came into England, which indeed Secretary Cecil had reason to resent, as too much
trenching on his office ; and therefore craved leave of the king that he might not attend beyond his moneth to prejudice the
other clerks, which was excused, and he
kept still at court.

These sufficiencies of his enabled him in
those times of gaining, with much repute
and direct honesty, to purchase large possessions.

as secre-
tary.

After Cecils death, the place of Secretary
was joyned in two principals; and not long
after he was one of them, and so continued
with honourable esteem of all men, until
that malice and revenge, two violent passions, over-ruling the weaker sexe concerning his wife and daughter, involved him into their quarrel, the chiefe and only cause
of his ruine. He had by his wife sons and
daughters; his eldest married unto the Lord

His ingage-
ment with
his wife
and daugh-
ter

Baron Rosse, (in right of a grand-mother,)
the son of Thomas, Earle of Exeter, by a
former venter; and upon the credit of Sir
Thomas Lake, he was sent Embassadour
Extraordinary into Spaine, in a very gallant equipage, with some hopes of his own
to continue leiger, to save charges of trans-
mitting any other.

In his absence, there fell out an extreame
deadly fewd (tis no matter for what) be- against the Countesse of Exeter.
tweene the Lady Lake and the Countesse
of Exeter. A youthful widow she had bin
and virtuous, and so became bedfellow to
this aged, gowty, diseased, but noble earle;
and that preferment had made her subject
to envy and malice.

Home comes the Lord Rosse from his
embassy, when being fallen into some neglect of his wife and his kindred, I conceive
upon refusal of an increase of allowance to
her settlement of joynture, which was promised to be compleated at his returne.

Not long he staies in England, but away
he gets into Italy, turnes a professed Ro-

mane catholick, being cousened into that religion by his publick confident, Gonda-more.

The accusation.

In this his last absence, (never to returne,) the mother and daughter accuse the countesse of former incontinencie with the Lord Rosse whilst he was here, and that therefore, upon his wives discovery, he was fled from hence, and from her marriage-bed, with other devised calumnies, by several designes and contrivements, to have poison-ed the mother and daughter.

This quarrel was soone blazoned at court to the king's eare, who, as privately as could be, singly examines each party. The countesse, with teares and imprecations, professeth her innocency, which, to oppose, the mother Lake and her daughter counterfeit her hand to a whole sheet of paper; wherein they make the countesse, with much contrition, to acknowledge her selfe guilty, craves pardon for attempting to poison them, and desires friendship with them all.

The king gets sight of this, as in favour
to them, and demands the place, time, and
occasion when this should be writ. They
tell him, that all the parties met in a visit at
Wimbleton, (the house of the Lord of Exeter,) where, in dispute of their differences,
she confesses her guilt of attempting their
poison; and being desirous of absolution
and friendship, (being required thereto,)
consents to set down all circumstances
therein, under her own hand, which presently she writ at the window, in the upper
end of the great chamber, at Wimbleton,
in presence of the mother and daughter,
the Lord Rosse, and one Diego, a Spaniard,
his confiding servant. But now they being
gone and at Rome, the king forthwith sends
Mr Dendy, (one of his serjeants at armes,
sometime a domestick of the Earl of Ex-
eters, an honest and worthy gentleman,) post
to Rome, who speedily returnes with Rosse
and Diego's hand, and other testimonialls,
confirming, that all the said accusation and
confession, suspitions, and papers, concern-

ing the countesse, were notorious, false, and
scandalous, and confirmes it by receiving
the hoast, in assurance of her honour and
his innocency. The king well satisfyed,
sends to the countesse, friends, and trus-
ties, for her jointure and estate ; who, comparing many of her letters with this writing,
do conclude it counterfeit.

Then he tells the mother and daughter,
that this writing being denied by her, and
their testimonies being parties, would not
prevaile with any belief ; but any other additionall witnesse would give it sufficient
credit. To which they assure him, that one
Sarah Swarton, their chamberesse, stood
behind the hanging, at the entrance of the
room, and heard the countesse read over
what she had writ ; and her also they procure to swear unto this before the king. :

To make further tryal, the king, in a
hunting journy, at New Park, neer Wimbleton, gallops thither, viewes the room ;
observing the great distance of the window
from the lower end of the room, and pla-

cing himself behind the hanging, and so other lords in turn, they could not hear one speak aloud from the window.

Then the house-keeper was called, who protested those hangings had constantly furnisht that room for thirty years, which the king observed to be two foot short of the ground, and might discover the woman if hidden behind them. I may present also the king saying, " Oaths cannot confound my sight."

Besides all this, the mother and daughter counterfeit another writing, a confession of one Luke Hutton, acknowledging for 40*l.* annuity, the countesse hired him to poison them; which man, with wonderful providence, was found out privately, and denies it to the king.

And thus prepared, the king sends for Sir Thomas Lake, whom, in truth, he very much valued; tells him the danger to imbark himself in this quarrel, advising him to leave them to the law, being now ready for the Star-Chamber. He humbly thank-

ed his majestie, but could not refuse to be
a father and a husband, and so puts his
name with theirs in a crosse bill, which at
the hearing, took up five several daies, the
king sitting in judgement. But the former
comes to
hearing
in Star-
Chamber, testimonies, and some private confessions
of the Lady Rosse and Sarah Wharton,
which the king kept in private from publick proceedings, made the cause for some
of the daies of triall appeare doubtful to
the court untill the king's discovery, which
concluded the sentence, and was pronounced upon severall censures. Sir Thomas
Lake and his lady fined 10,000*l*. to the
king, 5000*l*. to the countesse, 50*l*. to Hutton; Sara Wharton to be whipt at a carts
taile about the streets, and to do penance
at Saint Martin's church; the Lady Rosse,
for confessing the truth and plot in the
midst of the triall, was pardoned by the
major voices from penall sentence.

and sen-
tenced. The king, I remember, compared their
crimes to the first plot of the first sin in
Paradise; the Lady Lake to the serpent,

her daughter unto Eve, and Sir Thomas to poor Adam, whom he thought in his conscience that his love to his wife had beguiled him. I am sure he paid for all, which, as he told me, cost him 30,000*l.*, and the losse of his masters favour and offices of gaine and honour; but truly with much pitty and compassion of the court.

Our pamphleter enters upon the Scots, p. 57, and would cousen us to credit their story, where he begins a division between the English and them at court, and goes smoothly on to the middle of these last times, when it seems he writ this: "And," as he saies, "saw all our happinesse derivative from their favours by their own valour and bravery of spirit." Good man, he beleeves what he thought he saw; but wanting the eye of faith to foresee this great alteration, which he lived not to find, but we now to feele: "Our late gude presbyterian brethren turne false loones, and become the the traiterous rebells to that reformation, which not long ago they professed, and he

Pamp. 57. concerning the Scots.

Pamp. 58.

and others beleeved, and so disunited the
union of all our quiet and happines."

Pamp. 60.
Scandal
upon Earle
of Salis-
bury.
He tells us of a trick, that the Earle of
Salisbury had to compound with the Scots
courtiers for their books of fee-farmes which
they bought at 100*l.* per annum for a thousand pound; then would he fill up these
bookes with prime land worth 20,000*l.*

A pretty trick indeed to make himselfe
Lord Paramount of the best lands in England; but it had bin a gainful trade of our
author to have turned informer to the state
in the particulars of these tricks; and so
the return of these lands so deceitfully got
would prove now as hard a bargain to his
son, (as the lord-like purchasers of debenturs
have done lately,) and to his son that may
succeed him.

Remar. 3.
We are come to the consideration of the
third remark in the preface; and so we fall
Pamp. 61.
Robert
Carre and
Sir Tho.
Overbury.
in the history of Robert Car, after Earle of
Summerset, and intermixed with that of Sir
Thomas Overbury.

Robert Car was a Scottishman, of no

eminent birth, but a gentleman, and had
bin a page of honor to the king in Scotland; and, in truth, he became the first favorite that we find, that is, one whom the
king fancied meerly for his fashion, upon
no other score nor plot of design. His confident was one Sir Thomas Overbury, a man
of good parts, whom our author hath well
characterized; and his policy was to please
the English, by entertaining them his do-
mestiques.

There was amongst other persons of honor and quality in court, a young lady of
great birth and beauty, Fra. the daughter
of Thomas Howard, then Earle of Suffolk,
and Lord Treasurer of England, married
in under-age unto the late and last Earle
of Essex.

Of him, common fame had an opinion,
(grounded upon his own suspition,) of his
insufficiency to content a wife; and the
effects of this narration, with the sequell of
his life, and conversation with his second
wife, is so notorious, as might sparc me and

the reader our severall labours for any other convincing arguments. But with his first, when both were of years to expect the event and blessing of their marriage-bed, he was alwaies observed to avoid the company of ladies, and so much to neglect his own, that to wish a maid into a mischief, was to commend her to my Lord of Essex; which increased the jealousie of such men whose interests were to observe him, that he preferred the occasion himself to a separation. And which indeed, from publique fame, begat private disputation amongst civilians of the legality thereof, wherein those lawyers are boundlesse.

This case followed the heeles of a former nullity, fresh in memory, between the Lord Rich and his fair lady, by mutual consent; but because the Earle of Devonshire married her whilst her husband lived, the king was so much displeased thereat, as it broke the earl's heart: for his majesty told him, that he had purchased a fair woman with

a black soul.' And this is a known truth,
that before Viscount Rochford (for so was

· ' This was the celebrated Sir Charles Blunt, Lord
Mountjoy, and Earl of Devonshire, who fought a duel
with Essex, on account of having been graced with a
favour by Queen Elizabeth. See volume i. page 47.
He greatly injured his reputation by the alliance mentioned in the text, and it was probably upon the un-
easiness it occasioned him that he conceived the discontent, which, according to Moryson, his secretary,
affected him during the two years preceding his death.

" It was undoubtedly upon account of this dishonourable action that the author of a letter to Mr Winwood
made use of these harsh expressions: ' The Earl of Devonshire left this life—soon and early for his years, but
late enough for himself; and happy had he been if he
had gone two or three years since, before the world was
weary of him, or that he had left that scandall behind
him.' The person, it seems, who married them was W.
Laud, then chaplain to the Earl of Devonshire, and afterward Archbishop of Canterbury, for which he was
severely reflected upon by Archbishop Abbot, in the
following words: ' It was an observation what a sweet
man this was like to be, that the first observable act he
did was the marrying of the Earl of D—— to the Lady
R——, when it was notorious to the world that she
had another husband, and the same a nobleman, who
had divers children living by her. King James did for
many years take this so ill, that he would never hear
of any great preferment of him.' Mr Laud knew not,

Carre lately created) had made any address to this lady, her own friends, in justice and honour to her birth, exposed her to the plaint of her husband, and to the severest triall in a course of judicature.

And 'tis as true that the king knew hereof, our pamphlet saies: [A party in this baudy businesse,] for what was legall for the meanest subject, could not in justice be denied unto her; which, in fine, sentenced them both, by divine and civil canon, loose from their matrimoniall bands.

And because the nullity gave freedome to either, and so the means to the countesses after-marriage, with the sad occasions of all the sequell mishaps and suspected scandalls, so untruly expressed by the pamphlet; I have with some diligence labour-

as he pretended, that she was then the wife of the Lord Rich; and therefore looked upon that action as one of the greatest misfortunes of his life, and set down the day into the catalogue of days of special observance to him, both in his diary and the manuscript book of his private devotions."—*Biogr. Brit.* *Ed.* 1780, *ii.* 375. *note E.*

ed out the truth, precisely and punctually as it was acted, and proceeded by commission delegative, not easily now otherwayes to be brought to light.

Upon Petition of the Earle of Suffolke and his Daughter Frances to the King.

Proceedings of nullity.

That whereas his daughter Frances, Countesse of Essex, had been married many years unto Robert, Earle of Essex, in hope of comfortable effects to them, which contrarywise, by reason of certaine latent and secret imperfections and impediments of the said earl, disabling him in the rights of marriage, and most unwillingly discovered to him by his daughter; which longer by him to conceale, without remedy of law, and the practice of all Christian policy, in like cases, might prove very prejudiciall.

And therefore pray the king,

To commit this cause of nullity of matrimony, which she is forced to prosecute against the said earle, to some grave and worthy persons, by commission under the great seale of England, as is usual, &c.

Which accordingly was granted unto foure bishops, two privy counsellers, learn-ed in the law, and to foure other civill law-yers ; with clause to proceed, *Cum omni, qua poterint, celeritate, et expeditione, Sum-marie, ac de plano, sine strepitu, ac figura judicii, sola rei et facti veritate inspecta, et mera æquitate attenta.* And with this clause also, *Quorum vos præfat. Reverendissimum patrem Cant. Archi-episcopum, Reverendis-simum patrem Lond. Episcop. et Iul. Cæsar. Mil. aut duo vestrorum, inferenda sententia, interesse volumus.* But for some exceptions concerning the *quorum* by the commission-ers in the words *sententia esse,* not *interesse,* a second commission was granted and ad-joyned two bishops more, with this *Quo-rum. quorum ex vobis præfat. Re. Pa. Georg. Cant. Archiepis. Ioh. Lond. Episc. Tho. Win-ton Episc. Launcelot Eliens. Episc. Richard Covent. et Lichs. Episc. Ioh. Roff. Episc.*

Iulio Cæsare, Tho. Parry Mil. in ferenda sententia, tres esse volumus.

Upon this, the lady procures processe The ladies libell. against the earl to answer her in a cause of nullity of matrimony.

The earl appears before the commissioners by this proctor, and she gives in her libell, viz.

That the earl and the lady, six years since, in January, anno dom. 1606, were married, her age then 13, and his 14, and now she is 22, and he 23 years old.

That for three years since the marriage, and he 18 years old, they both did cohabit as married folke in one bed, naked, and alone, indeavouring to have carnall knowledge each of others body.

Notwithstanding, the earl neither did, nor could ever know her carnally; he being before and since possessed with perpetuall incurable impediment and impotency, at least in respect of her.

That the lady was, and is apt and fit,

without any defect, and is yet a virgin, and carnally unknown by any man.

That the earl hath confessed often times to persons of great credit, and his neerest friends, that he was never able carnally to know her, though he had often attempted and used his utmost indeavour.

And therefore prayeth the commissioners, upon due proof hereof, to pronounce for the invalidity and nullity of the marriage.

The earl, by his proctor, denies the said contents, *contestatio litis negativè*.

His answer upon oath.

His answer is required by oath, by second process, where, in open court, his oath was administered with so great care and effectuall words, to minde him of all circumstances, as the like hath been seldome observed.

Viva voce.

The earl confesseth the marriage and circumstance, (as in the libell,) and were not absent above three moneths the one from the other in any of the said three years.

That for one whole yeare of the three he

did attempt divers times carnally to know her; but the other two years he lay in bed with her nightly, but found no motion to copulation with her.

That in the first year she shewed willing-ness and readiness thereto.

That he did never carnally know her, but did not find any impediment in himself, but was not able to penetrate or injoy her.

And beleeveth, that before and after the marriage, he found in himself ability to other women, and hath sometimes felt mo-tions that way.

But being asked, Whether he found in himself a perpetuall and incurable impedi-ment towards her? he answered, "That in two or three years last he hath had no mo-tion to her, and believeth he never shall, nor that she is apt as other women; and that she is *virgo integra et incorrupta.*

And confesseth, that he hath often be-fore persons of credit confessed thus much.

Notwithstanding this his oath, she pro-duced sundry witnesses of the marriage, time, age, cohabitation at bed and at board, as before in the libell, &c.

So then that period of time, limited by the civill and canon law, proved his cohabitation and condormition for consummation.

The next was, that notwithstanding she remained *Virgo integra, incorrupta :* But, because the earl beleeved not the lady to be fit and apt for copulation, therefore her counsell desired, *Matronas aliquas probas et honestas, fide dignas, et in ea parte peritas, per dominos assignari, ad inspiciendum corpus dictae dominae.*

Whereupon it was decreed,

That six midwives, of the best note, and ten other noble matrons, fearing God, and mothers of children, out of which themselves would choose two midwives and three matrons, and out of which the delegates did select five, *ut sequitur.*

Tunc domini, viz. Arch. Cant. Lond. Eliens. Coventry et Lichs. Cæsar, Parry, Dun, Bennet, Edwards, *habita inter eos private delibe-*

12

ratione, ex numero matronarum prædict. eli-
gerunt ; the Lady Martha Terwhite, wife of
Sir Ph. Terwhite, Baronet ; the Lady Alice
Carew, wife of Sir Mathew ; the Lady Da-
lison, wife of Sir Roger. *Et insupplementum*
casu earum impedire, the Lady Anne Waller,
widdow, *et ex obstetricum numero, &c. Mar-*
garatam Mercer, et Christianam Chest. Et as-
signarunt procuratorem dictæ dominæ Fran-
ci. ad sustendum cujus modi inspectatrices, co-
ram Reverendissimo patre. Lond. Episc. Julio.
Cæsar, et Daniele Dun, &c. Inter cæteros no-
minat. isto die, inter horas quintam et sextam
post meridiem, juramentum in hac parte subdi-
turas, atque inspectione facta fideliter relatu-
ras, earum judicium juxta earum scientiam et
experientiam, &c. Coram dictis dominis, de-
legatis, sic ut præfertur, assignatis, quam
cito fieri possit, ante horam quartam, post me-
ridiem diei Jovis prox. alioquin, ad comparen-
dum, hoc in loco coram Comissariis, dicto die
Jovis, inter horas quartam et sextam post me-
ridiem ejusdem diei earum judicium in hac
parte, tunc relaturas, et interessendum diebus
hora et loco, respective prædict. ad videndum

*inspectatrices prædictas, juramento in hac
parte onerari. Nec non quibuscunque aliis
diebus, hora et loco prædictos dominos com-
missarios nominat. dictis inspectatricibus ad
referend. earum judicium assignatum.*

Accordingly, between the hours of five
and six in the afternoon that day, were presented before the said delegates, London,
Cæsar, *et* Dun; the said Lady Terwhite,
Lady Carew, Lady Anne Waller, Margaret
Mercer, and Christian Chest, midwives,
sworn *ad inquirend. et inspect.*

1. Whether the Lady Frances were a woman, apt and fit for carnall copulation,
without any defect that might disable her
to that purpose.

2. Whether she were a virgin unknown
carnally by any man.

Whereupon they went from the presence
of the commissioners into the next room
where the lady was, accompanied then with
the councell of both sides; into which room
was no entrance but at one dore, whereout
the councell came forth, and only the lady
left with the said women, who, after some

convenient time, returned their report under their hands ; the commissioners having first sequestred from their presence the councell of the earl and lady, who had been present in all these passages, and all other persons except the register, that so the ladies and midwives might more freely deliver their secret reasons, &c. though it was not fit to insert them in the record.

And this is their sum of their relation, viz.

1. That they believed the said lady fitted with abilities to have carnall copulation, and apt to have children.

2. That she is a virgin incorrupted.

And to coroborate all this, the lady in open court produced seven women of her consanguinity.

That, in as much as the truth of all was best known to her selfe, she might by vertue of her oath discover the same, and her oath should be no further regarded than it was confirmed by the oathes of these her kinswomen.

The law presuming that such kindred should be best acquainted with the inward secrets of their kinswoman.

In order, hereto, the Lady Frances, in open court, had an oath administered to her, with all the like grave admonition as before to the earl.

And so she affirmed,

That since the earl was 18 years old, for three years, he and she had divers times layn naked in bed all night; and sundry times there the earl had attempted, and indevoured to consummate marriage with her, and she accordingly yielded, and willing thereto, and yet he never had copulation with her.

And then these seven noble women, viz. Katherine, Countesse of Suffolke; Frances, Countesse of Kildare; Elizabeth, Lady Walden; Elizabeth, Lady Knevet; Lady Katherin Thinn, Mistris Katherine Fines, Mistris Dorothy Neal, her kinswomen, being charged by the court to speak without partiality what they beleeved as to the ladies deposition, they did all depose, that they believed the same to be true.

1. And in particular, that *post plenam pubertatem utriusque*, they both endeavoured copulation.

2. That, notwithstanding this cohabitation and ability of his part, *per inspestatrices*, she remained a virgin incorrupted.

3. That the earl had judicially sworne, that he never had, nor could, nor should ever know her carnally.

And this the law being, that *impotentia coeundi in viro*, howsoever, whether by naturall defect or accidentall means; and whether absolute towards all, or respective to his wife alone, if it precede matrimony, and be perpetuall, as by law is presumed, when by three yeares continuance, after the mans age of 18 years, there having been *nil ad copulam*, the marriage not consummated; the law allowing the said proofs, &c. was abundantly sufficient to convince the said earle of impotency.

Because, *canonum statuta custodiri de-*

bent ab omnibus ; et nemo in actionibus, vel judiciis ecclesiasticis, suo sensu, sed eorum aut horitate duci debet.

The said reverend and grave judges delegates gave this sentence unanimously, as followeth :

" Idcirco nos episcopi, &c. in dicta causa iudices, delegati, et commissarii, Christi nomine (primitus) invocato, et ipsum solum deum, oculis nostris præponentes, et habentes, deque, et cum consilio iurisperitor cum quibus in hac parte communicavimus ; matureque, deliberavimus præfatum dominum Comitem Essex, dictam dominam Franciscam, ob aliquod latens, et incurabile impedimentum perpetuum prædictum contractum, et solemnizationem, præcedens, citra solemnizationem, et contractum prædictum, nunquam carnaliter cognovisse, aut carnaliter eandem, cognoscere potuisse. aut posse, et eundem dominum comitem quod carnale copulam, cum eadem domina Francisca, exercend. omnino inhabilem, et impotentem fuisse, et esse : Pronuncia-

mus, decernimus, et declaramus præfatum
prætensum matrimonium, sic inter prædictum virum Robertum Devoreaux, Comitem
Essex, et prædictam prænobilem fæminam,
Franciscam Howard, de facto contractum,
et solemnizatum, omniaque exinde sequentia, ratione præmissorum, omnino invali-
dum, ac nullum, nulla fuisse, et esse, viri-
busque juris caruisse, et carere debere ;
atque nullo et nullis ; et invalido et invali-
dis ; ad omnem iuris effectum, etiamque
pronunciamus decernimus et declaramus,
dictum matrimonium prætensum, omniaque ex inde sequentia, cassamus, anulla-
mus, et irritamus ; memoratamque Dominam Franciscam Howard, ab aliquo vincu-
lo, hujusmodi prætensi matrimonii, inter
eam, et dictum dominum Robertum Comitem (ut præfatur) de facto contracti, et so-
lemnizati, liberam, et solutam fuisse, et
esse. Et sic tam liberam, et solutam insu-
per pronunciamus, decernimus et declaramus. Eademque dominam Franciscam, ab
eodem domino Comite Essex, quoad vin-

culum matrimonii prætensi prædicti, omniaque, ex inde sequentia, liberandam et divortiandam fore debere, pronunciamus, et sic liberamus, et divortiamus; eosdem quo ad transitum ad alias nuptias, conscientiis suis, in domino relinquere per hanc nostram sententiam definitam, sive hoc nostrum finale decretum, quam sive, quod secimus, et promulgamus in his scriptis."

And these records extant doe mention the proceedings (you see) modest and legall, parallel with any former of the like kind, though our pamphleter, with his baudy tale, pleaseth himself to defame those reverend bishops, whose dignities gave them place of judges, acting no more or otherwayes than the ecclesiasticall canons in such cases prescribe. *Nemine contradicente.*

Pamp. 78.   " Yes," sayes he, " Archbishop Abbot, who was therefore excluded the councell table, and so dyed in disgrace of that king, though in favour with the King of kings."

The truth is otherwise; for the archbishop (Providence permitting) ayming with

a crossebow to strike a deere, killed his
game keeper; for which act, having his
hand in blood, by the canons of the church,
he cannot be admitted to officiate at the
altar; and so he not being admitted to the
full use of his spiritual calling, himself forbore the councell table, as he told me in
these words: " Since they will have it so,
that I am uncapable of the one, I shall
spare myself the trouble of the other."

But he enjoyed the benefit of that see
whilst he lived, and retyred in that time
(most constant) to his palace at Lambeth.

Much displeased he was (as I well remember) with the court and clergy, and
upon that score. And forsooth, to justifie
that his function was not weakened by his
mischance quarrelling with the canons, he
fell upon down-right puritan tenents, whieh
gave occasion to many discontents of our
church and state, to visit him so frequent,
that they called themselves Nicodemites,
and his disciples.

And I observed very often, perhaps therefore (for I could not meet with a better reason) that the archbishop, constantly with candell light in his chamber and study, made it midnight at noon day.

And here he began to be the first man of eminency in our church, a ringleader of that faction, for I can name those then his private disciples, which lately appear desperate proselites. And thus he lived, but died not in displeasure of King James; for the pamphlet perswades us afterwards to believe him to be the kings confesser, living long after in the late kings time, from whom no evill resentment could passe in relation to this former story, it being buried in oblivion to him and all good men, till that our pamphletter rakes in the embers to light his owne candel.

Pamp. 175.

And thus, after all the former proceedings and the nullity pronounced, a marriage was solemnised with Viscount Rochford, then Earl of Somerset.

And truly here I should be unwilling to prosecute this story, but our pamphletters

foule mouth leads me back to Master Copinger, whose birth, breeding, and behaviour, deserves no lesse of fame, than to
leave him quiet in the silent grave. [But
he knew him otherwise deserving.] I am
sure many men now living know that our
author may give himselfe Copingers character; faces about, and in truth you have
him to a haires bredth.

Master Copinger had been heretofore
master of a larger fortune, which yet fell
not so low, as to turne baud for want of
better maintenance. Indeed he was entertained a dependent on Rochford, a favourite, and Lord Chamberlaine, and so no
dishonour for him or other men of better
ranke and birth than our authors family,
to be near attending so great a person as
gentleman of his bed chamber; and thereby the more proper to be trusted with the
secrets and civilities of his masters lawfull
affection and addresse to so great a lady,
which might then well become him, or any
other honest man to advance; and I may

Pamp. 66.
Mr Cop-
pinger.

believe he afforded the conveniency of his own house for their meeting and consent of marriage, which was not long after solem- nized with much honour and magnificence; and Sir Thomas Overbury congratulating the ceremony with as publique profession as others in court expressed. And it con- cerned this great favourite to look upon him with respect of preferment; and as he failed not the meanest, so it became him to advance his confident Overbury, most eminent, whose character our phamphlet- ter hath more deservedly hit upon than any other.

And therefore it was his own seeking, as best fitting his excellent parts to present the kings person in embassie to France, which to my knowledge he accepted, and seemingly prepared to advance.

Conceiting, perhaps, that the power which he usurped over Somerset, and the interests of eithers affection, (which Over- bury knew best how to master,) could not endure absence without much regret, which

Marginal notes:
Sir Tho- mas Over- bury.

Pamp. 65.

69.

accordingly had for some time the true effects, as Overbury intended.

But when Somerset had wisely considered, that there would be no great loss of so loose a friend, then Overbury would not goe; no, though I know his instructions were drawn, and additionalls thereto, by his own consent.

And this was a just and true ground for the king and councell to punish so great insolency with imprisonment in the Tower, which Somerset heartily endeavoured in due time to release.

But Overbury (to shadow his own demerits) devised the reason and cause from his disaffection of the former marriage, and which he published with much dishonor, though not the tythe which is studied in our pamphleters libell. For which the malice of women (as it often meets) sought revenge by poyson to punish him to the death; and for which fact they were arraigned, and some suffered death.

In prosecution of which, it behoved the kings piety and justice to be severe and

serious, without any king-craft ; and therefore needed not such an additiohall false-
hood, (as to kneel down to the judges,)
when then, as usuall, he gave them their
charge upon their *itinerate circuits.*[1]

[1] Roger Coke, in his " Detection," is very minute in
his detailing the discovery of Overbury's murder, and
there may be some advantage in comparing his account with that given by Welldon, and by the author
of Aulicus Coquinariæ.

" Sir Thomas Overbury's murder had been about
twenty months concealed, when, about the middle of
August, it was brought to light ; but the manner how
was variously rumoured : some talked, that Sir Thomas his servant gave notice of it to Sir Edward Coke ;
others, that my Lord of Canterbury had got knowledge
of it, and made it known to Sir Ralph Winwood, one
of the Secretaries of State ; and that, by searching in a
certain place, he should find a trunk, wherein were papers, which would disclose the whole business, which
Sir Ralph did, and found it so.

" The king at this time was gone to hunt at Royston,
and Somerset with him ; and when the king had been
there about a week, next day he designed to proceed
to Newmarket, and Somerset to return to London ;
when Sir Ralph came to Royston, and acquainted the
king with what he had discovered about Sir Thomas
Overbury's murder, the king was so surprised herewith,
that he posted away a messenger to Sir Edward Coke
to apprehend the earl. I speak this with confidence,
because I had it from one of Sir Edward's sons.

For then the truth of Overburies poison-
ing was but suspected; and therefore it was

" Sir Edward lay then at the Temple, and measured
out his time at regular hours, two whereof were to go
to bed at nine o'clock, and in the morning to rise at
three; at this time Sir-Edward's son and some others
were in Sir Edward's lodging, but not in bed, when the
messenger, about one in the morning, knocked at the
door, where the son met him, and knew him: Says he,
' I come from the king, and must immediately speak
with your father.'—' If you come from ten kings,' he
answered, ' you shall not; for I know my father's disposition to be such, that if he be disturbed in his sleep,
he will not be fit for any business; but if you will do
as we do, you shall be welcome, and about two hours
hence my father will rise, and you then may do as you
please,' to which he assented.

" At three, Sir Edward rung a little bell, to give no
tice to his servant to come to him, and then the messenger went to him, and gave him the king's letter;
and Sir Edward immediately made a warrant to apprehend Somerset, and sent to the king that he would wait
upon him that day.

The messenger went back post to Royston, and arrived there about ten in the morning; the king had a
loathsome way of lolling his arms about his favourites
necks, and kissing them; and in this posture the messenger found the king with Somerset, saying, ' When
shall I see thee again?' Somerset then designing for
London, when he was arrested by Sir Edward's warrant.
Somerset exclaimed, that never such an affront was offered to a peer of England in the presence of the king.

not unnaturall nor wonderous for the king
to take his leave of his favorite and friend
with expressions of great kindness, who
yet in justice he exposed to persecution.

And truly in this much forced story of
our author, take him at his own dimension,
an ingenious good nature may find out
much strugling in the king to make justice
and mercy kiss each other.

I was present at their arraignments, and
the pictures, puppets, for magick spells,
were no other but severall French babies,

'Nay, man,' said the king, 'if Coke sends for me I must
go;' and when he was gone, 'Now the deel go with
thee,' said the king, 'for I will never see thy face more.'

"About three in the afternoon, the Chief Justice
came to Royston; and so soon as he had seen the king,
the king told him that he was acquainted with the most
wicked murder by Somerset and his wife that was ever
perpetrated, upon Sir Thomas Overbury, and that they
had made him a pimp to carry on their bawdry and
murder; and therefore commanded the Chief Justice
with all the scrutiny possible, to search into the bottom of the conspiracy, and to spare no man however
great soever; concluding, 'God's curse be upon you
and yours, if you spare any of them; and God's curse
be upon me and mine if I pardon any of them.'—COKE's
Detection, ut supra.

some naked, others clothed ; which were
usuall then, and so are now a dayes, to
teach us the fashions for dresse of ladies
tyring and apparrell.'

---

^a Our author dismisses this story of *diablerie*, which
was an ingredient in many trials of the time, with
more philosophy and good sense than is used upon the
same occasion by another historian, more infected by
the superstition of the period.

" There was also shewed in court certain pictures of
a man and woman in copulation, made in lead, as also
the mould in brasse, wherein they were cast; a black
scarfe also, full of white crosses, which Mrs Turner had
in her custody ; at the shewing of these, and inchanted
papers, and other pictures in court, there was heard a
cracke from the scaffolds, which caused great fear, tu-
mult, and confusion among the spectators, and throughout the hall, every one fearing hurt, as if the devil had
been present, and grown angry to have his workman-
ship shewed by such as were not his own scholars; and
this terror coming about a quarter of an hour after silence proclaimed, the rest of the cunning tricks were
likewise shewed.

" Dr Forman's wife being administratix of her husband, found letters in packets, by which much was discovered ; she was in court, and deposed, that Mrs Turner came to her house immediately after her husband's
death, and did demand certain pictures which were in
her husband's study ; namely, one picture in wax, very
sumptuously apparelled in silkes and sattins, and also
one other, sitting in form of a naked woman, spreading

And indeed Foremans book was brought
forth, wherein the mountebanck had formerly, for his own advantage and credit,
sawcily inserted the countesses name, so
of many others that came to seek fortunes,
which she cleared by her own protestation
and Foremans confession that she was never with him. '

and laying forth her hair in a looking glasse, which
Mrs Turner did confidently affirm to be in a box, and
that she knew in what part of the roome of the study
they were.

"Mrs Forman further deposeth, that Mrs Turner and
her husband would be sometimes three or four hours
locked up in his study together; she did depose farther,
that her husband had a ring would open like a watch.

"There was also a note shewed in court, made by
Dr Forman, and written in parchment, signifying what
ladies loved what lords in the court; but the Lord Chief
Justice would not suffer it to be read openly in the court."
—*Narrative History of King James for the first fourteen
Years*, 1651, apud *Somers' Tracts, second edit.* ii. 332.

ᶻ The best account of this knave Foreman is to be
found in the Life of his fellow-cheat William Lilly, who
thus recounts his parentage and marvellous feats:

"He was a chandler's son in the city of Westminster; he travelled into Holland for a month in 1580,
purposely to be instructed in astrology and more occult sciences; as also in physick, taking his degree of

4

Sir Thomas Monson was brought to the
bar and began his tryall, but was remitted

doctor beyond seas: being sufficiently furnished and
instructed with what he desired, he returned into England towards the latter end of the reign of Queen Elizabeth, and flourished until that year of King James,
wherein the Countess of Essex, the Earl of Somerset,
and Sir Thomas Overbury's matters were questioned.
He lived in Lambeth with a very good report of the
neighbourhood, especially of the poor, unto whom he
was charitable. He was a person that, in horary questions, (especially thefts,) was very judicious and fortunate; so also in sicknesses, which indeed was his master-piece. In resolving questions about marriage, he
had good success: in other questions very moderate.
He was a person of indefatigable pains. I have seen
sometimes half one sheet of paper wrote of his judgement upon one question; in writing whereof he used
much tautology, as you may see yourself, most excellent esquire, if you read a great book of Dr Flood's,
which you have, who had all that book from the manuscripts of Forman; for I have seen the same, word
for word, in English manuscript, formerly belonging to
Dr Willoughby of Gloucestershire. Had Forman lived
to have methodised his own papers, I doubt not but he
would have advanced the jatromathematical part thereof very completely; for he was very observant, and kept
notes of the success of his judgments, as in many of
his figures I have observed. I very well remember to
have read in one of his manuscripts what followeth:
' Being in bed one morning,' says he, ' I was desirous
to know whether I should ever be a lord, earl, or knight;

to the Tower with as much civility as is
usuall to other prisoners.

whereupon I set a figure :' by which he concluded, that
within two years time he should be a lord or great
man. ' But,' says he, ' before the two years were expired, the doctors put me in Newgate, and nothing
came.' Not long after he was desirous to know the
same things concerning his honour or greatship. Another figure was set, and that promised him to be a great
lord within one year; but he sets down that in that
year he had no preferment at all, ' only I became acquainted with a merchant's wife, by whom I got well.'
There is another figure concerning one Sir —— Ayre,
his going into Turkey, whether it would be a good
voyage or not. The doctor repeats all his astrological
reasons, and musters them together; and then gave his
judgment it would be a fortunate voyage. But under
this figure, he concludes, ' This proved not so, for he
was taken prisoner by pirates ere he arrived in Turkey,
and lost all.' He set several questions to know if he
should attain the philosophers stone, and the figures,
according to his straining, did seem to signify as much;
and then he tuggs upon the aspects and configurations,
and elected a fit time to begin his operation; but by
and by, in conclusion, he adds, ' So the work went very
forward; but upon the □ of ☉, the setting glass broke,
and I lost all my pains.' He sets down five or six such
judgments, but still complains all came to nothing, upon the malignant aspects of ♄ and ♂. Although some
of his astrological judgments did fail, more particularly those concerning himself, he being no way capable
of such preferment as he ambitiously desired; yet I

And sir George More, then lieutenant of
the tower, took him from the bar, and both

shall repeat some other of his judgments, which did
not fail, being performed by conference with spirits.
My mistress went unto him to know when her husband,
then in Cumberland, would return, he having promised
to be at home near the time of the question; after some
consideration, he told her to this effect : ' Margery,
(for so her name was,) thy husband will not be at home
these eighteen days; his kindred have vexed him, and
he is come away from them in much anger : he is now
in Carlisle, and hath but three-pence in his purse.' And
when he came home, he confessed all to be true ; and
that, upon leaving his kindred, he had but three-pence
in his purse. I shall relate but one story more, and
then his death.

" One Coleman, clerk to Sir Thomas Beaumont, of
Leicestershire, having had some liberal favours both
from his lady and her daughters, bragged of it, &c.
The knight brought him into the Star-chamber, had
his servant sentenced to be pilloried, whipped, and afterwards, during his life, to be imprisoned. The sentence was executed in London, and was to be in Leicestershire ; two keepers were to convey Coleman from
the Fleet to Leicester. My mistress taking consideration of Coleman, and the miseries he was to suffer, went
presently to Forman, acquainted him therewith; who,
after consideration, swore Coleman had lain both with
mother and daughters; and besides, said,   -   -   -
    -   -   -   -   -   -   -   -   -
    -   -   -   -   -   -   -   -
    -   -   -   -   -   -   -   ,

together were carried in his coach to the
Tower. I say the truth, for I saw it.

-   -   -   -   -   -   -   -   -
-   -   -   -   -   -   -   -   -
-   -   -   -   -   -   -   'They
intend in Leicester to whip him to death; but I assure
thee, Margery, he shall never come there; yet they
set forward to-morrow,' says he, and so his two keepers
did, Coleman's legs being locked with an iron chain
under the horses belly. In this nature they travelled
the first and second day; on the third day, the two
keepers seeing their prisoner's civility the two preceding days, did not lock his chain under the horses belly
as formerly, but locked it only to one side. In this
posture they rode some miles beyond Northampton,
when, on a sudden, one of the keepers had a necessity
to undress, and so the other and Coleman stood still;
by and by the other keeper desired Coleman to hold
his horse, for he had occasion also. Coleman immediately took out one of their swords, and ran through two
of the horses, killing them stark dead; gets upon the
other with one of their swords; ' Farewell, gentlemen,'
quoth he, ' tell my master I have no mind to be whipped in Leicestershire,' and so went his way. The two
keepers in all haste went to a gentleman's house, near
at hand, complaining of their misfortune, and desired
of him to pursue their prisoner, which he with much
civility granted; but ere the horses could be got ready,
the mistress of the house came down, and enquiring
what the matter was, went to the stable, and commanded
the horses to be unsaddled, with this sharp speech: ' Let

But I cannot pick out the meaning why
so much pains is taken to tell out Mon-

the Lady Beaumont and her daughters live honestly;
none of my horses shall go forth upon this occasion.'
" I could relate many such stories of his perform-
ances ; as also what he wrote in a book left behind him,
viz. ' This I made the devil write with his own hand,
in Lambeth Fields, 1596, in June or July, as I now remember.' He professed to his wife there would be
much trouble about Carr and the Countess of Essex,
who frequently resorted unto him, and from whose
company he would sometimes lock himself in his study
a whole day. Now we come to his death, which happened as follows :—The Sunday before he died, his wife
and he being at supper in their garden-house, she being pleasant, told him, that she had been informed he
could resolve whether man or wife should die first;
' Whether shall I,' quoth she, ' bury you or no ?'—' Oh,
Trunco, (for so he called her,) thou wilt bury me, but
thou wilt much repent it.' —' Yea, but how long first ?'
' I shall die,' said he, ' ere Thursday night.' Monday
came, all was well ; Tuesday came, he not sick ; Wed-
nesday came, and still he was well ; with which his impertinent wife did much twit him ; Thursday came, and
dinner was ended, he very well ; he went down to the
water-side, and took a pair of oars to go to some build-
ings he was in hand with in Puddle-dock. Being in
the middle of the Thames, he presently fell down, only
saying, ' An impost, an impost,' and so died, a most
sad storm of wind immediately following. He died
worth one thousand two hundred pounds, and left only

sons tale, was he guilty or no; by the story
he had hard measure: so perhaps had some
of the others, for he was a creature of that
family; and yet for some, no doubt private, respects of our author, for he was his
companion, he is in and out, and out and
in, and in and out again.

Pamph.
115.
And now comes Somerset, who he sayes,
being warned to his tryal, absolutely refused, and was assured by the king never
to come to any. When was this assurance;
for he tells us, at their parting at Royston,
they never met after, but we must conceive
it by message.

one son, called Clement. All his rarities, secret manuscripts, of what quality soever, Dr Napper of Lind-
ford, in Buckinghamshire, had, who had been a long
time his scholar; and of whom Forman used to say,
he would be a dunce: yet in circumstance of time, he
proved a singular astrologer and physician. Sir Richard, now living, has all those rarities in his possession,
which were Forman's, being kinsman and heir to
Dr Napper. [His son, Thomas Napper, Esq. most ge-
nerously gave most of these manuscripts to Elias Ashmole, Esq."]—LILLY's *History of his Life and Times.*
Lond. 1774. 8.

And why for this must More, a wise man, be at his wits end.

The warrant for tryall came over night late, and it is so usual as it never failes, that the lieutenant of the Tower hath freedome of accesse to waken his soveraign at any hour.

The importance of his place and trust having that consequence annexed ; and in speciall to give knowledge of warrants, either of tryalls or of execution of prisoners. And this of course he did, when the king, in tears, is told a tale in his eare, that none knew, but he that was furthest off.

A trick of wit brings him to the barre, and a desperate plot by two men placed at his elbow, with clokes to clap over him, made him calm at his tryall. And thus it was, that the lieutenant stood on his right, and the gentleman jaylor on his left hand, with clokes on their backs, but not on their armes, might colour our authors conceipt. — It had appeared a mad president, when a prisoner at his tryall, upon life or death,

hath freedome to speak for himself in publique course of justice, to be snatched from
the bar, and from the power of the judge,
at the pleasure of a jaylor. But, to make
out this monument, the king rewards him
with 1500l. And for a truth More tells all
this to the author, of whom himself confesses he had no assurance of his honesty
nor I believe any body else.

The conclusion of all is, that due execution was done upon Sir Jervice Ellowayes,
Mrs Turner, Weston, and Franklyn. Monson cleared, the countesse and earl reprieved, (our author and most men cleer him
of the poyson, and condemn him only in
the high point of friendship, for suffering
his imprisonment,) which he could not release, and the countesse only guilty of con-
nivance. [1]

Pamph.
119.

---

[1] Northampton's accession to this infernal murder, is
too plainly proved by the following letters, addressed
to Elwaies, the lieutenant of the Tower, respecting the
disposal of the body. The first, which was obviously
designed to be ostensible, is signed by Northampton,
and couched in a stile of hypocritical ambiguity ; sug-

And now comes this.

Our prefacers third remarke to the judgment seat for sentence. Let him pick out a greater president in any history, more remarke than this of the king, to make good this his former protestation, wherein by the

gesting to Elwaies, at the same time he seems to desire the honours of a public funeral for Overbury, a sufficient apology for evading his own request. The second note is, for very obvious reasons, left unsigned, and, betrays all the hurry and anxiety of guilt. And Northampton being allowed guilty, how shall we excuse Somerset, whose name he uses so suspiciously?

The Earl of Northampton to Sir Gervaise Helwise, Lieutenant of the Tower.

Worthy Mr Lieutenant,

My Lord of Rochester, desiring to do the last honour to his deceased friend, requires me to desire you to deliver the body of Sir Thomas Overbury, to any friend of his that desires it, to do him honour at his funeral. Herein my lord declares the constancy of his affection to the dead, and the meaning that he had in my knowledge, to have given his strongest strajne at this time of the king's being at Tiballds for the delivery. I fear no impediment to this honourable desire of my lords, but the unsweetness of the body, because it was reported that he had some issues, and in that case the keeping of him above must needs give more offence then it

way he may take leave, to be allowed his owne even conscience, for justice and mercy both.

can do honour. My fear is also, that the body is already buried upon that cause whereof I write; which being so, it is too late to set out solemnity.

Thus with my kindest commendations I ende, and reste   Your affectionate and assured friend,

H. Northampton.

POSTSCRIPT.

You see my lord's earnest desire, with my concurring care, that all respect be had to him that may be for the credit of his memory; but yet I wish with all that you do very discreetly enforme yourself whether this grace hath been afforded formerly to close prisoners, or whether you may grant my request in this case, who speak out of the sense of my lord's affection, though I be a counsellor, is without offence or prejudice. For I would be loath to drawe either you or myself into censure now I have well thought of the matter, though it be a work of charity.

Upon the back of this letter are the following words in Sir Gervaise Helwis's own hand :

So soon as Sir Thomas Overbury was departed, I wrot unto my lord of Northampton ; and because my experience could not direct me, I desired to know what I should do with the body, acquainting his lordship with his issues, as Weston had informed me, and other foulness of his body, which was then accounted the

Which, no doubt, hath found acceptance
at Gods tribunall, in behalfe of him and

pox. My lord wrot unto me, that I should first have
his body viewed by a jewry, and I well remember his
lordship advised me to send for Sir John Lidcote to see
the body, and to suffer as many els of his friends to see
it as would, and presently to bury it in the body of the
quire, for the body would not keep. Notwithstanding
Sir Thomas Overbury dying about five in the morning
I kept his body unburied until three or four of the clock
in the afternoon. The next day Sir John Lidcote came
thither; I could not get him to bestow a coffin nor a
winding-sheet upon him. The coffin I bestowed; but
who did wind him I know not. For indeed the body
was very noysome; so that, notwithstanding my lord's
direction, by reason of the danger of keeping the body,
I kept it over long, as we all felt.

GER. HELWYSSE.

The Earl of Northampton to the Lieutenant of the Tower.

Worthy Mr Lieutenant,

Let me intreat you to call Lidcote and some of his
friends, if so many come, to view the body, if they have
not already done it; and so soon as it is viewed, without staying the coming of a messenger from the court,
in any case see it enterr'd in the body of the chappel
within the Tower instantly.

If they have viewed, then bury it by and by; for it
is time, considering the humours of that damned crew
that only desire means to move pity and raise scandals.

his, his own death being ordinary, not forced by any poyson. And his posterity in due time, by our Saviours merits, shall be gathered up in the mystery of everlasting salvation.

Pamp. 82.
Palsgrave
But by the way how smoothly we are told a story of the pittifull Palsgrave; how he married a kings daughter, with much joy, and great misfortune to all the princes of Christendom; but fayling of that, and all the rest, how he was cast out, he and his to beg their bread; but had his father-in-law been half so wise, (with our authors good counsell to boot,) and had he bought swords, with a quarter expence of words,

Let no man's instance move you to stay in any case, and bring me these letters when I next see you.

Fail not a jote herein as you love your friends; nor after Lidcote and his friends have viewed, stay one minute, but let the priest be ready; and if Lidcote be not there, send for him speedily, pretending that the body will not tarry.

In post-haste at 12.

Yours ever.

WINWOOD's *Memorials,* ii. 481, 482.

he had bin —— What? as his sonne that succeeds him, Palsgrave.

But we hasten, having much matter to meddle with, confusedly put together in our pamphlet; which wee must take leave to separate for each single story; and remind back, the death of that heroick Prince Henry, in the midst of Somerset's greatnes, who, had he liv'd to have bin king, would no doubt (with our authors leave) have been so gracious as to leave alive one Howard to pisse against the wall; when, as with reverence to his memory, it was a notorious truth, that he made court to the Countesse of Essex before any other lady then living. '

Prince
Henry.

The 4th
Remarke
in the pre-
face.

Pamph.58.

¹ On the subject of the amours of Prince Henry, his reverend historian is not very luminous. It is believed that a jealousy of Car's favour with Lady Essex occasioned the prince's aversion to that favourite, whom upon one occasion he threatened to strike with his racquet, while they played at tennis together.—See vol. I. page 266.

" With regard to any unlawful passion for women, to the temptation of which the prince's youth and situation peculiarly exposed him, his historian; who knew him

But he is dead, (and poysøned too, as we shall have it in his following discourse,) and yet speaks not one word more of him afterwards.

and observed him much, assures us, that, having been present at great feasts made in the prince's house, to which he invited the most beautiful ladies of the court and city, he could not discover by his highness's behaviour, eyes or countenance the least appearance of a particular inclination to any one of them; nor was he at any other time witness of such words, or actions, as could justly be a ground of the least suspicion of his virtue. Though he observes, that some persons of that time, measuring the prince by themselves, were pleased to conceive and report otherwise of him. It is indeed asserted as a notorious truth by the writer of *Aulicus Coquinariæ*, believed upon good grounds to be William Saunderson, Esq. author of the Complete History of Mary Queen of Scotland, and his son and successor King James, that the prince made court to the Countess of Essex, afterwards divorced from the Earl, and married to the Viscount Rochester, before any other lady then living. And Arthur Wilson mentions the many amorous glances which the prince gave her, till, discovering that she was captivated with the growing fortunes of Lord Rochester, and grounded more hope upon him than the uncertain and hopeless love of his highness, he soon slighted her. The learned and pious antiquary Sir Simonds d'Ewes, in a manuscript life of himself, written with his own hand, and brought down to the

1

Prince Henry was borne in Scotland, at Striveling Castle, in February 1594, the. first sonne unto King James and Queene Anne.

His breeding apted his excellent inclination to all exercises of honor and arts of knowledge, which gave him fame, the

year 1637, is positive that, notwithstanding the inestimable Prince Henry's martial desires and initiation into the ways of godliness," the countess, " being set on by the Earl of Northampton, her father's uncle, first caught his eye and heart, and afterwards prostituted herself to him, who first reaped the fruits of her virginity. But those sparks of grace, which even then began to shew their lustre in him, with those more heroic innate qualities derived from virtue, which gave the law to his more advised actions, soon raised him out of the slumber of that distemper, and taught him to reject her following temptations with indignation and superciliousness." But these authorities ought to have little weight, to the prejudice of the prince's character against the direct testimony in his favour from so well-informed a writer as Sir Charles Cornwallis.—BIRCH's *Life of Prince Henry, p.* 402.—Wilson informs us, that Lady Essex, having dropped her glove at a masque, a courtier, thinking to please the prince, picked it up and presented it to him, who replied haughtily " He scorned it, since it had been stretched by another."

most exquisite hopefull prince in Christendome.

His sick-
ness.
In the nineteenth yeare of his-age, appeared the first symptome of change, from
a full round face and pleasant disposition,
to be paler and sharpe, more sad and retired; often complaining of a giddy heavi-
nesse in his for-head, which was somewhat
eased by bleeding at the nose; and that
suddenly stopping, was the first of his distemper, and brought him to extraordinary
qualms, which his physicians recovered
with strong waters.

About this time, severall ambassadors
extraordinary being dispatched home, he
retired to his house at Richmond, pleasant-
ly seated by the Thames river, which invited him to learn to swim in the evenings
after a full supper, the first immediate pernicious cause of stopping that gentle flux
of blood, which thereby putrifying, might
ingender that fatall feaver that accompanied him to his grave. His active body
used violent exercises; for at this time be-

ing to meet the king at Bever, in Notting-
hamshire, he rode it in two dayes, neer a
hundred miles, in the extremity of heat in
summer; for he set out early, and came to
Sir Oliver Cromwells, neer Huntingden, ' by
ten a clock before noon, neer 60 miles,
and the next day betimes to Bever, 40
miles.

There and at other places, all that progress, he accustomed to feasting, hunting,
and other sports of balloon and tennis, with
too much violence.

And now returned to Richmond, in the
fall of the leaf, he complained afresh of his
pain in the head, with increase of a meager complexion, inclining to feverish ; and
then for the rareness thereof called the new
disease.

Which increasing, the 10th of October ⟨Takes his chamber,⟩
he took his chamber, and began councel
with his physician, Doctor Hammond, an
honest and worthily learned man; three

' Uncle to the Protector, whom he lived to see in possession of supreme authority : but his principles would
not permit him to profit by his nephew's elevation.

dayes after he fell into a loosness (by cold)
15 times a day.

Then removes to London, to St James's,
contrary to all advise; and (with a spirit
above his indisposition) gives leave to his
physician to go to his own home.

And so allowes himselfe too much liberty, in accompanying the Palsgrave, and
Count Henry of Nassaw, (who was come
hither upon fame to see him) in a great
match at tennis in his shirt, that winter season, his looks then presaging sickness. And
on Sunday the 25th of October, he heard a
sermon, the text in Job; " Man that is born
of a woman, is of short continuance, and is
full of trouble." After that, he presently
went to Whitehall, and heard another sermon before the king, and after dinner being ill, craves leave to retire to his own
court, where instantly he fell into sudden
sicknes, faintings, and after that a shaking,
with great heat and head-ach, that left him
not whilst he had life.

and his
bed.

Instantly he takes his bed, continuing all
that night in great drought and little rest;

the next day head-ache increasing, his body costive, pulse high, his water thyn and whittish.

Doctor Mayern prescribes him a glister; after which he rose, played at cards that and the next day, but looked pale, spake hollow, dead sunk eyes, with great drought.

And therefore Mr Nasmith should have let him blood by Mayerns counsell; but the other physicians disagreeing, it was deferred; yet he rose all this day, had his fit first cold, then a dry great heat.

On his 4th day comes Doctor Butler, (that famous man of Cambridge,) who approved what had bin ministred, gave hopes of recovery, and allowed of what should be given him.

Mayern, Hammond and Butler, desired the assistance of more doctors; but the prince would not, to avoid confusion in counsell. His head-ache, drought, and other accidents increased.

This evening there appeared, two hours after sun set, a lunar rainbow, directly cross over the house, very ominous.

The sixth and seventh increasing his disease.

The eighth his physicians bleed the median of his right arm, eight ounces, thin and putride: after which he found ease, with great hopes; and was visited by king, queen, duke, palsgrave and sister.

His disease. The ninth worse than before, and therefore Doctor Atkins assisted their opinions, That his disease was a corrupt putrid feaver, seated under the liver, in the first passage. The malignity, by reason of the putrefaction, (in the highest degree) was venemous.

The tenth increasing convulsions, greater ravings, and feaver violent; and therefore Mayern advised more bleeding, but the rest would not, but applyed pigeons and cupping glasses to draw away the pain.

The eleventh small hopes, all accidents violently increasing, no applications giving ease, his chaplains continuing their daily devotions by his bed side, the Archbishop of Canterbury, and Doctor Melborn, Dean of Rochester, and others, with whom he daily prayed.

The twelfth no hope. The king with excessive grief removes to Kensington House.

There were added Doctor Palmer and Doctor Guifford, all imaginable helps, ordialls, diaphoretick, and quintessentiall spirits, and a water from Sir Walter Raleigh, prisoner in the Tower; all these were by consent administred without any effect.

And so he died at eight a clock at night, Friday the sixth of November, 1612. His death.

The corps laid upon a table, the fairest, cleerest, and best proportioned, without any spot or blemish. Corps laid out,

The next day was solemnly appointed for imbowelling the corps, in the presence of some of the counsell, all the physicians, chirurgions, apothecaries, and the Palsgraves physician.

And this is the true copy of their view, under their hands as followeth :— and viewed by certificate.

The skin, as of others blackish, but no way spotted with blacknesse, or pale marks, Skin.

much less purpled, like flea bites, could shew any contagion, or pestilenticall venome.

Kidnies.   About the place of his kidnies, hipps, and behind his thighs, full of rednesse, and, because of his continuall lying upon his back, his belly somewhat swollen and stretched out.

Stomach.   The stomach whole and handsom within and without, having never in all his sicknesse been troubled with vomiting, lothing, or yelping, or any other accidents which could shew any taint.

Liver.   The liver marked with small spots above, and in the lower parts with small lines.

Gall.   The gall bladder, void of any humour, full of wind.

Spleen.   The spleen on the top and in the lower end, blackish, filled with black heavy blood.

Kidnies.   The kidnies without any blemish.

Midriffe,   The midrife, under the filme or membraine
Heart.   containing the heart, (wherein a little moysture) spotted with black leadish colour by reason of the brusing.

The lungs, the greatest part black, the Lungs. rest all spotted with black, imbrewed and full of adust blood, with a corrupt and thick serocity, which, by a vent made in the lungs, came out foming in great abundance. In which doing, and cutting a small skin which invironeth the heart to shew the same, the chirurgian by chance cutting the trunck of the great veine, the most part of the blood issued out into the chest, leaving the lower veins empty; upon sight whereof, they concluded an extream heat and fullnesse, and the same more appeared that the windpipe, with the throat and tongue, were Throat. covered with thick blacknesse.

The tongue cleft and dry in many places Tongue.

The hinder veins, called piamater, in the Piamater. inmost filme of the braine, swolne, abundance of blood, more than naturall.

The substance of the braine, faire and Braine. cleere; but the ventricks thereof full of cleere water, in great abundance, which was engendred by reason of the feaver maligne, divers humors being gathered together of a long time before, he not being subject to any dangerous sicknesse by birth.

Without poyson. The other part, by reason of the convulsions, resoundings, and benummings, and of the fullnesse, choaking the naturall heat, and destroying the vitalls by their malignity, have convayed him to the grave without any token or accident of poyson.

His admirable patience in all his sicknesse might deceive the physicians, never dreaming danger.

The urines shewd none; and the unknown state of his greatest griefe lay closely rooted in his head, which in the opening was discovered.

And vainly surmised. But the picture of death, by a strange extraordinary countenance, from the beginning possessing him, hath been the cause that some vainely rumored that he was poysoned.

By sent. But no symptome appearing, it is surmised that he might be poysoned by a sent.

But indeed he died in the rage of a malicious extraordinary burning fever.

The seventh of december, he was interred at Westminster, 1612.

His mottos, *Fax mentis, Honestæ Gloria.*
Juvat ire per Altum.

He was comely tall, five foot eight inches high, strong and well made, somewhat broad shoulders, a small waste, amiable with majesty; his haire aborne colour, long faced, and broad for-head, a pearcing grave eye, a gracious smile, but with a frowne, danting. *Description, and*

Courteous and affable, naturall shamefast and modest, patient and slow to anger, mercifull and judicious in punishing offenders; quick to conceive, yet not rash, very constant in resolves, wonderfull secret of any trust even from his youth; his corage prince-like, fearless, noble, undaunted, saying that there should be nothing impossible to him that had bin done by another: most religious and Christian, protesting his great desire to compose differences in religion. *Character.*

In a word, he was never heard by any body living to swear an oath, and it was re-

membred at his funerall sermon by the
archbishop, that he being commended by
one for not replying with passion in play,
or swearing to the truth, he should answer
that he knew no game, or value to be won
or lost, that could be worth an oath.

To say no more, such and so many were
his virtues that they covered sin.

Pamp. 85. We are told by our pamphlet, that his
death was foretold by Bruce, who was therefore banished: and if so, he deserved rather
ther to be hanged.

But, in truth, he was not banished at all,
but wisely removed himself into Germany,
where his profession of prophesying gained
most profit; and from whence all Christendome are filled with such lying foretel-
lings. But in this particular he needed not
much art or devills help to say, that Salisburies crazy body should yeeld to nature
before Prince Henry's.

Pamph. 68. And this true story of Prince Henry
may answer the fourth remarke in the preface, that he came not to untimely death.

Sir Arthur Ingram and Sir Lionell Cranfield our pamphlet couples upon the score
of merchants; though the latter being of
merit, and was ranked with the peers.

Ingram was bred a merchant, and for his
wit and wealth imployed as a customer;
and afterwards came to that esteem, as to
be preferred cofferer in the kings house, and
with much reason and policy so to be. For
the vast expence of the state, kept the treasury dry; especially the needfull disbursements of the court, divided into severalls of
king, queen, prince, princess, and palsgrave
and duke. And at this time also of the
marriage, and who more proper to assist,
(the revenue failing) but such able men as
these, who could, and honestly might, discover the cunning craft of the cosening
merchant. And it was high time so to doe,
or the customers had ingrosed all the wealth
of the commonweal.

Though our pamphlet bestowes on them Pamph. 87
the characters of evill birds defiling their
own nests, what is our auther then, who

defiled the court that gave him breeding, defamed the king that gave him bread ?

And this I know, that the king, most prudent, put this course in practice at court, somewhat differing, I confess, in the line of ascent to the household preferment, which rises by order and succession.

This man, Sir Arthur Ingram, a stranger in court, stept in to discover the concealments of the Green Cloth also, and when this tyde had its ebb, it returned again to its wonted chanell. And it is true, that the king shifted the fault upon his favorit; an ordinary fate, which often follows them, to beare the burthen of their masters mistakes: which yet was but an experiment, proper enough for the Lord Chamberlain to put in practice.

Sir Lionell Cranfield.

He being layd aside, Sir Lionell Cranfield came into publick upon such like design, but in a nobler way.

I find him of an antient family in Glocestershire, as by their bearing of arms in the Heralds Office appears.

6

This gentleman, a brother unto Sir Randall Cranfield, who inherited his fathers possessions there, and in other counties of good value, and in Kent, neighbouring our authors habitation.

He was bred a merchant adventurer in London, and by his extraordinary quali-ties, and the blessing of God upon his indeavours in that most commendable way of adventure (besides his great understanding in the affairs of the customes) became usefull to the state.

And first had the honour of knighthood, then the custody of the kings wardrobes, afterwards Master of the Court of Wards and Liveries; and, lastly, succeeded Suffolke in the place of Treasurer of England, and in that time created Earle of Middlesex.

In all which offices of trust, I never knew then, nor can find since, any suspicion, unlesse in that of the treasurer; the ground whereof is hinted unto us by our author. But in truth in this he hath but scummed

Pamph.
165.

the pot to cleere the broth. For indeed, who more fit (for the reasons I have shewed) than this man of experience in stating the accompts for the revenues of the state, which I know he improved, and not unlikely thereby purchased envy for his eminency. And to say truth, according to his place, he did indeavor to husband the same to piece out with the expence, which the princes journey into Spain had wonderfully and unnecessarily exhausted; as by the printed accompt thereof lately divulged by parliament doth manifestly appeare. Then which no better evidence can be produced to acquit the treasurer, together with what the pamphletter publishes as a supposed crime, his refusall to supply that journey, and Buckinghams folly and prodigallity; and this he did deny, as the duty of his office required, and which he well understood, as being of counsell, and acted as a counsellour in that undertaking, to my knowledge, and as indeed being then the statesman at the counsell table.

Pamph. 166.

But his refusall of supplying Buckingham, upon that score only, wrought him
no doubt, at his returne home, the treasurers
great enemy.

And whom he opposed, a small accusation might serve to turne any man out of
all, as he did him.

And yet, to the honour of his memory,
though they raked into all his actions, and
racked all mens discoveries to the height of
information, the power of Buckingham could
never produce any crime, though mightely
attempted, against his exact accompts in
that boundlesse trust of the tempting treasury.

And in spite of malice, though they divested him of that office, yet he lived long
after in peace, wealth, and honour; and
died since these times of inquiry, leaving
to his heire, his honors untaint with a plentifull estate to all his children, enabling
them to beare up the worthy character of
their fathers meritts.

And thus, having digressed in our matter beyond our time, we returne to the first
appearance of our new favorite, George
Villiers, who was of an ancient family in
Leicestershire. His father, Sir Edward Villiers, begat him upon a second wife, Mary
Beomont, of noble birth, whom for her
beauty and goodnesse he married. He had
by her three sonnes, John Viscount Pur-
beck, George Duke of Buckingham, and
Christopher Earle of Anglesey, and one
daughter, Susan Countesse of Denbigh.

Our pamphlet tells us, That he come
over by chānce from his French travells,
and sought his preferment in marriage with
any body, but mist of his match, for want
of a hundred marks joynture; and so pieces
him for the court, (like in the story of
Dametus' Caparisons,') borrowing of every
one piecemeal to put him forward for the
kings favourite.

The truth is thus: His mother, a widow,

George
Villiers, 89.
His discent.

Page 90.

* A clown in Sir Philip Sidney's Arcadia, who is armed for a mock combat.

was lately married unto Sir Thomas Compton, second brother to the Lord Compton, who by chance falling upon a wonderfull match (for matchless wealth,) with Alderman Sir John Spencer's daughter and heir. [1]

[1] Of this Compton, Wilson has recorded an early adventure, which seems worthy of notiee. Slugs and a sawpit have been often mentioned, but I believe this is the ouly instance in which the latter has been really chosen as a scene of combat. "And now we have named Sir Thomas Compton, there will follow a story of his youthful actions, which, though done long since, will not be uncomely to crowd in here. He had the remark of a slow-spirited man when he was young, and truly his wife made him retain it to the last. But such as found him so in those vigorous days of duelling, would trample on his easiness; and there could not a worse character be imprinted on any man than to be termed a coward. Among the rest, one Bird, a roaring captain, was the more bold and insolent against him, because he found him slow and backward, (which is a baseness of an overbearing nature,) and his provocations were so great, that some of Compton's friends taking notice of him, told him, it were better to die nobly once than live infamously ever; and wrought so upon his cold temper, that the next affront that this bold Bird put upon him, he was heartened into the courage to send him a challenge. Bird, a great massy fellow, confident of his own strength (disdaining Compton, being less both in stature and courage,) told the second

And his father then lately dead, this lord
was master of all, which was of more than

that brought the challenge, in a vapouring manner,
that he would not stir a foot to encounter Compton,
unless he would meet him in a sawpit, where he might
be sure Compton could not run away from him, The
second, that looked upon this as a rodomontado fancy,
told him, that if he would appoint the place, Compton
should not fail to meet him. Bird making choice both
of the place and weapon, (which in the vain formality
of fighters was in the election of the challenged,) he
chose a sawpit and a single sword; where, according
to the time appointed, they met. Being together in the
pit, with swords drawn, and stript ready for the encounter, ' Now, Compton, said Bird, thou shalt not escape
from me;' and hovering his sword over his head in a
disdainful manner, said, ' Come, Compton, let's see
what you can do now.' Compton, attending his business
with a watchful eye, seeing Bird's sword hovering over
him, ran under it in upon him, and in a moment run
him through the body; so that his pride fell to the
ground, and there did spraul out its last vanity; which
should teach us that strong presumption is the greatest
weakness; and it's far from wisdom in the most arro-
gant strength to slight and disdain the meanest adver-
sary. There is yet in bleeding memory, (even in these
times of just severity against this impious duelling,) one
of the same family of the Comptons, in some part guilty of Bird's crime; for the provoker to such horrid en-
counters seldom escapes, the divine justice permitting
such violent madness to tend to its own destruction."—
WILSON, _ut supra_, p. 727.

credible ; and so might be enabled bountifully to set up a kinsman, without help or alms of the parish.

And it was plotted long before, and Villiers sent for to the same purpose. And this indeed was done by practise of some English lords.

And I can tell him the time and place. There was a great but private entertainment at supper, at Baynards Castle, by the family of Herberts, Hartford, and Bedford, and some others; by the way in Fleet-street, hung out Somersets picture, at a painters stall; which one of the lords envying, bad his footman fling dirt in the face, which he did; and gave me occasion thereby to ask my companion upon what score that was done. He told me that this meeting would discover : and truly I waited neer and opportune, and so was acquainted with the design to bring in Villiers. And thus backt, our new favourite needed not to borrow, nor to seek out many bravoes to second his quarrels, which at first I confess he met with.'

For, having bought the place of cup-bearer to the king, his right was to have the upper end of the table at the reversion of the kings diet, only during his monethly waiting. But he, not so perfect a courtier in the orders of the house, set himself first out of his month when it was not his due; and was told of it, and so removed : which was not done with over much kindnesse, for indeed the other was Somersets creature.

But not long after, this party, by chance rather than by designe, spilt upon Villiers

---

' As King James returned from his visit to Scotland, in 1617, the dispute between the rising and falling favourite had nearly been brought to a bloody issue. For Ker, a bastard of the house of Fernihirst, having resolved to avenge the quarrel of his kinsman Somerset, came to Carlisle armed, and determined to assassinate Buckingham. His design was betrayed by one to whom he had communicated his purpose, and shewed the gun with which he meant to execute it. But as he fiercely and stubbornly denied the charge, he escaped after a long and severe imprisonment.

6

cloaths as he carried meat to the kings table; and returning to dinner, Villiers gave
him a box on the eare; for which the custome of the court was to have his hand cut
off, and which belonged to Somerset, as
chamberlain, to prosecute the execution,
as he did. And here the kings mercifull *Favorite.*
pardon, without any satisfaction to the party, made him appear a budding favorite.

And now we are fallen upon a story of *Pamph.91.*
fooling and fidling, sometime used for
courtlike recreations I confesse, but alwayes
with so much wit as might well become the *Not Ger-*
exercise of an academy; which our author *biers.*
misconstrues and calls a brothelry, to
usher in the new favourite, and to out the
old one, whose misfortunes with his lady,
break out, even now, as we have told of before.

And now indeed all the browse boughs *[Pamph.*
cut downe or removed to plain the stemm, *18.*
our favourite appears like a proper palm.

His first step into honourable office was *Admirale.*
in the admiralty, to succeed a good and

gallant old Lord of Nottingham, who being almost bed ridd, made sute to the king, that himself might dispose his place as a legacy in his life-time upon Villiers, which was so done; and who, to my knowledge, went in person to acknowledge the kindnesse, and presented his young lady with a very noble and valuable reward, which my Lord Compton paid for, and besides a pension therefore during his life. ' And all this was done with so much love and liking, that I have often observed Villiers his great civility to him ever after, at each meeting to call him father, and bend his knee, without the least regret of the lord that gained more than he lost by the bargain, and did not cost the king a penny.

And because Sir Robert Mansell (a dependant of Nottingham) had the place of vice-admirall at pleasure only, Villiers (for his lords sake) continued him by patent during life.

For which courtesie, the good old man came himself to give thanks, (as I remem-

ber,) the last complement his age gave him
leave to offer.

And thus was this office of honor and
safety to the kingdom, ordered from the
command of a decrepid old man to a proper young lord, and strengthned with the
abilities of an experienced assistant, with- Pamph.
out deserving the least quarrelling item of 175.
our carping pamphleter.

The next in our way, is that of the Lord Chancel-
Egerton ; he was Chancellor of England, lor Eger-
a man very aged, and now with sicknesse ton.
fallen on his death-bed. Pamph.
12½.

The term come, and the seal to be disposed ; in order thereunto, the king sent
Secretary Winwood (not Bacon) for the
seal, with this message : That himself would
be his under-keeper, and not to dispose it
whilst he lived, to bear the name of Chancellor. Nor did any receive the seale out
of the kings sight till Egerton was dead,
which followed soon after.

Sir Francis Bacon succeeded him in the Chancel-
Chancery. He was Attorney Generall, and lor Bacon.

as others by that place, and the usuall way
of preferment, (time without memory) come
to high office of judicature, either in Chancery, or to the other benches, so did he
rise.

He was a man of excellent parts, of all
other learning, as of that of the law ; and
as proper for that place as any man of the
gown. His merits made him so then, which
in after-time his vices blemished, and he
justly removed to his private studies, which
render him to the world full of worth ; and
with the small charity of our author, might
merit the bayes before any man of that
age.

And so we shall spare our labor to observe his entrance into that honor, by the
idle message from Buckingham, made up
Pamph.
127. only by our authors mouth, who tells us
of his growings, heighth, and pride ; particularly intimated afterwards to the king in
Scotland, by letters from Winwood, which
Pamph.
131. the king read unto our author ; at which,
he sayes, they were very merry.   Good

God ! the king opens his bosome to him at that instant, (not usuall to any of the Green-cloth,) when this man, so vilely studied and plotted his soveraigns and that king-doms dishonor, for which he was turned out of the court. Was the king so gracious *Vide pre-face.* to him, and he so graceless then and since in the pamphlet to defame him and his posterity ? He that eats of his bread lifts up his hand to destroy him.

And afterwards we are told his downfall, which, he says, at last humbled him to a horse-boy.

He did (as became him to do to the House of Peers) prostrate himself and sins, which ingeniously he acknowledged, cra-ving pardon of God and them, promising with Gods mercy to amend his life; which he made good to the worlds eye, those ex-cellent works contrived in his retirements doe manifest.

And let me give this light to his better character, from an observation of the late king, then prince. Returning from hunting, he espied a coach, attended with a goodly troop of horsemen, who, it seems, were gathered together to wait upon the chancellour to his house at Gorembury, at the time of his declension.

At which the prince smiled : " Well, do we what we can," said he, " this man scornes to go out like a snuffe."[1] Commending his undaunted spirit and excellent parts, not without some regrett that such a man should be falling off; and all this much differing from our authors character of him.

Pamph. 129. Those times are complained of. What base courses our favourite took to raise moneys for advance of his beggerly kindred. Heretofore we are told that the great men mastered all, and now the affairs are managed with beggerly fellows; and

---

[1] Gondomar found that Bacon had the same spirit, when, haughtily taunting him in his misfortunes, he wished him ironical a merry Easter, " And to you, Signior, I wish a good Passover," alluding to his supposed Jewish descent,—the most deep affront that could be given to a Spaniard,—and perhaps to his speedy dismissal from England.

concludes against himselfe, that riches make men cowards, and poverty valiant.

'Tis true, plenty makes men proude, and industry brings a man to honour. Had our author lived to these our dayes, and observed as much now as he pried into then, he must have spoke other language, unlesse (as likely he could) hold with the hare and run with the hounds.

We all know the Duke of Buckingham had many kindred, for his family were antient, and dispersed by time into severall matches with the gentry, who, no doubt, did addresse to the favourite for preferment. And what strange or new advice was it in him to raise them that were neere in blood by noble and worthy wayes as he did; and if our author had liked to lick after the kitchen maid, had it been handsome for a kinsman to have kickt at his kindnesse?

Good God! what a summary bead-roll [Pamph. 129, 130.] of pensioners are listed in our authors account; sure he became register to the revenue of that rabble. Chancellour, attorney, deans, bishops, treasurers, rich and poore, raking upon the rates of offices, bishopricks, deaneries, with fines and pensions. "Otherwise," he sayes, "it had been impossible that three kingdomes could have maintained his beggerly kindred."

Pamph. 7.
Oh, but he must tell us he made them all lords, which got him much hatred; he did so, and he did well. He made his two brothers peers, his mother and sister countesses; the rest of his kindred, by his countenance, got means to live like their birthrights, being a race handsome and beautifull.

And yet let me tell him, I have been often present, when it hath been urged as a crime to this great man the neglect of his owne, when the discourse hath been prest for preferment of his friends; and this I know, for I acted therein. The late king, in honour of Buckinghams memory, supplied the necessities of his kindred, which his untimely death left without support.

As for the base observations through and through the pamphlet, though I lived in the shadow of the court reasonable years to see many turns of state, yet I confesse my time other wayes diverted than to rake after so much ribaldry and beastly bawdery, as now to question this his peeping, pimping, into each petticoat placket; and for his sufficiency therein, he might have been made master of the game.

In Bacons place, comes to preferment Doctor Williams, by the title of Keeper of the Seal during pleasure, which the chancellor hath for life. He was also Dean of Westminster and Bishop of Lincolne, " Brought in," sayes he, " to serve turns to do that which no layman was found bad enough to undertake." Pamph. 139. Doctor Williams, Lord Keeper.

Former ages held it more consonant to reason to trust the conscience of the clergy with the case of the laymen, they best knowing a case of conscience.

And antiently the civill law was alwayes judged by the ministers of the church, and the chancery and courts of equity in charge of a divine minister.

So ran that channell till Bacons father had it from a bishop, and now a bishop has it again.

And had King James lived to have effected his desires, the clergy had fixed firm footing in courts of judicature, out of the rode of the common law.

And this was the true cause of Williams initiation thither; how he fell from that and other his wayes since, from worse to worst of all, we leave him, if he be living, to lead a better life, and make a godly end. Amen.

Pamph.
143.
Spanish
match.
Fift re-
mark.

'Tis no new matter to tell us, that the Spanish jesuit is more than our match in the intricate way of treaty, being enabled to out-wit us and all the world besides ; of which we made tryall, upon trust of our emissaries, and now the king was minded to put it to the touch.

And so resolved, that the prince, with Buckingham and Cottington, and a domestick of the dukes, should hazard a journey into Spain, being invited thither by secret intimation of Sir Walter Aston, ambassador extraordinary, with the Earl of Bristow, lieger, which was to put period to that business of a marriage that had lasted long enough in design to weary both parties. Nor was it held such a ranting journey by wise men, that knew more perhaps than our author would make us beleeve he did.

For the great busines inclusive with the match was to get render of the Palatinate, which this way or none was to be expected.

And it appeared afterwards, that though the Spaniard did pretend it, yet he had other overtures with the house of Austria as a double bow-string.

All which we suspected before, and therefore it was a prince-like boldnesse, to bring it to issue by himselfe, or to break the bonds asunder; which, at his being there, he soon discovered, and so returned.

Wherein Bristoll, a suspected pensioner to that state, did not so timely unmask the

Spanish counsells to the princes advantage as he might and ought to have done; for which neglect, it had like to have cost him his life when he came home to the true examination.

Pamph. 146. But evermore we must expect a bawdy tale in our authors stories; which to all men that know the retired custome of the Spanish (much more of the grandees ladies) from conversing or sight of their owne, either kindred or friends, (much more of strangers,) must needs discredit this tale of Buckingham, with Olyvares countess, as absurd and feigned.

Nor hath our author either courtship or civill breeding otherwise to understand what the princes behaviour should have been towards so great a person as the infanta of Spain, but to allow him his cap on his head, and privacy in her cabinet.

But above all the strains of impudency, give me leave to marke out the infamy which he endeavours (oh horrid!) to cast on King James, as of many other which

he asperts him, so this sans-parell, intimating thus much, that not glutted with the Pamph. 149.
blood of his dear and eldest son, that most
incomparable Prince Henry, for whose
death he should cunningly dissemble with
a feigned sorrow. So now to adde to that,
and for hatred to Buckingham, whom the
world knew he could have blasted with
his breath, he should think it no ill bargain
to lose this prince, his only son and successor to all his crowns.

And to illustrate the kings wearinesse of Pamph. 150.
Buckingham, he tells us a tale of the lieger
Spanish ambassador Marquesa d'Innocessa,
and a Spanish confessor Padre Maiestre,
" which," he sayes, " was sent to reveal to
the king what he had received under seal
of confession, and on pain of damnation
never to utter, which was, that the king 153.
should be murthered by Buckingham, or
some body else, or no body at all."

Then the kings passion hereupon, with- 154.
out any other proceeding to secure his own
life, that was so fearfull to lose it.

And then that the duke being challenged
with the truth, durst not fight in his own
defence, which certainly had he bin so
wicked to designe, the devil might have
assisted him with courage to have countenanced it.

Pamph.
155.
Indeed there was a letter of complaint
sent to Spain, by advice of the whole councell here, to demand of that king how far
he had commissioned his ambassador in an
affair of consequence, which letter was inclosed and returned to him with peremptory command, to give satisfaction to the
prince and duke, or to be subject to worse
construction ; which, to my knowledge, the
ambassador did recant, (for I copyed the
transactions,) and with much adoe, begged
favour of the prince to be reconciled upon
submission, which the prince in honour
was pleased to accept, or it might have
cost Inocossa his head at his coming home.'

* The following account of the discovery of the Spanish intrigue against Buckingham, and its being coun-
teracted, is taken from the Life of the Lord Keeper

. The former story is interlaced with observation, how Buckingham shifted from

Williams, the principal agent in the whole transaction. It is confirmed, partially at least, by the papers in the Cabala, which refer to the subject.

" A paper of informations or complaints against the parliament and Buckingham, was put into the kings pocket unobserved; and in the postscript it was prayed, That Don Francisco Carondolet, secretary to the Marquis Iniosa, might be brought to the king when he and the prince were sitting in the House of Peers, to satisfy such doubts as his majesty might raise. This sleight was performed by the Earl of Kelly, who told their errand so spitefully, that the king was much troubled about it, and it struck especially at the marquis; whom, though he defended in some particulars against any of the Spanish, yet he complained that he had noted a turbulent spirit in him of late, and knew not how to mitigate it. In this humour he took coach with the prince for Windsor; and when Buckingham, who attended, offered to step in, the king found a slight excuse to leave him behind, who begged in vain with tears to know the cause of his majesty's displeasure. Williams, who spared no cost to procure intelligence, had notice by his scout of the information, went immediately to the marquis, who was retired melancholy to Wallingford-house, where he acquainted him with what he had discovered; and bid him go to Windsor, and never leave his majesty, to prevent any more mischief, in persuading his majesty to break thoroughly with the parliament, and upon their dissolution, to send the marquis to the Tower. Bucking-

trusting the king, as knowing his desire to
be rid of him; a d so the duke wrought

ham takes the advice, and on Saturday tells the story
to the prince at Windsor, who was early on Monday
morning at the House of Lords; and when the keeper
came thither, took him aside into the lobby, thanked
him for the warning given to Buckingham, and begged
him to search further into the plot against that favourite. Williams answered, 'That he knew some in the
Spanish ambassador's house had been preparing mischief, and infused into his majesty about four days past.'
The prince replied, ' I expected better from you ; for
if that be the picture-drawer's shop, no counsellor in
the kingdom is better acquainted than yourself with
the work and the workmen.'—' I might have been,'
says the keeper, ' and I am panged like a woman in
travail, till I know what misshapen figure they are
drawing; but your highnes and the marquis have made
it a crime to send unto that house ; it is a month since
I have forbid the servants of that family to come to
me.'—' But, sir,' answered the prince, ' I will make
that passage open to you without offence, and inter-
pose any way to bring us out of this wood; only, before we part, keep not from me how you came to know
or imagine that the Spanish agents had charged Buckingham to my father with high misdemeanours, or perhaps disloyalty. I would hear you to that point, that
I may compare it with some parcels of my intelligence.'
—' Sir,' says the keeper, ' I will go in directly with
you. Another perhaps would blush when I tell you
what heifer I plough with; but knowing mine inno-
cence, the worst that can happen is to be laughed at.

himself into the princes poor spirit, with
much regret of the old king and every body

Your highness hath often seen Don Francisco Carondolet; he loves me because he is a scholar, for he is
Arch-Deacon of Cambray, and sometimes we are pleasant together, for he is a Walloon by birth, and not a
Castilian. I have discovered him to be a wanton and
an humble servant to some of our English beauties;
but, above all, to one of that craft in Mark-lane; a wit
she is, and one that must be courted with news and oc-
currences at home and abroad, as well as with gifts. I
have a friend that bribed her in my name to send me
a faithful account of such tidings as her paramour Carondolet brings to her. All that I intrusted the marquis with came out of her chamber; and she hath well
earned a piece of plate or two from me; and shall not
go unrecompenced for these secrets about which your
highness do use me, if the drab can help me in it;
truly, sir, this is my dark lanthorn, and I am not ashamed to require of a Dalilah to resolve a riddle; for in
my studies of divinity I have gleaned up this maxim,
licet uti altero peccato. Though the devil make her a
sinner, I may make good use of her sin.'—' Yea,' says
the prince merrily, ' do you deal in such ware ?'—' In
good faith,' replied the keeper, ' I never saw her face.'
He then left the prince, and got Carondolet's under-
secretary, whose lodging he knew, seized as a Romish
priest. This brought Carondolet to him to beg his
secretary's discharge; To which, says the keeper,
' would you have me run such a hazard to set a priest
at liberty, a dead man by our statutes, when the eyes
of parliament are so vigilant upon the breach of justice,

else, especially when he should rather have
called to mind the bravery of his brother
who hated the whole family, " although,"

especially in this kind, to the grievance of our godly
men, who detest them that come hither out of the seminaries above all malefactors, because they come
to pervert them who have lived in the bosom of our
church ?'—' My lord,' said Francisco, ' let not the
dread of this parliament trouble you ; I can tell you,
if you ha'n't heard it, that it is upon expiration.' He
afterwards fished out of the secretary the heads of all
the articles in the paper slipt, as above mentioned, into the king's pocket. He did not stay for the copy·of
them, which was brought to him four days after, but
immediately drew the heads, then discovered to him
into such a form, as it should appear to be copied from
the original; and gave all to the prince, of whom he
desired secrecy, having put his life into the hands of
his highness, first for searching into the king's coun-
cils, and then discovering them ; and for further security, he ordered Carondolet out of the kingdom immediately, that he might not be produced to confront
him, if the matter should come to be questioned. Dr
Hacket observes, that this story accounts for the king's
reconciliation to the parliament, as well as why his majesty never offered afterwards to retrieve the Spanish
match, and furnishes a reason why King Charles the
following year readily entered into a war with Spain.
But our chief motive for inserting it here is, that it
agrees with one. part of our author's character represented by Lord Clarendon."—*Biogr. Brit.* p. 4283,
note II.

he sayes, " none of them had ever offended him."

Certainly Buckingham was not in being when Prince Henry died ; and if he were, he was more brave indeed than to hate the family that never did him hurt. But sure our author meant Somersets ladies family Howards ; for he tells us before, that Prince Henry would not leave one of them to pisse against the wall, (the male ones he means.)

And taking occasion before to smell out something of suspition of poyson in Prince Henries death, we are promised in his page 84, that his discourse following will tell you the truth thereof, and yet he never speaks word of him, no more nor otherwise than in this place.

Our author proceeds and says, " Now that we have heard what made the king hate Buckingham, wee shall know the reason of Buckinghams extreame hatred to the king, which is believed to be the cause of his so speedy death."

_More poyson yet ?

Pamph.
84.

Pamph.
156.

But first we proceed to the story of Yelverton.

Pamph.
156.
Sir H.
Yelverton,
Attorney
Generall.

Sir H. Yelverton was Attorney Generall; and by his place of imployment, it was his duty to manage the charge of impeachment against Somerset, or any subject whatsoever without dispute, which he refused, as receiving that place by his favour; and this contempt to the kings service, (not without suspition of concealment of some passages concerning Overburies death.) He was for these reasons (and deservedly) by the whole councell, committed to the Tower, close prisoner.

Where, we are to be perswaded, the Lieutenant Balfore admits the duke to treat with him in private, and then to peece out a peace between them.

Certainly Yelverton had law to teach him, or any other prisoner of reason, that this was treason in Balfore, and in the duke to attempt. And therefore to cleer it, Balfore himself hath vowed to a prisoner, sometime under his guard, that there was never

6

any such act done by the duke, or by his permission to any body else.

But afterwards, upon Yelvertons humble submission for his former fault, and his innocency cleared in the other suspitions, he was set at liberty ; and in truth, according to the merit of the man otherwayes, he was afterwards trusted with the judgment seat.

And what was this secret information which we are told he should tell the duke, forsooth, that which the king spake in parliament, not to spare any that was dearest or lay in his bosome, by which he pointed to you, (meaning the duke.)

And must Buckingham adventure his and the lieutenants head to learn this news, which no doubt the duke heard before, being then at the king's elbow.

After this impertinent digression, or great Pamph. 161. secret, he discovers (which none ever dreamed of) a wonderfull failing of the Spaniards both wisdom and gravity. And why gravity, forsooth ? That which had bin against all humanity, commerce, and custome of nations, the Spaniard mist of the advantage to imprison the prince, a sure pledge, no doubt, for the Spaniard to have gotten the heir-dome of England.

And this he tells us, for truth, out of their own confessions; but they were caught with a trick, having the princes faith, and his proxy to boot, remaining with Digby, which might cosen them into this kindnes to let him come home again. Where, at a conference of both houses of parliament, Bristoll is blamed, and (it being truth) the prince owns it, and Bristoll is sent for by authority, otherwise it had bin petty treason in him to return home from his commission.

Pamph. 163. The king of Spain (he sayes) disswades Bristolls return, as doubting the successe, (as well he might, knowing him to be his pensioner,) who for his sake is like to suffer.

But he being come and convented before the parliament, endeavors to cleer himself, with a single copy of a paper (and a

bawdy tale to boot) against Buckingham,
but forbore to tell it out for offending their
chast ears.

In this the author is so ingenious, as to Pamph. 165.
be judged by the reader what a horrible
wound Bristoll gave the prince or Buckingham, and yet by his confession the wisdome of the house committed Bristoll to
the Tower; but some days after (not the
next day) he was set at liberty, nor durst
any bring him to further tryall.

He was committed for his contempt, and
might have lain there longer prisoner; but
the duke made means for his release, lest
it should move a jealousie that it was his
designe thereby to delay the tryall; which,
to my knowledge, was earnestly pursued
by the duke, and had that parliament lasted, might have been a dear bargain for
Bristoll.

In this parliament, our author observes Pamph. 168.
the princes early hours to act by, where (he
says) he discerned so much juggling to

serve his own ends, that being afterwards
come to be king, he could not affect them.

A notable note, he calls that parliament
jugglers, and gives it a reason why the late
king must needs disaffect all other parliaments that succeeded.

Pamph.
169. · Then have we a discovery of our authors
owne making, which is intended (he sayes)
as a caution to all statesmen, with a singular commendation of the wisdome of the late
Earl of Salisbury, whom before throughout
his pamphlet he loads with singular disgraces.

He tells us of a treaty heretofore with
Spain for a match with Prince Henry,
where the jugling was discovered that there
was no such intention, and that the duke
of Lerma, the favorite of Spain, leaves the
Spanish ambassador here in the lurch to
answer for all ; who, in a great snuff against
those that sent him thither, prostrates his
commission and letters of credit (under the
king his masters hand and seale) at the foot

of our councell table, and so returnes home, and yet was not hanged for his labour, but lived and died, *bonus legatus*.

And thus our author having hunted the king hitherto, blowes his death at parting, " which," he sayes, " began with a fever, but ended by a poysoned plaister, applied by Buckingham ; for which, being questioned the very next parliament, it was hastily dissolved for his sake, only to save his life."

Pamph. 1:1. King James's sickness.

In the entrance of the spring, the king was seized with a tertian ague, which to another constitution, might not prove pestilentiall.

But all men then knew his impatience in any pain, and alwayes utter enmity to any physick ; so that nothing was administered to give him ease in his fits.

Which at length grew violent, and in those maladies every one is apt to offer advice, with such prescriptions as have been helpfull unto others ; and, in truth, those as various as the disease is common.

So it was remembered (by a noble, vertuous, and untaint lady, for honour and honesty, yet living) of a present ease, by a
plaister approved upon severall persons,
which, because the ingredients were harm-
less and ordinary, it was forthwith compounded, and ready for application; not
without serious resolution, to present it to
the physicians consent.

But the king, fallen into slumber, about
noone the physicians took opportunity to
retire, having watched all night till that
time.

When, in the interim of their absence, the
king wakes, and falls from a change of his
fit to timelier effect than heretofore it usually happened; which to allay, this playster
was offered, and put to his stomach.

But it wrought no mitigation, and therefore it was removed by the doctors; who
being come, were much offended that any
one durst assume this boldness without
their consents.

But by examination, they were assured

of the composition, and a peece thereof
eaten downe by the countesse that made
it;' and the playster it selfe then in being
for further tryall of any suspition of poyson; which, if not satisfactory, it must and
ought to lodge upon their score. Sir Mathew Lister, Doctor Chambers, and others,
who were afterwards examined herein, with
very great satisfaction to clear that calumny, and are yet living to evince each ones
suspition.

It was indeed remembred the next parliament following, and whereof the duke
was accused, as a boldness unpardonable;
but in the charge, (which, as I remember,
Littleton managed at a conference in the
Painted Chamber,) it was not urged as poysonous, but only criminous.

But ere the king dyed, it is told us, that ^Pamph.
Buckingham was accused to his face by an   174.

' The Countess of Buckingham, mother of the favourite, was the person who administered this suspicious
plaister. See Dr Eglisham's story about it in the next
tract.

honest servant of the kings, (name him if
you can,) who valiantly tript up the dukes
heels, (that his pate rung noone,) for which
he called upon the gasping king (no body
being by) for justice. And though speech-
lesse, we are told, what he would have said,
viz. not wrongfully accused.

Pamph.
176.
And here observe, he makes Archbishop
Abbot the kings confessor at his death,
" who before," he sayes, (p. 78,) " lived in
disgrace, and excluded the counsell table ;
and died in disgrace of this king on earth,
175. but in favour of the King of kings." Bishop Williams, then Lord Keeper, was the
other confessor, and in the mouths of two
witnesses consists the truth. What regret
and jealousie remaines then in our authors
heart, that some mischief should lye hid
in the secrets of the sacrament of confession, which he could not learn to out-live
the honour and fame of his sacred soveraign.

How hath our author patched up a pamphlet of state notions, picked up from the

gleanings of some smell-feast guests, at his table diet, afforded him by the bounty of his soveraign master? and which this man hath, as a rapsodie, mingled with misconstruction, incertainties, improbabilities, impossibilities, in as much he can to poyson the memory of his majesty, and blanch the government of the state and court, wherein his fore-fathers and himselfe tooke life and livings in the advance of his family, with some repute and fortune to be what they are.

But he is dead, peace be upon his grave.

CONCLUSION.

AND thus have we done with our pamphleter and his book, my pen being dulled with disdain, to deal with such a subject, were it not to enlighten good men with the knowledge of a truth, before that either age or longer time had wasted with too much oblivion, or that the negligence of others of any (more able I confesse) had given but too much way to confirm the ignorant.

What I have don may seem defective in some part to some persons, whose eminence in court, and years of experience, could have limmed the originalls with a bolder pencill.

However, I have adventured upon this copy, not to discolour truth by any concealement.

A hard taske, I confesse, when modesty forbidds the defacement of persons departed to their graves of rest, whom living, we should not dare to look in the face, and whose posterities enjoy the merits of their parents vertues.

To them I submit, craving pardon, that without their leave I have bin bold to speak in their cause, which might better become greater abilityes to plead.

CHARACTER.

It may merit dispute whether I shall quarrell with the character of King James, or let
it alone, as the pamphletter hath described
him, which (he says) is easier to doe, than
to take his picture; and he gives the reason for it, his character was obvious to every
eye; I am sure his outward observations
are so, infering that his picture was inward:
it is true indeed, his best peece was his inside, which wise men admired. [1]

---

[1] Ben Jonson has, in one of his masques, introduced
a gypsy fortune-teller, who describes James very hap-
pily and somewhat freely, by his leading propensities and
peculiarities of taste. The captain of the gang of gyp-

Was ever a prince thus limn'd out to posterity by his quilted doublets and full stuft breeches; who reads his court needs none of this character, so like they are in belying. But I spare the author, and pitty the publisher. —— The deficiency of the one could

sies pitches upon the king, among the crowd of spectators.

> *Captain.* Bless my masters, the old and the young,
> From the gall of the heart and the stroke of the tongue.
> With you, lucky bird, I begin, let me see,
> I aim at the best, and I trow you are he:
> Here's some luck already, if I understand
> The grounds of mine art; here's a gentleman's hand.
> I'll kiss it for luckysake: you shall, by this line,
> Love a horse and a hound, but no part of a swine.
> To hunt the brave stag, not so much for your food,
> As the weal of your body, and the health o'your blood.
> You're a man of good means, and have territories store,
> Both by sea and by land; and were born, sir, to more,
> Which you, like a lord, and the prince of your peace
> Content with your havings, despise to encrease:
> You are no great wencher I see by your table,
> Although your Mons Veneris says you are able:
> You live chaste and single, and have buried your wife,
> And mean not to marry by the line of your life.
> Whence he that conjectures your quality learns
> You're an honest good man, and take care of your barns.
> Your Mercuries hill too, a wit doth betoken,
> Some book-craft you have, and are pretty well spoken.
> But stay, in your Jupiter's mount, what's here?
> A king! a monarch! what wonders appear!
> High, bountiful, just; a Jove for your parts,
> A master of men, and that reign in their hearts.
> *Masque of the Gypsies metamorphosed.*

not make out the other ; for it becomes the wit of man in truth to apprehend king James, whose wisdome in his sovereignty had esteem beyond any contemporary potentate with his reign. Take him in his turn, who had to do with all about him ; for at his entrance into his inheritance he was engaged to go through with the difficulties, in order as he found them, or to make bargain with all the better to conserve it.

Had he not done so he might have found little leisure to live in peace, and to enjoy his realms as he did, with as much quiet as ever any king upon earth since the story of Solomon,' and yet, in the like example with us, fell to distraction in his son that succeeded. Compare them together, and find me a parallell with more even conclusion.

I know it were to be wished, that in evill effects we could find out the true cause, but like blind men, we grope and catch hold

---

' Who bent all his counsels and endeavours to promote that now exploded motto of *Beati Pacifici*.

of the neerest, not looking up to him who
ballanceth counsell with his hand, and dis-
poseth the successe in the future, not alwayes by the failings of the former.

In the government of his birth-place at
home, what wisdome was there not to preserve himselfe from jealousie of his predecessor, of being too hasty an inheritour
here; what jesuiticall plots in the many
against Queen Elizabeth, as defender of
the protestant faith, which, because Providence protected her to the last, was not revived with more cunning designs upon him
who was to act over her part, with disadvantage against fresh plots to oppose him.

What emissaries and secret dispatches by
severall princes addressed to prepare and
gain him as an advance to eithers interest.

With what amaze to all Christendome,
how he could so easily enter his possessions,
and then to amaze them all, how to deal
with him.

How he was welcommed and caressed,

9

by ambassadors of each potentate, upon severall designs of their own.

What contracts were made and to be made amongst his neighbours, upon sundry overtures, in case he should doe even any thing but what he did, with what difficulty to any other, he maintained himselfe in peace against the envy of them all.

How was he by consanguinity imbroyled in his son in law's too hasty accession to the kingdome of Bohemia, when as a wise king he forewarned and prophesied his destruction and Christendoms distraction.

What ambassies publick, and messengers private, he wisely disposed for advantage of his and the peoples interest.

How he managed the generall affairs of the church protestant as a wise patriarch against the plots of the pope.

How far his reputation reacht out to forraign princes far off.

How from abroad and at home he enriched his subjects, and encreased his own revenue.

What did he not doe without the pike if not with his pen.

How he preserved himself with friendship of all.

And thus in particular to put down in print is the work of a weighty pen.

But to take his true dimension we have no scale.

Nor can it be done, without much dishonor, to patch him up in a petit pamphlet: we shall remit it to mature deliberation.

And for the present leave him so great a king to his continued memory, by his own excellent impressions in print, that fame him to posterity, whom we did not value, because we could not comprehend.

EPITAPH UPON KING JAMES HIS DEATH.

WRITTEN BY THE REVEREND DIVINE, DR MORLEY, C. C. C. OXON.

---

*The following Epitaph, which contains some happy lines,
seems not ill-calculated to close the charitable character
of James I., drawn by the Author of the preceding Tract.*

ALL who have eyes awake and weep,
For he whose waking wrought our sleep
Is fallen asleep himself, and never
Shall wake again till wak'd for ever:
Deaths iron hand hath clos'd those eyes
Which were at once three kingdoms spies,
Both to foresee, and to prevent
Dangers as soon as they were meant.
That head, whose working brain alone
Wrought all mens quiet but its own,
Now lies at rest.   O let him have
The peace he lent us, in his grave.
If that no Naboth all his reign
Was for his fruitful vineyard slain;

If no Uriah lost his life
Because he had too fair a wife;
Then let no Shimei's curses wound
His honour, or profane his ground.
Let no black-mouth'd, no rank-breath'd cur,
Peaceful James his ashes stir.
Princes are gods; O do not then
Rake in their graves to prove them men.
For two and twenty years long care;
For providing such an heir,
Who to the peace we had before
May add twice two and twenty more;
For his days travels, and night watches,
For his craz'd sleep, stol'n by snatches,
For two fair kingdoms joyn'd in one;
For all he did or meant t'have done;
Do this for him, write on his dust,
James the peaceful and the just.

THE
DIVINE CATASTROPHE
OF
THE KINGLY FAMILY
OF
THE HOUSE OF STUARTS:
OR
A SHORT HISTORY
OF THE
RISE, REIGN, AND RUINE THEREOF.

WHEREIN THE MOST SECRET AND CHAMBER-
ABOMINATIONS OF THE TWO LAST KINGS ARE DISCOVERED,
DIVINE JUSTICE IN KING CHARLES HIS OVERTHROW VINDICATED,
AND THE PARLIAMENTS PROCEEDINGS AGAINST
HIM CLEARLY JUSTIFIED.

BY

SIR EDWARD PEYTON, KNIGHT AND BARONET,

A DILIGENT OBSERVER OF THOSE TIMES.

INTRODUCTION.

Sir Edward Peyton, author of the following piece
of secret history, was representative of the ancient and honourable family of Peyton, of Isleham. His father, Sir John Peyton, of Isleham,
was Lord of Peyton-Hall, Isleham, Wiker, and
Wicksho; was sheriff of the counties of Cambridge and Huntingdon 25th Elizabeth; represented Huntingdon shire in parliament; was
again High Sheriff 1st James I., and received
the new honour of baronetage from that monarch. Sir Edward Peyton, our author, was bred
at St Edmundsbury, and finished his education
at Cambridge. He was knighted at Whitehall,
4th February, 1610, during his father's life, and
was then denominated of Great Bradley, in Suffolk. He served in parliament from 18th James I.
to the 3d Charles I., as one of the members for
the county of Cambridge. About this time also

he was Custos Rotulorum for the county of Cambridge; but notwithstanding he held the office under the great seal, he was deprived of it in an arbitrary manner, by the intrigues of the favourite Duke of Buckingham, and it was granted to Sir John Cuts. After this affront, Sir Edward Peyton seems to have been uniform in his opposition to Charles I. He drew his pen against that monarch on his rash attempt to seize the persons of the five members in 1641, and exerted all his influence in behalf of the parliament. But, though attached to the victorious party, he did not escape great loss during the civil wars. He was taken prisoner either at the battle of Edgehill, or shortly afterwards in the castle of Banbury. As the king had resolved, in order to strike terror into his opponents, to impeach the principal among them of high treason, Sir Robert Heath, who had been made Lord Chief Justice of the King's Bench for this very purpose, seems to have attainted Sir Edward Peyton among others. But the king's weak circumstances rendered this accusation an empty and ineffectual threatening. Meanwhile, it would appear, that our author's property was plundered by both parties; for he complains in the fol-

lowing treatise, that at Broadchoak, in Wiltshire,
four hundred pounds worth of his household stuff
was seized by the royalist garrison of Langford,
which was never restored to him, although the
place was afterwards taken by Cromwell. In
short, as he could not, it would seem, serve his
party very effectually, his attachment, as usually
happens in such cases, did not save him from
neglect and injury. At the close of the civil
war, in which so many followers of the successful side had made their fortune, Sir Edward Peyton was so much impoverished, that he was obliged to sell Isleham, the ancient patrimony of his
family. His eldest son, John Peyton, was in-
duced to join in the sale, reserving annuities for
his father's life and his own. And thus this ancient family was totally ruined. The account
of the family of Peyton in the Baronetage of
England, from which, as well as from Wood's
Athenæ, and the author's own notices, these particulars are extracted, proceeds to inform us further :—" This Sir Edward first married Matilda,
daughter of Robert Livesay of Tooting, in com.
Surr. Esq., by whom he had issue John and Edward, who was a clergyman, and left two sons,
Robert and George. His second wife was ——,

daughter of —— Timilthrop : by this venter, he
had a son Thomas, who married Elizabeth, eldest daughter and co-heiress of Sir William Yelverton, from whom descends the family of Peyton, now remaining at Rougham, in com. Norf.
He died at Wicken, in Cambridgeshire, in the
beginning of the year 1657."

The " Divine Catastrophe of the Kingly
House of Stuarts" was published in 1652, and
seems to have been intended as a propitiatory
offering to the rulers of the day. These were
the remains of the Long Parliament, (after its
repeated purgations,) on the one hand, and Cromwell and the army on the other. To each of
these the author brings his incense and oblation,
and augurs halcyon days free from oppression
and favouritism, just upon the very commence-
ment of a military despotic government. There
are some particular passages, from which we may
infer, either that Sir Edward Peyton was himself of
the more violent and fanatical independents, who
expected a theocracy similar to that of the Jews
under the law of Moses, or at least that he connected himself with those who held such opinions
so far as he judged necessary to conciliate their
protection. Of Cromwell and the army, he speaks

in terms of the highest deference, and of the exiled royal family in such a manner as was best calculated to support his own title-page, averring their catastrophe to be a judgment of God upon the crimes of their house. His account of the unfortunate race of Stuart before their accession to the crown of England, displays singular confusion and perversion of historical events. But in the points which are detailed as having occurred after the accession of James I., his evidence is worthy of attention, though always to be received as that of a prejudiced enemy of their dynasty. It is true that the over-zealous loyalty of Anthony Wood has termed his work " a most despicable and libellous book, full of lies, mistakes, and nonsense," and has stigmatised the author as guilty of great baseness and ingratitude ; yet, under the favour of this vehement loyalist, even such books are useful, as preserving the extreme charges of faction or of party against each other. It is of advantage for the present age to consider the arguments - by which their ancestors deemed themselves justified in emancipating themselves from a regular government, to submit their necks to the yoke of a military despot. Nor can it be denied that these Memoirs, amid a quantity of false argument and sophisticated history, contain many minute particulars, worthy of preservation respecting the politics and incidents in the court of the two first princes of the house of Stuart.

With respect to Sir Edward's principal argument against the exiled race of monarchs, that God had, by giving success to their enemies, declared himself against them, the publishers need only remark, that it would justify any successful usurpation in history, and that the reason must have been peculiarly acceptable to that prudential party of the day, who distinguished themselves by adhering uniformly to the party that was uppermost, and called their subservient truckling to authority, " a waiting upon Providence."

THE SUPREME AUTHORITY OF THIS NATION,

———

RIGHT HONORABLE SENATORS,
WANDERING in the circumference of my contemplations, to finde out what was most sutable to present to the supremacy of parliament, under such a divine revolution as God hath brought to pass instrumentally by your wisdom and direction, and his heavenly providence; in this wide field, the omnipotent guided my thoughts to dedicate a discourse to your honourable hands, concerning the fatal catastrophe of the last house had superintendencie over us to the

time the Almighty put the stern of this com-
mon-wealth into a parliamentary power,
which I most humbly wish our celestial
Creator to continue, till a snail be able to
creep over the whole globe of the earth.

In the mean while, I crave your pardon
that I have not so distinctly in order laid
down many remarkable passages worthy recite, my papers being remote a great distance from me: yet, by Gods grace, I have
composed a little enchiridion of divers remarkable events have happened 'out, to.
prove Gods just revenging hand on the family of the kingly Stuarts of Scotland, and
justified your proceedings, and proved that
the heavie weight of sin hath given a down-
fal justly imposed by providence from
above; my observations reaching no higher
then from the King of Scots being taken
prisoner at Muscleborough-field, ' in Edward the Sixth his reign.

* We shall find below that the supposed captivity of
James V. at the battle of Musselborough, or Pinkie, is
improved into his being slain there. The battle of Musselborough was fought 1547. James V. died in 1542.

Now, therefore, I thrice humbly desire your patronage, especially finding by experience the composition and stile of this present narrative will incur the displeasure and hatred of most in this state :' yet I value it not, being prompt by a higher power then that of man, which points out by a divine finger the overthrow of all men exalted above all that is called God, whose ruine will be the bridge to let into the stage of the world the heavenly government of Christ, which shall continue for ever, ' maugre the malice of the universe.

* This is a singular acknowledgement that an attachment to the House of Stuart pervaded the bulk of the nation, which later historians have thought proper to controvert, although here admitted by an author who sets forth as the determined enemy of that dynasty.

* It is uncertain if Peyton, who, according to Wood, was bred a presbyterian, had become a fifth Monarchy Man, or Millenarian, as they were otherwise termed. These persons held that their duty was to be regulated by their own interpretation of the Apocalypse, and consequently studied future events more than moral obligation, and regarded the prophecies of scripture (their own vain imaginations being interpreter,) more than its holy precepts, which cannot be misunderstood. Vane

Wherefore I most humbly implore the thrice honourable parliament to accept of this as a testimony of my fidelity to the present government; which I pray God to bless and maintain, to advance his glory, and bring the whole nation to a most happie condition, which now the present symptomes thereof shew plainly a new approach of a great tranquillity, not onely to this, but to the three nations in generall.

EDW. PEYTON.

and Harrington were of this sect, and their mode of arguing may be gathered from the celebrated answer of Col. Overton, who being, at the Restoration, summoned to surrender the town of Hull, of which he was governour, announced in reply his intention to keep the place till the coming of Christ!—a melancholy instance of stupid fanaticism venting itself in open blasphemy.

RISE, REIGN, AND RUINE

OF

THE KINGLY FAMILY

OF

THE STUARTS.

SINCE Great Britain hath been elevated all
along the stems of Plantagenet, Theodor
or Tedor, [1] and Stuart, to so high a tree of
tyranny as she was afore the late wars; the
princes had designes proportionable to a
way of making themselves absolute gover-
nours; which overture hath appeared more

---

[1] Commonly called Tudor.

or less, according to the humour of times
and inclination of the guiders of the stern: .
for some indued with ability and craftiness
necessary to settle an usurped ambition,
whilst the people were willing to beare the
load of that burden, have made a progress
so politickly to bring their aime to the mark
shot at, that they have so subtilly dissem-
bled the enterprise, as no notice or scandal
arrived at their doors, nor impatience to
the three countreys of England, Ireland,
and (since the access of the family of the
Stuarts) to Scotland, untill King James,
for hatred of his mothers death, plotted the
ruine of parliaments, ' which ratified Queen
Maries execution; and left it as his testa-

' This is ascribing James's dislike to parliaments to
rather a more respectable, though a much more wrong-
headed opinion, than he was capable of adopting. He
has been usually censured for the apathy with which he
passed over his mother's death,—an apathy, however,
which probably paved his way to the crown of England.
He only hated parliaments as a check upon the prerogative, of which he was a zealous defender in theory,
though in practice he was often forced to relax his tenets.

ment for his successor to follow; dictating,
not long afore his death, to Williams, Archbishop of York, the course he should steer
to bring his counsel to conclusion. This
devillish advice thrust on this wilful prince
with an inconsiderate fury; and, inflamed
with that fire, to settle to himself and his
successors an unbridled power of dominion;
which hurried him on with the whirlwinde
of passion, to discover the mistery which
ought to have been concealed till the designe should be accomplished. Wherefore,
of this number in our days was Charles the
First, who, from the beginning of his government, blaming the moderation of his predecessors, resolved to go a way contrary to
the stream of a pious rule, and the command of God; and act, during his time,
that which God would not suffer to be done
in many ages past. And because the pre-
tention is always encumbred when the object cannot be attained, by wicked advice
perceiving he had not so well marched to
accomplish his drifts, with the just power

of parliaments, which might sound a trumpet in the behalf of a commonwealth, by
advice of his antecedent and his wicked adherents, laboured to raze out the memory,
breaking up two parliaments; and, not satisfied therewith, to practise tyranny, kept
the nation neer fourteen yeers without such
most lawful assemblies, where the rights of
the nation might be discovered, and true
liberty appear. This he did, that the power
of law, and property of the subjects estates,
might be inclosed in his sole arbitrary brest.
To that purpose, he made his sycophants
of the council-table judges of the right of
his people, the Star-chamber the execution-
ers of his unbridled will, and the high-commission the destroyers of piety and religion:
which three, though he revoked by acts, yet
being angry with himself for so doing, he
raised a war to make abortive all he had
done, by an armed power, although he
seemed willing to affect it afore: therefore,
pursuing the former series of his will for a
law, Charles quarrels first with the gentry

1

and people about coat, conduct, and ship-
money, and plotted with his wicked council
that a thousand Germane horse, in the nature of Trayle Battoun, ' should take every
one denied to give him money, or that
would not subscribe to his endless will and
easeless power, to be hurried to prison,
there to end their days; (some of them being so barbarously used.) This unjust resolution he took upon him, unless they
yeelded to his unsatiable desires: by which
means the eyes of many of the triple na-

ı The commission of Trail Baston, (the derivation of
which name is disputed,) was introduced in the latter
part of Edward I.'s reign, for the reformation of real
or pretended abuses in the administration of justice.
As so broad an authority gave pretence for many abuses,
it was much murmured against even in that reign when
the prerogative was less jealously watched, and when, as
the power of administering justice was ultimately derived
from the sovereign, his interference to correct abuses in
that department seemed more plausible. An attempt to
engage foreign mercenaries, though undertaken in a he-
sitating manner, and soon abandoned, did not tend to re-
concile the people of Charles I. to such a measure at a
time when the independence of justice upon the will
of the sovereign was much better understood.

tions were sealed, as pigeons are used for traines to devouring hawkes to plume and prey on. This struck such a pannick fear, that they imagined all power consisted in the diadem, to be at his mercy, because they were ignorant of their rights, which were usually discovered in parliaments by some practised in the records. But behold ! God raised up some heroes within the doors of the representative, and without, to awaken the people from a deep sleep; or, rather, to cure them of a disease of lethargy : who, rouzing like lions let loose out of a den,[1] opposed this most wicked oppression; by which way they certainly fulfilled Gods determination upon the seventh conjunction of Saturn and Jupiter (being sabbattical) since the beginning of the world, to bring down the mountain of monarchy, which had continued more then five hundred yeers;

---

[1] This passage seems to have been in Akenside's recollection in his Ode on the 30th January :—

Then like a lion from his den
Arose the multitude of men,
The injured people rose.

to depress the extortion practised in Europe
from Charlemain's age; a symptome and
harbinger for France, Spaine, Germany,
Turky, and papacy, to change from an unbridled power to an aristocratical or plebeian way of rule, which will better advance the kingdom of Jesus Christ thorow
the universe: whereby it appears, that England, (by Gods assistance) may be the elder
brother, to bring to pass so mighty an alteration on the stage of Christendom.

By divers ungodly sophisms of state,
for the space of ten years, King Charles raised up innumerable projectors and ungodly burdens, to enthral the nations by an
arbitrary sway; imposing monopolies and
many unlawful taxes, under which they remained without remedy of relief; the eyes
and eares of all in high authority being
blinde and deaf, not to hear nor see petitions of just complaints, insomuch that the
people generally cried out, Where are our
laws? and demanded if all justice were
banished out of their quarters; and, with

eyes lift up to heaven, desired that those caterpillers might not swell too big, like a spleen, to bring a consumption to the whole body; praying also that their empty purses might not be filled with blood, although their eyes with tears.

Now this miserable condition (perceived by the wrinkles sorrow made on the brow of our disordered affaires, all wise counsels banished, and the reputation of a pious state withered) was augmented by King Charles his imposing the Common-Book of Prayer on the Scots, (wherein God seemed to be deaf a time, for the sins of this nation, multiplied against the Divine Majesty; yet at last heard the prayers of the saints, that the Scotish men could not endure this imposition so diametrically opposite to the kirk and disposition of the nation.)

This stratagem was by the artifice of Laud, Archbishop of Canterbury, to bring into the country episcopal government, to unite both kingdoms in one forme of church, in something agreeable with Rome, as a bridge over which he might bring both people to popery, to ingratiate himself with the pope for a cardinal's cap.

Lo how Charles and Scotland differed in this wide field of behaviour ! the interest of the king made will a law, and the other avoided such a slavery : the issue was, (growing by this edict obstinate,) they could not endure it. But King Charles persisted in his wilful determination to finde out this subject to work the effects of his indignation upon ; so that this occasion was fitly presented to his wishes, to raise an armed power to subdue them to his unbridled pleasure. But when this war exenterated his coffers, for lack of money he was constrained, *nolens volens,* to call a parliament, by the advice of the former wicked counseller, who perswaded him to it; making the king believe that at his pleasure he might on all occasions break the neck of such assemblies. In the mean while, the enterprise was hatched on the basis of a contrariety of inclination, by which he might set a bone to divide and governe both; because that nation, by the immense bounty of King James, was grown exceeding rich; which sowed seeds of envy in England to oppose the Scot. But by this parliament, God (who hath sole power in sublunaries,) turned this cross blow to the good of both, to enlarge the gospel of Jesus Christ, and for the liberty of England and Scotland.

But because the errand of my discourse is not solely to shew the abuses of state, but rather, by reckoning up a brief catalogue of some, to demonstrate and delineate the just judgment of God on the family of these Stuarts, for cruelties and murthers one of another, that we may raise up our praises to God, who, out of the ashes of intended ruine, hath made the source of so glorious a state, as now is planted on our English stage, wherein God findes this commonwealth very consistent with his adequate glory in consummating the fulness of the Gentiles, and calling home of the Jews, foretold in the Scriptures, to be performed in the latter ages of the world ; to the intent promises and prophecies should be accomplished, for the dominion of Christ to extend to the ends of the earth, that those who sit in darkness, and in the shadow of death, may be brought into a more perspicuous light, to follow the steps Christ hath traced out for all to walk in ; which the over-grown pride of kings and emperours would not submit to.

Therefore, to demonstrate and observe how the almighty hand of God hath determined the extirpation of the royal stock of the Stuarts, for murthering one of another, for their prophane government, and wanton lasciviousness of those imps ingrafted in that stock, I am forced to raise the fabrick of this relation higher by the fourth story, and last staire of the great grand-father of Charles the First, who was slain at Muscleborough-field ' by the English army,

* The author is as inconsistent with himself as with fact. James V. was, page 310, said to be taken prisoner at Musselborough-field, which was fought three years after he had died of a broken heart, for loss of

under the command of the Earl of Arundel and Surrey. This king, I say, left a
sole daughter, Mary Stuart, inheritrix of
that realm ; who, when she attained of vi-
ripotency, was sought for a consort to the
dolphin of France, which title of right belongs to the first son of the king of that
crown. This prince, after the marriage,
ended his days by a shiver of a launce at
the sport of tourney in Paris.[*]

A match contrived by the French for the
Scots to be goads in our sides, to hinder
our invading of France, to which we had
a just title.

But this Mary, deprived of her mate by
this sad accident, living some few years in

the battle of Solway, fought in 1542. From the mention of an Earl of Surrey, it would seem Sir Edward
Peyton had confused the battle of Pinkey (or Musselborough) with that of Flodden, where James IV. really
fell.

[*] Another gross blunder, confounding the death of
Francis II. of France, husband of Mary Queen of Scotland, with that of Henry II. killed at a tournament by
a splinter from the lance of the Compte de Montgo-
merie.

the French court, where she was educated
in the school of Venus, proved an apt scholar in that wanton academy; and affecting
in her inclination to be more absolute in
her passion of love, to chuse without con-
troul a paramour sutable, when, how long,
and how she pleased, grew weary of the delights of Paris, desiring variety, returned
into Scotland, where she had more power;
(she being constant in nothing but incons-
tancy,) a place where the amorous way was
much in esteeme, though the church-go-
vernment somewhat hindered it, which was
then not of such force as since.

This princess cast her glances everywhere
about, to finde a beauty fit for her imbrace,
and at last fixt her liking on the Lord Darnely, of the house and family of the Stuarts
of Boote in Scotland; whose ancestors were
there famous, contesting long ago for the
king with one Wallis in their home-bred
broiles, who sided with the people.' To say

* This seems to allude to a dispute, real or supposed,
said to have happened between the Steward of Scot-

truth, this lord was a goodly and amiable person, fit for any compeership how great soever: but after some time, this princess (soon satiated) grew weary of the conjunction, by reason of a servant she entertained, called David Ritsoe, an Italian musician, who excelled in the airs of Italy above others in that faculty; who, inchanting the queen with his voice, made her think there was no happiness but in his approach into her cabinet, (a place wherein she continually resided;) but from thence the Lord Darnely was banished above nine months, divorced from her in jóy, although he sought divers means in vaine.

At last, for a medicine to remedy his discontent, one Douglas ' administred phy-

---

land and Sir William Wallace, about leading the van of the Scottish army at the fatal battle of Falkirk, 1298.

' The Earl of Morton would seem to be meant, were it not that this confused historian afterwards mentions him as privy to the amours of the queen and Rizzio, and favouring them. We must therefore be contented to suppose he means George Douglas the bastard, who struck the first blow at Rizzio, and is said thereby

sick for his cure, to amove Ritsoe from the
queen, and put the lord her husband into
her armes. So violent was the ingrediente,
that Ritsoe was taken from this princess
by twelve armed lords, and their retinue,
who put her into the lords armes, killing
Ritsoe, laid his dead body on the same
trunk that was his bed the first night he
arrived to the queens service. But there
was much adoe afore this tragedy was acted.
To understand this better, this Douglas, an
agent for the twelve banished lords out of
Scotland to return, could not effect it, unless the Lord Darnely undertook the accomplishment upon the former condition,
to dispatch Ritsoe from court.

But they being jealous of Darnelys promise, not fixt in other puntilios, would not
believe him, till, pricking his fingers, he
wrote an assurance under his hand with
blood, in a paper, really to effect it; which

---

to have verified the prediction of a soothsayer, who had
bid him beware of the bastard, which warning he mis-
interpreted as referring to James, Earl of Murray.

was acted when the queen leaned on Rit-
soes shoulder, at the game of primero with
the Earl of Morton, Chancellor of Scotland,
who cherished this unlawfull familiarity;
a verity justified on oath by Darnely, and
one of the twelve lords, the Lord Ruthin
at his execution on the scaffold, a place
where dying men speak true. '

This lady very sorrowful, retiring to Stir-
lin castle, shortly after was brought abed
of King James, but took no delight in her
husbands company; for the Lord Both-
wel became a new corival in her affection,
who both consented (as Germanicus wife
with Serjanus, after she had been lascivious
with him) to blow up her husbands body

* Lord Ruthven escaped into England, and died of
a slow fever at Berwick. His confession (not made at
the gallows however) is extant in history. Had Sir
Edward taken the trouble to consult what he ventures
to quote, we should have been spared the trouble of
some of these notes. It is scarcely necessary to say that
Morton, whom he is pleased to represent as playing at
primero with Rizzio, and cherishing his familiarity with
the queen, was his most determined enemy, and actual-
ly secured the court and gates of the palace with a body
of armed men while the murder was perpetrated.

with gun-powder, who was cast dead on a tree next morning; a spectacle made Scotland amazed at so fearful a murder. By this most wicked designe, she grew so contemptible to her realm, that she was fain to flee to Queen Elizabeth for succour; but, lo! some yeers afore severall treasons were here discovered, that this Mary set the traytors awork to take away our late queens life, who were afore condemned for traytors, and suffered death; for this Mary was the next pretender to the crown from Henry the Seventh : but God prevented it by her privy council, (counted the wisest of all Europe,) who counselled Elizabeth to condemn her, to free England from treasons against her person.

But the sage princess conjectured, if the death should be by her edict, it might raise the hatred of forraine princes against her; and therefore caused the sentence onely to be ratified by act of parliament, the vote of the whole realm, insomuch that a mock secretary (called Davison) was chosen to

go to Fotheringham, where she was rewarded with a hatchet,—a just judgement of
God on her. [1]

After this, King James (being about six-
teen years old) was crowned, and had for
tutor one Bohannon, called amongst us
Buchanan ; a learned divine, and wise, to
train up young princes, whose books are
famous through this part of the world.

This prudent schoolmaster, observing the
young prince's facility to signe any grant
for his servants without reading, by which
means he had pardoned many murthers,
and passed other instruments of damnable consequence to the commonwealth, in
which this tutor imitated Theodosius's godly fraud, to discerne the hearts of his courtiers soundness in religion ; who, having
taken great pains with the king from his
childhood, desired a boon, which King
James was willing to grant; therefore one
morning, the king going out early a hunt-

[1] The author forgets to add, that Davison was rewarded by banishment for this good service.

ing, Buchanan brought an absolute resig-
nation of his kingdom, with all immunities
to it, which was signed without aspect.
At night, returning from field-sports, retiring usually afore supper to read some profitable author, which his schoolmaster chose;
all shut out of the chamber, Buchanan sate
down in the king's chair, and told him that
he was king, giving him the writing to peruse, which reading, he shed tears for his
folly; yet Buchanan after comforted him,
and charged his scholar not to signe any
grant but what was just; and so threw the
grant of all Scotland into the fire.

About this time Queen Anne was brought
out of Denmark for a match;[1] a lady of

[1] James himself set sail to bring home his bride with a
spirit of enterprize and gallantry which seemed no part
of his character. Nevertheless, lest his subjects should
mistake him, he left behind him a manifesto of the reasons for his conduct, which forms perhaps the most extraordinary proclamation upon record. It exists in an
ancient abridgement of the records of the Scottish Privy
Council, from 1562, to 1684, in the possession of Alexander Boswell, Esq. of Auchinleck, and has been trans-
ferred by him to the notes upon a beautiful poem, printed,

a goodly presence, beautiful eyes, and
strong to be joined with a prince, young,

but not published, entitled, "Clan-Alpine's Vow." The
king's main object in this wonderful production seems
to have been, to convince his subjects, in the first place,
that he was not in reality the driveller and idiot whom
they might take him for, "led about by his chancellor
by the nose," as his majesty deigns to word it, "like an
ass or a bairn." Secondly, he is anxious to assure them,
that this extraordinary effort did not arise from feeling
in himself any particular deficiency in the virtue of
continence, but was merely undertaken in tender care
for the public weal. It seems somewhat hard that this
latter circumstance should have been assumed as matter of vituperation by Sir Edward Peyton. We take
the liberty of subjoining James's proclamation, as the
most singular illustration of his feelings and mode of
reasoning that has ever been given to the public.

"In respect, I know that the motion of my voyage at
this time will be diversly skansit upon, the misinter-
preting whereof may tend, as well to my great dishonour, as to the wrangous blame of inoccents; I have
thereupon bein moved to set down the present declara-
tion with my own hand, hereby to resolve all good subjects, first, of the causes briefly that moved me to take
this purpose in heid; and nixt, in that fashion I resolved myself thereof. As to the causes, I doubt not but
it [is] manifestly known to all how far I was generally
found fault with by all men, for the delaying so long of
my marriage; the reasons were, that I was alane, without fader or moder, brither or sister, king of this realme,
and heir apperand of England. This my nakedness

and weak in constitution; an union unsutable for a virago to couple with a spiny

made me to be weak, and my enemies stark; ane man
was as na man, and the want of hope of succession
breads disdain; yea, my lang delay bread in the breasts
of many a great jealousie of my inhability, as gif I were
a barran stock; thir reasons, and innumerable others
hourly objected, moved me to heasten the treatie of
my marriage; for as to my own nature, God is my witness I could have abstained langer, nor the well of my
patrie could have permitted. I am known, God be
praised, not to be very intemperately rash nor concety
in my weichtiest affairs, nather use I to be sa carried
away with passion, as I refused to hear reason. This
treaty then being perfyted, and the queen my bed-fel-
low coming on her journey, how the contrarious winds
stayed her, and where she was driven, it is mair nor notorious to all men; and that it was necessarlie conclu-
dit be the estates, that it behoved necessarlie to be performed this year. I remit it to themselves, who concluded the same in the spring, at the earl marshall's
directing; the word then coming to me, that she was
stayed from coming through by the contrarious tem-
pests of winds, and that her ships were not able to per-
fite her voyage this year, throw the great hurt they had
received; remembering myself of her inhability on the
ane part to come, and of the foresaid resolution of the
estates on the other, the like whereof I had often solemnly avowed; I upon the instant, yea, very moment,
resolved to make possible on my part that which was
impossible on hirs; the place that I resolved this in was
Craigmillar, not ane of the haill council being present

and thin creature; a course made her fancy
work as a fat¹ for to further a female con-

there; and as I took my resolution only of self, as I am
a true prince, sa advised with myself only what way to
follow furth the same; whereupon I thought first to
have had the colour of the Earl of Bothwell's parting,
whom first I employed to have made the voyage, as
well in respect of his office, as likewise the rest of the
council being absent all that hail day. After I came to
Edinburgh, the chancellor and the justice clerk being
yet unreturned out of Lauder, and the haill rest of the
officers of estate being all at their own houses, the clerk
of register being only excepted; but fra I saw this voyage impossible to be perficted by the Earl of Bothwell,
in respect of the coistes he had bestowed upon the preparation of my marriage, whereby he was unable to
make it with sic expedition and honour as the estate
of that affair and his person did require. I was then
forced to seek some other way, and to abide the coun-
cils assembling; who, being conveined, found sic difficulties in rieking out a number of ships for her convoy; for sal I give it out who should be the person of
the ambassade, as I was compelled to make them the
mair earnest to avow, in great vehemence, that gif there
could be gotten na other to gang, I should gang myself allane, gif it were but in ane ship; but gif all men
(said I) had been as well willed as became them, I needed not to be in that strait. Thir speeches moved the
chancellor upon three respects to make his offer of going; first, taking these speeches of evil will unto him,
because all men knows how he has been this lang time

¹ Now spelled *vat.*

tent, and placed in her delight one Master Stuart, of the house the Earle of Murry.

slandered for over great slawness in the matter of my marriage; nixt his zeal to my service, seeing me sa earnest; and last, the fear he had that I should have performed my speeches, gif na better could have been. Fra the time of the making of this offer, I have ever kept my intention of my goeing as closs as possible I could from all men; because I thought ay it was enough for me to put my foot in the ship when all things were ready, without speiring farder, as I kept it generally closs from all men; so I say, upon mine honour, I kept it sa from the chancellor, as I was never want to doe any secrets of my weightiest affairs; two reasons moving me thereto: first, because I know that gif I made him on the council thereof, he had been blamed of puting it in my head, which had not been his duty; for it becomes no subjects to give princes advice in sic matters; and therfor, remembering that invious and unjust burding he dayly bears of leading me by the nose, as it were, to all his appetaytes, as if I were ane unreasonable creature, or a bairne that could doe nothing of myself, I thought it pitty then to be the occasion of the heaping of further unjust slander upon his head; the other reason was, that as I perceived it was for the staying of me that he made the offer of his goeing, sa was I assured, that, upon knowledge of my goeing, he would ather altogether have stayed himself, or at least lingered as long as he could, thinking it over great a burden for him to overtake my convoy, as I know upon the rumours of my goeing, he has said no less to sundry of his friends. This far I speak for his part, as well for

9

His haunting her chamber too sedulously
bred such a jealousie in King James, for
to impart his thoughts to Marquess Hunt-
ly, and get dispatched this Stuart out of
the way, burning his house and himself in
it. After whose death, the queen found

my own honour's sake, that I be not unjustly slandered
as an irresolute asse, who can do nothing of himself;
as also, that the honesty and innocency of that man be
not unjustly and untruly reported and reproched; and
as for my part, what moved me, ye may judge by that
whilk I have already said, besides the shortnes of the
way, the suretie of the passage being clean of all sands,
foirlands, or sic like dangers; the harbouries in these
parts sa suir, and na foreyn fleits resorting upon these
seas: it is my pleasure then, that na man grudge or
murmure at thir my proceedings; but let every man
live a peaceable and queit life, without offending of
any; and that all men conform themselves to the directions in my proclamation, while my return, which
I promise shall be, God willing, within the space of 20
days, wind and weather serveing; that all men assure
themselves, that whasoever contraveins my directions
in my absence, I will think it a sufficient proof that he
bears na love in his heart towards me; and be the con-
trair, these will I only have respect to at my return,
that reverences my commandment and will in my absence.   Farewell.   JAMES R."

    The Earl of Murray, fondly called by the common
people the " Bonnie Earl," was distinguished by his

others to satisfie her unruly appetite,; as,
namely, the Earle of Gowry, a lord of a

feats of gallantry and address; and, according to popular tradition, was really regarded by Queen Anne of
Denmark with more than prudent distinction. The
popular ballad of "Child Waters," was supposed to refer to his catastrophe; and another, which may be termed a Lament for him, concludes,

> O the Bonny Earl of Murray,
> He was the queen's love.

Yet it would be absurd to impute his catastrophe to
the king's jealousy as the direct cause. Murray had
been summoned to Edinburgh from the north, in order
that the king might accommodate a feudal quarrel between him and his powerful neighbour, the Earl of
Huntley. In the meanwhile, an attempt was made by
the seditious Earl of Bothwell, upon James's person in
his own palace. This attempt, it was pretended, was
aided or abetted by the Earl of Murray, and the king
dispatched Huntley with a charge to bring him to his
presence. The intrusting this commission to a hostile
and rival baron is the most suspicious part of the king's
conduct, and argues him to have been at least indiffer-
ent as to the consequences that might have been fore-
seen. Murray, when summoned, stood in his defence,
and a shot from his house of Dunnibrisell killed one
of Huntley's friends. They then fired the house; Dunbar, the sheriff of Murray, rushed first out, with the generous intention of sacrificing himself to preserve his
friend. But as Murray himself burst through the flames,
his long hair caught fire, and by its light, he was traced
down to the rocks at the sea-side, and slain with

comly visage, good stature, and of an at-
tracting allurement; who, upon King James
suspition of often society with the queen,
converted to the poyson of hatred the friendship and love of the earl; causing Ramsey,
after Earl of Holderness, with others, to
murther Gowry in his own house; giving
it out for a stale, that the earl, with others,
would have killed him; and, to make his
falshood appear odious in shape of truth,

repeated wounds. John Gordon, of Buckie, who
struck the first blow, insisted that Huntley should stab
the earl also; and, as he wounded him in the face,
Murray said, while expiring, "Ye hae spoiled a better
face than your ain." The whole seems to have been
one of the bursts of feudal revenge common to the
age and country; though, if the king's jealousy were
really public, Huntley might consider it as an encou-
ragement to the slaughter. He fled, however, when
the deed was done; and one of his party, who was left
behind wounded, was brought to Edinburgh, and instantly executed. Huntley took refuge in the castle of
Ravenscrag, belonging to Lord Sinclair, who paid him
the *naive* compliment, that the earl was welcome to his
house, but would have been much more welcome to
have gone past it. He escorted him, however, to the
highlands. But the Earl of Huntley, confiding in his
favour with the king, returned to court shortly after
wards, and was only punished by a short imprisonment.

appointed the fifth of August a solemn day, of thanksgiving for his supposed delivery; and in this mocked the God of heaven.[1]

After this the queen entertained into her service one Mr Beely, a Dane, to whom she bore an affection. This gentleman came with her into England, and grew more entire in her thoughts, with whom I had a familiarity to be a commissioner for him in a grant his mistress procured for him of King James, of felons goods in divers counties; who, in great secrecie, discovered to me, he was natural father of King Charles; but waxing old, the queen took two proper gentlemen of the house of Bohannon to her service: these being partners in her affection, fell out in a duell, and killed one another for priority in her love.[2]

---

[1] Mr Pinkerton, who adopted in part, at least, this theory of the Gowrie conspiracy, was disposed to think the younger brother Alexander Ruthven was the paramour of Queen Anne.

[2] There is no hint of any such rivalry or duel in Buchanan of Auchmar's account of the branches of his own name; and it seems an anecdote which, if true, could hardly have escaped his attention.

Not long after Gowries death, Prince Henry was born at Edinburgh; whereupon Queen Elizabeth sent the Earl of Sussex ambassadour, to congratulate this birth, and be godfather, with a gallant retinue; but Scotland being poor, and the king wanting money to discharge the glory of such a royal entertainment, the Earl of Orkney, a bastard of the former king's, pawned his estate in the islands of Scotland, to raise a great sum to discharge the christening.[1] Behold how King James did not onely disengage this morgage, but suffered this earl to die in prison at Blackness, near Edinburgh-castle; an ingratitude indelible for after-ages to detest.

I omit the murders, inchantments, witcheries, committed by his predecessors, of weight enough without more to pull down that house.

But Henry the Fourth of France being

---

[1] An account of this christening, which was very splendid, occurs in Somers' Tracts, vol. ii. The fact, that the expence was defrayed by the Earl of Orkney, (Sir Robert Stuart of Strathdown,) rests upon Peyton's sole averment.

informed of this congratulation, and conceiving it to be a step to unite England and Scotland in one government, Elizabeth waxing old, sent a letter of incouragement to King James, to joyn with him in revenge of his mother's death; who replied, (as the true copy expressed,) that he would not fall at difference with Elizabeth, since he was now more secure in his throne then in his mother's time; intimating, he was not sorry for her removall, for her life might have procured his ruine. [*]

Elizabeth, after forty years reign, was moved by her privy council to settle King James for successor; who said, she would not erect a monument in her life for a follower to expect her end.

She was a lady adorned with majesty,

[*] This is so far accurate, that Henry IV. did send Mons. de la Bethune on an embassy to James VI., and that the circumstance excited Queen Elizabeth's anxiety. But the utmost exertions of Neville, then the English envoy at Edinburgh, could discover no other object than the renewal of the ancient league between France and Scotland, and of the exemptions and privileges of the Scottish nation in France.

learning, languages, wisdom, and piety;
yet fearful of death, for she hated any word
tended to it, as shall be manifest by Roger
Lord North, when, carving one day at dinner, the queen asked what that covered
dish was? he lifted up the cover, replied,
" Madam, it is a coffin;" a word moved
the queen to anger: " and are you such a
fool," said she, "to give a pie such a name?"[*]
This gave warning to the courtiers not to
use any word which mentioned her death.
But this prudent prince died after fourty-
four yeers compleat, and King James was
proclaimed about the last of March, 1602, 1603

[*] This family had the fortune to draw down singular
answers from their sovereigns. Lord North, in the
time of Charles II., when his brother, the celebrated
Lord Chief Justice North, was made Chancellor, thought
it his bounden duty to inform his majesty that his brother, although excellently well-intentioned, was not in
point of talents altogether qualified to hold that high
office; a confession, he said, which nothing but the
profound duty he owed his majesty, &c. &c. &c. could
have wrung from him. The witty monarch thanked
him with great composure, and said, " He had always
known there was one fool among the brothers, and he
was obliged to his lordship for shewing him which it
was."

King of England, by his privy council, assisted by the Lord Mayor of London, Sir
Robert Lee. In May after, he entered,
met with many nobles and gentlemen; the
sheriffs attending him in every county from
Berwick: so that there was a generall ap-
plause, and royal entertainment at his entrance into the Charter-House in London;
yet ominously attended with a great plague
of three thousand dying in a week in the
city. This union gave a grand expectation of tranquillity to both kingdoms. To
effect this better, he called a parliament,
which lasted seven yeers, and raised many
subsidies, with great sums left by his predecessor; which vast treasure was all bestowed on the needy Scots, who, like horse-
leeches, sucked the exchequer dry; so that
honour and offices were set to sale, to fill
the Scots purses, and empty the kingdoms
treasure.

This caused a by-word, that the exchequer reached from London to Edinburgh.
This was not sufficient to gorge their insa-

tiable requests, but many monoplies likewise were erected; myself after reporting thirty-two patents to the parliament, in decimo octavo Jacobi.

The queen, deprived of the nightly company of a husband, turned her delight to the prince, whom she respected above her other children; finding him too serious, diverted him from so much intensiveness, to an amorous gesture, in which the English court took great pride. To that purpose, she initiated him in the court of Cupid; as one night, she shut him under lock and key in a chamber, with a beautiful young lady now dead, which shewed her love to the sport; indeed, more like a bawd than a discreet mother, who is bound to season her children in virtue while young, that they may hold the taste in age; whose example in vertue or vice might draw a world to follow the pattern. But after,'

* Some trivial frolic seems to have been exaggerated into this infamous scandal. All must remember the horrible calumnies which were inserted in the charge

Prince Henry fell mortally sick of a supposed fever, but not without suspition of
poyson. A prince whom all Europe expected to be the promoter of some great
and famous action, because his inclination
was bent to the martial art above his yeers,
and also excelled in matters of state, both
in discourse and choice of ablest company;
which he much delighted in for advice and
counsel. This ripeness in judgement, and
dexterity in souldering to form models of
any sort of battels, stirred up King James to
suspect the prince might depose him; especially knowing he was not begot of his body.

This caused the Lord Saintcleare, then ambassadour in Denmark, not to be ashamed
to challenge Prince Henry to be his own
son, to English and Scots, there arrived;
so, that by some pill or other, the prince
came to his end. This was plainly shewed

against the unfortunate Marie Antoinette. As for
Prince Henry, he is said to have been very much master of his passions towards the female sex. See p. 239,
note.

when he was cut up to be imbalmed ; his brain was liver-hued and putrefied ; an argument of poison, as was affirmed by a most learned physician, Butler of Cambridge.'   Now King James, more addicted to love males then females, though for complement he visited Queen Anne, yet never lodged with her a night for many yeers. Whereupon, Gundamore observing how King James was addicted, told him that the Lady Hatton would not suffer the Lord Cook her husband to come into her fore-doore, nor he himself to come into her back-door ; Hatton and Ely houses joyning together where they dwelt, she denying him a passage backward to take air.

Now that the fruit of mortality might declare humane frailty, Queen Anne, who had trod so many stately footings in masks of court,' beauty fading, strength failing,

---

' See the Aulicus Coquinariæ for a confutation of this rumour.

' The following is a lively description of one of these celebrated entertainments :

and youth metamorphosed to yeers, health
to sickness, being haunted with a lingering

" At night we had the queen's maske in the banquet-
ting-house, or rather her pagent. There was a great
engine at the lower end of the room, which had motion,
and in it were the images of sea-horses, with other terrible fishes, which were ridden by Moors : The indeco-
rum was, that there was all fish and no water. At the
farther end there was a great shell, in form of a shallop,
wherein were four seats, on the lowest sat the queen
with my Lady Bedford ; on the rest were placed the Ladies Suffolk, Darby, Rich, Effingham, Ann Herbert,
Susan Herbert, Elizabeth Howard, Walsingham, and
Bevil. Their apparell was rich, but too light and curti-
zan-like for such great ones. Instead of vizzards, their
faces and arms up to the elbows were painted black,
which was disguise sufficient, for they were hard to be
known : but it became them nothing so well as their
red and white, and you cannot imagine a more ugly
sight than a troop of lean-cheek'd Moors. The Spanish
and Venetian ambassadors were both present, and sat
by the king in state; at which Monsieur Beaumont
quarrells so extreamly, that he saith the whole court is
Spanish. But by his favour he should fall out with
none but himself, for they were all indifferently invited
to come as friends to a private sport; which he refusing, the Spanish ambassador willingly accepted, and
being there, seeing no cause to the contrary, he put off
Don Taxis, and took upon him *el Senor Embaxador,*
wherein he outstript our little monsieur. He was privately at the first mask, and sate amongst his men disguised; at this he was taken out to dance, and footed

sickness, which contracted her end. For
Doctor Upton at his death, (not long afore
the queen's) declared a skeleton being in
her womb proves she was with childe, and
that physick had destroyed it, and so the
skeleton remained ; which was laboured to
be purged away, but all in vain, rotted in
her. Of this doctor there was a jealousie
of revealing it, for which his passage was
made to another world, as his tongue to me
at his death uttered ; who married my neer
kinswoman.

The queen departed, the king sold his
affections to Sir George Villiers, whom he
would tumble and kiss as a mistress. [a]

---

it like a lusty old gallant with his countrywoman. He
took out the queen, and forgot not to kiss her hand,
though there was danger it would have left a mark on
his lips. The night's work was concluded with a banquet in the great chamber, which was so furiously as-
saulted that down went table and tresses, before one bit
was touched. They say the Duke of Holst will come
upon us with an after-reckoning, and that we shall see
him on Candlemas night in a mask, as he hath shewed
himself a lusty reveller all this Christmas.—WINWOOD'S
Memorialls, II. 44.

[a] Weldon and Osborne have already borne testimony

This favourite had erected many monopolies; who, finding parliaments hindered his profit, caused his master to dissolve those patents, and break up the parliament of *decimo octavo;* raising a number of privy seals, which were borrowed and never paid.

to the odd familiarities which James used with his favourites, and which were, to say the least, most disgusting and unseemly. The following extract of a letter from Sir Dudley Carleton to Mr Winwood contains some curious particulars attending the marriage of Sir Philip Herbert, afterwards Earl of Montgomery, with his first lady. " There was no small loss that night in chaines and jewells, and many great ladies were made shorter by the skirts, and were well enough served that they could keep cut no better. The presents of plate and other things given by the noblemen were valued at 2,500*l.* but that which made it a good marriage, was a gift of the king's of 500*l.* land for the bride's jointure. They were lodged in the councill chamber, where the king, in his shirt and night-gown, gave them a *reveillé matin* before they were up, and spent a good time in or upon the bed, chuse which you will believe. No ceremony was omitted of bride-cakes, points, garters, and gloves, which have been ever since the livery of the court; and at night there was sewing into the sheet, casting of the bride's left hose, with many other petty sorceries."—WINWOOD's *Memorialls,* II. 43.

And, to adde to the iniquity of the times, divers incests were then pardoned: insomuch as two gentlemen, who married two sisters one after another, got licence at New-Market not to be molested in the high-commission. But, above all, a godly minister in Lincolnshire was barbarously murthered by one Cartwright, whom King James pardoned.[1]

The reason of this murther was, for rebuking him of swearing, drunkenness, and whoring.

At this time were many pious divines silenced by the bishops, who inhibited preaching in the afternoon; divers exercises in several towns commanded down: an occasion bred much prophaness in England, King James allowing dancing about May-poles, and so winked at breaking the

---

[1] See an account of this murder in a scarce pamphlet, entitled, " The Life, Confession, and Hearty Repentance of Francis Cartwright, for his Bloudie Sinne in Killing of one Master Storr, Minister of Market Rason." 1621.

Sabbath; a vice God curseth every where in Scripture.'

What shall I say more? All impiety was incouraged in such a sort, that lawful marriages were divorced or multiplied; as, namely, the Countess of Essex from the Earl of Essex, late general for the parliament; alledging the lord had a defect, and was not able to perform the act of generation, (although the contrary was after proved,) to make a gap for Somerset's adultery, by a nullity which Bishop Bilson devised; a nickname being given for this to his son,

---

' The celebrated Baxter informs us, that in his youth he laboured under strong temptations from the vicinity of a May-pole to his father's house, round which the villagers danced every Sunday evening until it was dark. " And though one of my fathers own tenants was the piper, he could not restrain him nor break the sport. So that we could not read the Scripture in our family, without the great disturbance of the taber and pipe, and the noise in the street. Many times my mind was inclined to be among them, and sometimes I broke loose from conscience and joined with them, and the more I did it the more I was inclined to it. But when I heard them call my father *puritan*, it did much to cure me and alienate me from them."—*Life of Mr Richard Baxter, folio,* 1696.

who was rewarded with knighthood ; and therefore stiled by the people, Sir Nullity Bilson. This bishop maintained Christs personal descention into hell : an opinion disavowed by all orthodox divines. ' And many other false opinions were maintained in that age; as, that Solomon was damned, an amanuensis of the Scripture.

The second example is the Lord Riches Lady, named Penelope, who was divorced to make way for the Lo. Montjoy's lust, Earl of Devonshire. *

What shall I say more ? Did not King James his minions and favourites rule the kingdom in the person of the king, who were five in number, since his approach upon English ground ? to wit, Sir George

1 Thomas Bilson, Bishop of Worcester, a learned divine of the 17th century, maintained a controversy with the celebrated Hugh Broughton, upon the just interpretation of the word *Hades* as used in the Creed. The bishop contended that a literal descent of our Saviour into hell was to be understood, an opinion now disowned by the church.—See the last edition of Somers' Tracts, vol. II. p. i. for some account of this dispute.

* See Aulicus Coquinariæ, page 200, and note.

3

Humes, Earl of Dunbar, Sir Philip Herbert, after Earl of Montgomery and Pembrook, Sir James Hayes, Earl of Carlile, and Sir Robert Car, Earl of Sommerset, who defiled his hands in Overbury's death; that wicked divorce ushering the murther. This Sommerset being elected of the council, furnished his library onely with twenty playbooks and wanton romances, and had no other in his study.

A lord very like to give wise counsel! This lord, with the lady, were questioned for the murther; and the Lieutenant of the Tower, Sir George Elloways, was hanged but for concealing of it; King James being willing with this accusation, to make passage for another favourite, which was Sir George Villiers, after Duke of Buckingham, who by his greatness vitiated many gentile and noble virgins in birth, though vitious for yeelding to his lust; whose greatness opened the door to allure them more.[1]

[1] Some of Peyton's scandals are countenanced by graver historians:—

To please this favourite, King James gave way for the duke to entice others to his will. Two examples I will recite: first, the king entertained Sir John Crofts and

" For the Marquis himself, as he was a man of excellent symmetry, and proportion of parts, so he affected beauty, where he found it ; but yet he looks upon the whole race of women as inferior things, and uses them as if the sex were one, best pleased with all. And if his eye culled out a wanton beauty, he had his setters that could spread their nets, and point a meeting at some other house, where he should come (as by accident) and find accesses, while all his train attended at the door as if it were an honourable visit. The Earl of Rutland, of a noble family had but one daughter to be the mistress of his great fortune ; and he tempts her; carries her to his lodgings in Whitehall ; keeps her there for some time, and then returns her back again to her father. The stout old earl sent him this threatening message, That he had too much of the gentleman to suffer such an indignity ; and if he did not marry his daughter, to repair her honour, no greatness should protect him from his justice. Buckingham, that perhaps made it his design to get the father's good-will this way (being the greatest match in the kingdom) had no reason to dislike the union, therefore he quickly salved up the wound, before it grew to a quarrel : and if this marriage stopt the current of his sins, he had the less to answer for."—WILSON apud Kennet, ii. 728.

his daughter, a beautiful lass, at Newmarket, to sit at the table with the king.

This he did then, to procure Buckingham the easier to vitiate her: Secondly;
Mrs Dorothy Gawdy, being a rare creature, King James carried Buckingham to
Gulford, to have his will on that beauty:
but Sir Nicholas Bacon's sons conveyed
her out of a window into a private chamber, over the leads, and so disappointed the
duke of his wicked purpose. In which
cleanly conveyance, the author had a hand,
with the knights sons. Truly, that day a
sober man was hard to be seen, in king,
prince, and nobles.

Moreover, it was an art King James used
for these favourites, to be skreens to decline
the hatred of his people; when complained
of in parliament, and when questioned,
they were spunges to be squeezed to fill his
coffers.

One story I will relate more remarkable
then the rest; the king, very timerous of
death from the contrivings of pope and

Spaine, wrote a letter to the pope, that he
would tolerate popery when he brought
affaires to his bent in Great Britaine. The
letter, discovered by a lucky chance to the
seven yeers parliament, and complained of
in the remonstrance to the king, he made
the Scotish secretary own this act, and
affirm it was his, and not the kings; promising him to take him off at last with
advancement: but contrary, it occasioned
the secretaries ruine.[1]

---

[1] James had acknowledged, by public proclamation,
22d February, 1604, the obligations he lay under to
Clement VIII., and it would seem that his secretary,
Lord Balmerino, thought himself authorised to use
yet stronger language in a letter addressed to him. In
the traditional history, called "The Staggering State
of Scots Statesmen," the following account is given of
the secretary's disgrace:

"Mr James Elphingston, brother to the Lord Elphingston, was one of the octavians, and secretary after
the death of the said Mr Jon Lindsay, a man of a notable spirit and great gifts, as he gave proof at his being in England, as one of the commissioners for the
treaty of union, in anno 1605.

"He was in such favour with King James, that he
craved the reversion of Secretary Cecil's place, at the
king's coming to the crown of England, which was the

Here, by the way, I must play the cook,
to lard three several occurences, not im-

beginning of his overthrow; for the said Secretary
Cecil wrought so, that having procured a letter which
had come from King James, wherein he promised all
kindness to the Roman see and pope, if his holiness
would assist him to attain the crown of England; this
letter the said Secretary Cecil shewed in the king's presence in the council of England; whereupon, King
James fearing to displease the English nation, behoved
to disclaim the penning of this letter, and lay the blame
thereof on his secretary, who, a little before that, he
had made Lord Balmerino, to whom he wrote to come
to court; where, being come, for exoneration of the
king, he behoved to take on him the guilt of writing
that letter: and therefore was he sent back to Scotland with the Earl of Dunbar as prisoner, first to Edinburgh, with the people of which place he was little favoured, because he had acquired many lands about the
town, as Restalrig, Barnetoun, and mills of Leith; so
that John Henderson, the baillie, forced him to light
off his horse at the foot of Leith-wynd, albeit he had
the rose in his leg, and was very unable to walk, till he
came to the prison-house. Some days thereafter he
was accused of treason, and then sent prisoner to Falk-
land, and at last carried to St Andrews, and there sentenced to want the head, but no time prefixed when.

" Thereafter he got liberty to go to his own house
of Balmerino, where, being a widower, he got an ama-
torious portion of cantharides from a maid in his house,
called Young, (thereafter wife to Doctor Honeyman,)

pertinent to the matter in hand. The first was, that Secretary Winnode took a bribe of 20,000*l.* to redeliver the four cautionary townes in Holland to the Dutch; which we now may see might have curbed the states from prejudicing England. Another was, King James his weakness to give way to Gundamore to take away Sir Walter Rawliegh's life, who might have vexed Philip the Second of Spaine. A third was, to sell iron ordnance, and discover the art of their carriages, which all the world was ignorant of.

This last favourite, George, Duke of Buckingham, advanced to such power with his mother, rewarded the king with pyson, by a poysoning water, and a plaister made of the oyle of toads.

This duke, from a private gentleman, with an annuity of thirty pound a year

of which he died."—*Staggering State of Scots Statesmen, by John Scot of Scotstarvet. From an original MS. Edin.* 1754, 8. p. 59.

for life, was raised to such a mount of
glory and power, to be Master of Horse,
Master of the Wards and Liveries, Admiral of England, and Lord Warden of the
Cinqports. A lord tall of stature, amiable of
countenance; who, like a ravenous kyte,
ingrossed all into his hands, to inrich and
advance his kindred, and to place and dis-
place whom he listed.; so that this lord was
grown so potent, his master stood in awe
of him, in such sort, that when the king
was sick of the gout, he would remove him
from place to place at pleasure against the
kings will; who, to work his ends, wrought
into favour with the rising Phœbus, King
Charles. The king prying into this way
of his successor, set a bold courtier, Doctor Turner, afloat, to bring the Earl of Bristol (then out) to launch into favour; but the
duke complying with Turner, and perceiving
the plot against him, wrought by a coun-
termine by Charles, the chief engineer; but
the dukes drift was, after King James his
death, to make himself King of Ireland,

and therefore he was styled Prince of Ty-
peraria, an appendix to that throne.[1] This
made the duke swell like a toad to such a
monstrous proportion of greatness in vast
thoughts, as multiplying to an ocean from
the rivers of pride, power, and ambition,
he sate as a gyant on the shoulders of King
James, and drowned his power, limiting no
bounds to his overflowing will; whose vertue and good nature being corrupted by
so wicked a life, turned love into hatred,
obedience into rule : for, after he had dispatched the Duke of Richmond, Marquess
Hamilton, the Earl of Southampton and
his son, by poyson, (as by Doctor Egle-
stons relation[2] plainly appeared to the par-

[1] This seems absolute extravagance.

[2] Bishop Kennet gives the following account of Eglisham's evidence, which the reader, if he incline, may
consult at length in the Harleian Miscellany, or in Somers' Tracts :

" Dr Eglisham, one of the king's physitians, was
obliged to flee beyond seas for some expressions he
had muttered about the manner of his majesty's death,
and lived at Brussels many years after. It was there
he published a book to prove King James was poyson-

liament, whom he caused to be killed in forraine parts for discovering the villany.)

ed; giving a particular account of all the circumstances of his sickness, and laying his death upon the Duke of Buckingham and his mother. I have read the book some fifteen years ago, in the hands of Don Pedro Ronkillor, the Spanish ambassador, who told me it had been translated into High-Dutch, about the time Gustavus Adolphus was entering into Germany for recovering of the Palatinate; and that by a secret order of the court of Brussels, to throw dust upon the royal family of England. Among other remarkable passages I remember in the book, there is one about the plaister that was applied to the king's stomach. He says, it was given out to have been mithridate, and that one Dr Remington had sent it to the duke as a medicine, with which he had cured a great many agues in Essex. Now Eglisham denies it was mithridate, and says, ' Neither he, nor any other physitians could tell what it was.' He adds, ' that Sir Matthew Lister and he, being the week after the king's death at the Earl of Warwick's house, in Essex, they sent for Dr Remington, who lived hard by, and asked him, What kind of plaister it was he had sent to Buckingham for the cure of an ague, and whether he knew it was the king the duke designed it for?' Remington answered, ' that one Baker, a servant of the duke's, came to him in his master's name, and desired him if he had any certain specifick remedy against an ague to send it him;' and accordingly he sent him mithridate, spread upon leather, but knew not till then that it was designed for the king. ' But,' con-

Thus filled with venome of greatness, he made no bones to send his master packing to another world, as appeared plainly in parliament, by the witness of divers physitians : especially Doctor Ramsey, in full hearing at a committee. Wherefore, for this and other crimes he was impeached in the beginning of King Charles his government; and though King Charles was bound to prosecute King James and the other lords death, committed contrary to all the laws of God and nations; yet King Charles, to save the duke, dissolved the parliament, and never after had the truth tryed to clear himself from confederacy, or the duke from so hainous a scandal. Now

tinues Eglisham, ' Sir Matthew Lister and I shewing him a piece of the plaister we had kept after it was taken off, he seem'd greatly surprized, and offered to take his corporal oath, that it was none of what he had given Baker; nor did he know what kind of mixture it was.

" But the truth is, this book of Eglisham's is wrote with such an air of rancour and prejudice, that the manner of his narrative takes off much from the credit of what he writes."—WILSON, *ut supra*, p. 790, note by Kennet.

let all the world judge of Charles his carriage, whether he were not guilty of conniving at so foul a sin, though not of the death : so that covering his lyon-like disposition, with appearance of a lamb, he proved like Nero the tyrant, that in the parliament of the petition of right, shewing himself in his lively colours: for displaying the banner of tyranny, he put an end to the meeting, and imprisoned divers members, so that Sir John Elliott dyed, and the rest remained in durance, because they had been faithful to their countrey; and, to add to cruelty, he sent Sergeant Glanvile, Sir Peter Hayman, and Colonel Purify [1] into forraine parts, to consume their fortunes and hazard their lives, calling not a parliament long after.

By this time, sycophants so inlarged the monarchy without bounds, that there were exactions too many to be repeated in so

[1] Commonly spelled Purefoy; but probably Sir Edward preferred the fanatical to the Norman orthography.

little a volume as this ; and piety being intombed so many yeers, and so many pious
men silenced, caused nobility, gentry, and
all inferiours more licentious ; who, by insensible steps, grew atheistical. This was
connived at by many debauched in authority : so great a current of prophaness was
generally for want of ordinances, which
caused the people to perish in godliness.

The fault proceeded in both kings, but
especially from the first governing by young
counsellors, who had not vertue, but vanity ; this caused Gundamore (that cunning
Machiavil) to scoff at the counsellors of
state, telling King James he was the wisest
and happiest prince of Christendome, to
make privy counsellors sage at the age of
twenty-one, which his master (the King of
Spaine) could not till sixty. A jest pocket-
ed up by him, who loved commendation
and flattery more then truth ; by which he
was blinded, and saw not the hidden flour.
This prince (otherwise very much knowing)
mued in his English reign favourites to the

fifth coat: these nobles being addicted more to pleasure and delights then the school of prudence and wisdome; looking more at their own interest then the common good or piety of life, gave so vast a liberty to their lives, as made an abordment of looseness in many; insomuch that strictness of life (which our Saviour requires) was imputed a disgrace; and the vainest counted the wisest; the profanest, no hypocrite; and a puritan was stiled a *devil*:[a] so that by this time it was difficult to hear profitable sermons; the pulpits being stuffed more with eloquence then zeal to move the conscience; and the preachers were fitter for a stage then a pulpit. Thus begun goodness to dwindle, and vice to spread far and neer; vitious being counted the gallantest men.

But God opened Pembrook's heart to see the errours of youth.[b]

[a] King James used to term them, from their excess of rigour, Christians out of their wits.

[b] We have already had occasion to commemorate the wisdom, spirit, and gratitude of Philip, Earl of Pembroke and Montgomery. See vol. i. p. 220. But his

But, behold! the last was Sir George Villiers in number, but first in vice and villany, as by the former relation he appeared unmasked in his open colours; who mounted the highest steps of honour, and profited most in the academy of Nicholaus the Florentine, accompanied with a juncto of Achitopel-advisers, who spun the web of all his inhumane devices, and had none to intercept the contriving, but Felton, with a knife, to take away their general; which hindered further rallying his diabolical plots. This man imbargued us in an unnecessary war at the island of Rees, where many brave commanders ended their dayes by his unexperienced discipline in war; who, though advised by Burrows, guarded not a fort, which made the French masters of that island after he had taken it; and in his retreat from thence, placed his ensignes in the muskets, not the pikes.

Afore this, King Charles sought to marry

being converted to fanaticism, was probably, in Sir Edward Peyton's estimation, a cover for all sins.

with Mary of the house of Bourboune, and sent the Earl of Holland ordinary ambassador to France; who, with the assistance of the extraordinary Buckingham there, dispatched that overtuie by the aid of the queen-mother, with their alluring behaviour, which drew on the conclusion more then a team of horses or oxen could: a byword King James used to obtaine ends by female creatures.

To Dover Mary was brought, and so to Canterbury, where King Charles bedded her, without the ordinary religious forme of uniting.

This queen, some yeers after, shewed great modesty, although there lay a pad in the straw: for the Count of Soysons justified boldly and openly at the Louvre in Paris, that he was contracted before to her with divers witnesses; and so challenged her for his lawful wife before God.

Holland[1] of this advertised, sent Soysons

[1] Rich, Earl of Holland, beheaded in 1648, was, with Hay, Earl of Carlisle, ambassador at Paris for settling

12

a challenge to combat him ; but Soysons
was deaf of that eare, and never met : a
reason was, the court-faction for the marriage was too strong for him to maintaine
the truth with his sword : an occasion de-
monstrated more his fear of ruine then valour, and that his enemies power abated
the edge of his courage.

Whilst this match was a brewing, the
duke assayed to defile Lewis the Thirteenth's
bed by some accomplices, which then was
found out by the parliament in Paris : a
discovery instigated him to procure his
master to the French war, inhibiting the
Spanish marriage, because Count Olivares
had foysted into his bed a pocky courte-
san at Madrid, in stead of his lady, often
sollicited by Buckingham ; most of his wisdom consisting in such constuprations. So
that these bawdy transactions, in a pros-
pective-glass, may bring nearer to our me-
mories the fashion of Charles his reigne,

the marriage between Charles I. and Henrietta Maria.

how sin was hatched from an egg to a dragon, to devour holiness of life ; insomuch,
that the masks and playes at Whitehal were
used onely for incentives of lust : therefore
the courtiers invited the citizens wives to
those shews, on purpose to defile them in
such sort. There is not a lobby nor chamber (if it could speak) but would verify
this.'

* The comedies of the age have many allusions to
what is here more than intimated. Ben Jonson, in
the character of Robin Goodfellow, gives an account
of the various persons admitted to those court festivi-
ties :—" I watched what kind of persons the door most
opened to, and one of their shapes I would belie to get
in with. First, I came with authority, and said I was
an engineer, and belonged to the motions. They asked me if I were the fighting bear of last year, and laughed me out of that, and said the motions were ceased.
Then I took another figure of an old tire-woman ; but
tired under that too, for none of the masquers would
take note of me, the mark was out of my mouth. Then
I pretended to be a musician ; marry, I could not shew
mine instrument, and that bred a discord. Now there
was nothing left me that I could presently think on,
but a feather-maker of Black-friars ; and in that shape,
I told 'em, surely, I must come in, let it be open'd unto me ; but they all made as light of me as of my fea-
ther, and wondered how I would be a puritan, being of

King James dead, King Charles ascended the throne, with a dismal plague of

so vain a vocation. I answered, We are all masquers
sometimes; with which they knocked hypocrisy o' the
pate, and made room for a bombard-man, that brought
bouge for a country lady or two, that fainted, he said,
with fasting for the fine sight, since seven o'clock in
the morning. O, how it grieved me that I was prevented o' that shape, and had not touched on it in time, it
liked me so well. But I thought I would offer at it yet.
Marry, before I could procure my properties, alarum
came that some of the whimlens had too much; and
one shewed how fruitfully they had watered his head,
as he stood under the grices; and another came out
complaining of a cataract, shot into his eyes by a planet
as he was star-gazing. There was that device defeated.
By this time I saw a fine citizen's wife or two let in;
and that figure provoked me exceedingly to take it;
which I had no sooner done, but one o' the blackguard
had his hand in my vestry, and was groping of me as
nimbly as the Christmas cutpurse. He thought he
might be bold with me, because I had not a husband
to squeak to. I was glad to forgo my form, to be rid of
his hot steaming affection, it so smelt of the boyling
house. Forty other devices I had of waremen, and the
chandrie, and I know not what else; but all succeeded
alike. I offered money too, but that could not be done
so privately as it durst be taken for the danger of an
example. At last a troop of strangers came to the door,
with whom I made myself sure to enter; but before I
could mix they were all let in, and I left alone without,
for want of an interpreter. Which, when I was fain to

50,000 dying every week: God pointing
to us, as with a fescu, as a schoolmaster, to
warn us to repent of our abominable sins ;
if no admonition would reform us, he would
scourge us with an iron rod. Yet, in shew,
King Charles gave good hopes to his people of a vertuous reigne ; but finding the
sweetness of his invasselling the people,
King Charles paved his path by the steps
of his forerunner, who reigned twenty-three
yeers save one day : but Charles, instead
of pacing it, ran violently to destroy his
subjects, following too hastily his prece-
dents direction ; which brought him afore
his time to the block, the desert of tyrants.

be to myself a colossus, the company told me I had
English enough to carry me to bed; with which all
the other statues of flesh laughed. Never till then did
I know the want of an hook and a piece of beef, to
have baited three or four of those goodly wide mouths
with. In this despair, when all invention, and transla-
tion too, failed me, I e'en went back, and stuck to this
shape you see me in of mine own, with my broom and
my candles, and came on confidently, giving out I was
part o' the device."— *Love Restored, in a Masque at
Court, by Ben Jonson.*

12

Certainly those times differed much from these : for where it is falsely objected, that these days are more heretical ? I answer, by a general sale of heretical books ; then they sought to vitiate truth with greediness, the sole indeavour in the universities : now in these days, too curiously finding out truth, they mistake it unwillingly, and run upon some points of error, which this wise parliament labours to suppress, by placing pious and learned divines, (as speedily as they can,) men indued with the spirit of God, through their dominions : there being a wide difference 'twixt those do wilfully maintaine against knowledge, falshood, and the others that mistake the truth.

But in those times they studied erronious opinions, being incouraged by the bishops ; so that the students were ambitious to rake out of the ashes many heresies of Rome to maintain their lordships; as, namely, kneeling at the sacrament : they used arguments of the real presence of Christ, and to reverence Christ corporally present with the papists; when our Saviour used sitting, another gesture.

From this root sprang the Socinian damnable opinion, to make Christs death an imitation for all to follow, to bury in oblivion the great high-priesthood of Christ, and to advance their sacerdotal tyranny, and insult over the people by the power of spiritual courts, which exalted them above others; when Christ abased himself to be a saviour in his actions on earth; a carriage they ought to have used according to his example : by which meanes, the clergy were the eyes, eares, hands, legs, and, above all, the braine, to support the kings insupportable tyranny. To this head, I will reduce their idolatrous cringing to the altar, bowing at the name of Jesus, and making churches idolatrous; usually kneeling and praying in them, when no service of God was used : and their ———— reverence at the Eucharist was to no other purpose; but to support antichristian episcopacy; what honour was done in the church was placed

on them ; transferring the honour done
from the place to the persons administring
service : a cause made King Charles take
them into his intimacy, to support his absolute monarchy to do what he pleased with
subjects property, real, personal, and vital ;
as also finding the papacy conduced more
to regality, he favoured them more then
protestants : for when the justices in all
parts persecuted the papists upon the statutes, they were disgraced and removed,
and the protestants persecuted and punished, and the priests delivered out of prison.

In which rout, amongst others, was Secretary Windebank, a principal agent to
get in favour with Queen Mary ; insomuch,
that I knew divers papists brought out of
Newgate, and their pursuers punished.
This last-recited secretary was a creature
to Laud, both brothers in iniquity to accomplish such matters.

Did not King Charles his letter written
in Spaine to the pope shew his inclination
to set up popery, if the pope would grant

him a dispensation to marry the infanta?
Yea, certainly it cannot be denied by any
rational man; if he considers fully the bent
of those times, he must be convinced by a
truth I shall utter. When the king came,
from Greenwich with the queen on a Tuesday morning, a little afore the last parliament, she landed at Sommerset-house, where
she lodged; the king arrived at Whitehall,
a day he used to hear a sermon; the queen
drew him from the sermon to Sommerset-
house, insomuch, as a lord, to whom I gave
a visit, told me, (when he came not to the
preaching at twelve of the clock, long expected,) in anger, that the king was then
at mass, and reconciled to the pope; and
so this lord in haste went after mass-time to
Sommerset-house, and there dined '.

' Lilly, who was, like our author, a sufficiently prejudiced investigator of the actions of Charles I., clears
him from this scandal, and at the same time assigns an
admirable reason why the astrologer himself did not
honour the queen's devotions with his presence.

" He [King Charles] was ill thought of by many, especially the puritans, then so called, for suffering the
chapel at Somerset-house to be built for the queen,

It is therefore no marvel why the Almighty sent so much misery upon these three kingdomes, and wrought such a fatal catastrophe to turn the spoakes of the wheel upside down, raising the humble out of the dust, and abasing the proud and highminded.

By this, as by a prospective glass, we may behold how King Charles erected the fabrick of his potency, or rather the structure of his ill government. For it will appear plainly, that King Charles negotiated with the pope to reduce England to popery privately; therefore it is known to all, that King Charles entertained three nuncios from the pope, Gregorio. Pansano, Signeur Con, and another, under pretence to regulate the popish clergy, under

where mass was publickly said. Yet he was no papist, or favoured any of their tenets; nor do I remember any such thing was ever objected against him. Myself was once there to gaze whilst the priest was at high mass; the sexton and others thrust me out very uncivilly, for which I protested never to come there again."—LILLY's *Life of Charles I.*, apud *the Lives of Ashmole and Lilly.* London, 1774, 8. p. 190.

the Bishop of Calcedon,[1] appointed by
Barbareno, the popes nephew, protector of
the English catholicks, when the purpose
was to reduce to an union the protestant
clergy with the Roman. And was not Arthur Bret appointed to go embassador to
Rome from King Charles, who dyed by
the way: and after, there was sent Sir James
Hambleton, of the house of Abercorn.

To make a step further, I will inform the
reader: After Buckingham's death, the Earl
of Holland was highest in favour with King

---

[1] A schism between the catholic regular and secular
clergy in England broke forth with great violence, in
a controversy concerning the spiritual authority of Dr
Smith, titular Bishop of Chalcedon. To compose their
difference, the pope sent Gregorio Panzani, and others
as his envoys. They met with more attention and en-
couragement from the English clergy than was perhaps
prudent, and even returned to open a negotiation with
Laud for reconciling England with the church of Rome,
which he seems to have broken off *multum gemens*. See
in Somers' Tracts, vol. iv. a piece entitled, "The Pope's
Nuncios, or the Negotiation of Seignior Panzani, Seignior Con, &c. resident here in England with the Queen,
and treating about the Alteration of Religion with the
Archbishop of Canterbury and his Adherents, in the
Years of our Lord 1634, 1635, 1636," &c.

Charles, who bestowed on him neer one
hundred and fifty thousand pound in few
yeers ; and he was no less esteemed of the
queen, being her agent to receive moneys
forfeited, and compositions given her-by
her consort ; as, namely, to free Sir Giles
Alington's punishment for marrying his
neece, twelve thousand pound was paid to
Holland for the use of the queen ; they
sharing money and delights together.

This made the kings love of Holland not
alwayes firm ; for a suspition arose, as a
devil, to be the bane of friendship, which
thus happened ; such was the intirety twixt
the queen and this lord, she having sent
letters into France to one Monsieur de
Jerre, then in prison, she inclosed a letter
unsealed in Hollands letter sealed, which
was intercepted by the ambassador, the
Lord Jerome Weston, resident in France,
and sent to his father the Lord Treasurer,
by whom it was shewn to the king ; a matter made him so passionately jealous of
Holland, as he was confined to Kensing-

ton.[*] Whereupon, the queen was so discontented as she bedded not with the king
some nights ; and was so inraged for Hollands confinement, as, till the king released
him, she would not entertain him to her
bed : But, as nature is frail, so she flying
imbraces, made the husband more earnest
to peruse her fruition ; so that at last, Hollands enemies are chid, and he brought into favour. These are the devices of cunning dames, when silly men, being horn-
beaten, often times are cured without a
plaister : he had better have put them into his pocket. After this, the queen was
advertised of Charles his lubricity with divers ladies his mistresses ; which appeared,
because he was jealous of a lord handing a
countess he dearly loved through the court
of Whitehall, at which he shewed much indignation for a great time. In the mean-
time, there were not people wanting, who

* This may be accounted a piece of paltry scandal,
being utterly inconsistent with the character of Henrietta Maria.

nourished each in suspition ; so that both seeing themselves peccant, one had free-dome of mistresses, and the other of ser-vants.

Now I must crave your pardon, if I have not observed so punctually the times, this being rather a rhapsody then a continued history, and therefore I am constrained to patch up the post with the prior faults ; being all of one batch of tyranny ; as Ben. Volington, Will. Stroud, and Eliot, Mr Hambden, Sir John Corbet, Sir John He-vingham, were confined, for being faithfull in parliament. Moreover, for discovering the designe of a thousand German horse, the Earl of Sommerset, the Earl of Clare, dead ; Sir Robert Cotton, dead ; my Lord Saint John, Mr Seldon, and Mr James, were sent to the Tower. The occasion was this, as I re-member : Pickerni, Master-Falconer, found the written project in the kings cabinet, it being open, who took it out, and brought it to Sommerset, and so it came to the hands of Sir Robert and the other four usually meeting; but Sir Robert had a man would take his cups freely, and at a taverne told it to a false brother, who betrayed them all: for which cause, the five were brought *aurium tenus* into the Star-chamber, because it was discovered afore it was acted.

But it is more memorable how King Charles was angry with the parliament of the petitions of right, as he was so far from punishing Sir Richard Plumly for pulling a knight Hubard out of a coach, and beating him so that he dyed; and to shew his hatred to Hubard, who was one of them held the then speaker of the parliament, Sir John Finch, in the chair, that he advanced this Plumly to be Admiral of the Irish Seas, and made him a knight for his service for killing Hubard, when justly he should have questioned him for his life.

And to sound King Charles his heart, it is probable King Charles was in his heart a papist, by the queens perswasion, and her mother; for, after going from the parliament, he sent pardons for divers priests con-

demned; who ingeniously finding this would
make a rupture 'twixt king and parliament,
the prisoners petitioned the houses, sending the pardons to the house ; and desired,
rather then there should be a breach between them, to suffer death : for which
prudence the parliament would not let them
die.

In both these kings times swearing was
in such esteem, principally from King James
his example, cursing the people with all the
plagues of Egypt ; though King Charles
granted twelve pence an oath through the
kingdome to Robin Lashly, which was observed more to get money, then suppress
swearing : for such a negligence was in the
magistrates, seeing the great courtiers gar-
nished their mouthes with God-dammees,
as if they desired damnation rather then salvation. [1]

[1] The habit of swearing was inveterate among the Cavaliers, who affected to distinguish themselves by this
odious practice from their fanatical opponents. A contemporary poet, describing the military men of the civil
wars, addresses them thus :—

Bribery, the nurse of injustice, was so rife in those days, that right was not distributed to the owner: a vice augmented by knights of the post, very frequent in city and country.

And lawyers would take fees, and never plead for their clients; and sometimes on both sides; insomuch as in a suit depending 'twixt myself and my son, we gave fees to one and the same person. Wherefore

> Now, you wild blades that make loose inns your stage,
> To vapour forth the acts of this sad age,
> Your Edgehill fight, the Newberries and the west,
> And northern clashes where you still fought best,
> Your strange escapes, your dangers void of fear,
> When bullets flew between the head and ear,
> Your pia-maters rent perished your guts;
> Yet live as then ye had been but earthen buts,
> Whether you fought by *Damn-me* or the Spirit;
> To you I speak ——
>
> *The Legend of Captain Jones*, 1671.

Cromwell argued that the body of Scottish horse, by whom his quarters were beaten up near Musselburgh, about 30th July, 1650, were assisted by English cavaliers, because one who was dying said with his last gasp, " Damn-me, I'll go to my King."—See Relation of the Campaign in Scotland, in Original Memoirs during the Great Civil War. Edinburgh, 1806.

on these times God hath brought on us a lamentable war.

Now let all the world behold how King Charles violated the rights of parliament, coming into the house with great power to carry away the five members. To prove how great a breach of priviledge of parliament this was, the author hereof wrote a discourse against it, affixing his hand; it being taken in his waggon at Banbury by the kings party;[a] for which he was condemned to die by Sir Robert Heath,[b] and his estate given away.

I will not repeat how much he hath suffered for being faithful to parliaments, both afore and since the access of this; onely I

[a] The castle of Banbury surrenderred to Charles I. immediately after the battle of Edgehill.

[b] Sir Robert Heath, Attorney General, in the reign of James I., and Lord Chief Justice of the Common Pleas during the peaceful part of Charles I.'s reign, was, about the time that Charles took up arms, made Lord Chief Justice of the King's Bench, for the purpose of attainting of high treason the Earl of Essex and the principal followers of the parliament. It would seem he had exercised his functions upon our author.

will rehearse, that being taken prisoner by the cavaliers, he lost four hundred pounds in mony, apparel, waggon, and fourty horses: and likewise in Wiltshire at Broad Choak, in houshold stuff, four hundred pounds; which was carried into Langford, after a garrison taken by Colonel Ludlow, ' for the parliament; which he had never restored, although he often petitioned.

Another wrong long since he had: When Sir Robert Heath had inclosed two thousand acres of common, as Lord of Joham, one named Anne Dobbs was kept with bread and water in Cambridge castle, by a justice of peace, a creature of Sir Roberts, to confess the author of this discourse counselled her with others to pull down the enclosure taken from the common; by that means to take away his life as a rebel; when it was well known he had no hand in

' Langford House, near Salisbury, a garrison of the royalists, surrendered to Cromwell, shortly after the battle of Naseby. Colonel Ludlow was placed there as governor for the parliament.

it, but then was sitting in parliament as a member.

By this it appears, the king chose good judges and justices, which were so corrupt. The reason was, that the author being condemned, he might forfeit a mannor next adjacent. This justice of peace was a mortal enemy of his, Sir Robert Heath having bought four hundred pound a yeer of the justice, where the accused was lord, that Sir Robert might beg it of the king.

And if we examine the King of Denmark, brother of Queen Anne; the first time he was entertained into England, what debauchedness was exercised in his welcome to King James, to add punishment to the family! who both were so drunk at Theobalds, as our king was carried in the armes of the courtiers, when one cheated another of the bed-chamber, for getting a grant from King James, for that he would give him the best jewel in England for a jewel of a hundred pound, he promised him; and so put King James in his armes, and carried him to his lodging, and defrauded the bed-chamber-man, who had much ado to get the king into his bed. And Denmark was so disguised, as he would have lain with the Countess of Nottingham, making horns in derision at her husband the high Admiral of England ; which caused a deep discontent between them.* And generally the

* The most picturesque and witty account of the scandalous revels, during the reign of James I., occurs in the following contemporary letter :—

Sir John Harington to Mr Secretary Barlow, [*from London,*] 1606.

" My good Friend,

" In compliance with your asking, now, shall you accept my poor accounte of rich doings. I came here a day or two before the Danish king came, and from the day he did come, till this hour, I have been well nigh overwhelmed with carousal and sports of all kinds. The sports began each day in such manner and such sorte, as well nigh persuaded me of Mahomets paradise. We had women, and indeed wine too, of such plenty, as would have astonished each beholder. Our feasts were magnificent, and the two royal guests did most lovingly embrace each other at table. I think the Dane hath strangely wrought on our good English nobles; for those, whom I could never get to taste good liquor, now follow

courtiers were then so debauched in that
beastly sin, as at that time, in the way-

the fashion, and wallow in beastly delights. The ladies
abandon their sobriety, and are seen to roll about in in-
toxication. In good sooth, the parliament did kindly
to provide his majestie so seasonably with money, for
there have been no lack of good livinge; shews, sights,
and banquetings from morn to eve.

"One day, a great feast was held, and after dinner the
representation of Solomon his temple, and the coming
of the Queen of Sheba was made, or (as I may better
say,) was meant to have been made before their majesties by device of the Earl of Salisbury and others.
But, alas! as all earthly things do fail to poor mortals in
enjoyment, so did prove our presentment thereof. The
lady who did play the queen's part did carry most precious gifts to both their majesties; but forgetting the
steppes arising to the canopy, overset her caskets into
his Danish majesties lap, and fell at his feet, though I
rather think it was in his face. Much was the hurry
and confusion; cloths and napkins were at hand, to
make all clean. His majesty then got up, and would
dance with the Queen of Sheba; but he fell down, and
humbled himself before her, and was carried to an inner chamber, and laid on a bed of state, which was not
a little defiled with the presents of the queen, which
had been bestowed on his garments; such as wine,
cream, jelly, beverage, cakes, spices, and other good
matters. The entertainment and show went forward,
and most of the presenters went backward, or fell down;
wine did so occupy their upper chambers. Now did
appear in rich dress, Hope, Faith, and Charity. Hope

ters chamber at supper, a courtier was
found dead on the table, the wine foam-

did assay to speak, but wine rendered her endeavours
so feeble that she withdrew, and hoped the king would
excuse her brevity: Faith was then all alone, for I am
certain she was not joyned to good works, and left the
court in a staggering condition: Charity came to the
king's feet, and seemed to cover the multitude of sins
her sisters had committed; in some sorte she made obeysance, and brought giftes, but said she would return
home again, as there was no gift which heaven had not
already given his majesty. She then returned to Hope
and Faith, who were both sick and spewing in the lower
hall. Next came Victory, in bright armour, and presented a rich sword to the king, who did not accept it, but
put it by with his hand; and, by a strange medley of
versification, did endeavour to make suit to the king.
But Victory did not triumph long; for, after much lamentable utterance, she was led away like a silly captive,
and laid to sleep in the outer steps of the antichamber.
Now did Peace make entry, and strive to get foremoste
to the king; but I greive to tell how great wrath she did
discover unto those of her attendants; and, much contrary to her semblance, made rudely war with her olive
branch, and laid on the pates of those who did oppose
her coming.

" I have much marvelled at those strange pageantries,
and they do bring to my remembrance what passed of
this sort in our queens days; of which I was some time
an humble presenter and assistant: but I neer did see
such lack of good order, discretion, and sobriety as I
have now done. I have passed much time in seeing the

ing out of his mouth : a horrid sight to behold. [1]

royal sports of hunting and hawking, where the manners were such as made me devise the beasts were pursuing the sober creation, and not man in quest of exercise and food. I will now, in good sooth, declare to
you, who will not blab, that the gunpowder fright is
got out of all our heads, and we are going on hereabouts,
as if the devil was contriving every man to blow up
himself, by wild riot, excess, and devastation of time
and temperance. The great ladies do go well masked,
and indeed it be the only show of their modesty, to
conceal their countenance; but, alack! they meet
with such countenance to uphold their strange doings, that I marvel not at ought what happens. The
lord of the mansion is overwhelmed in preparations at
Theobald's, and doth marvelously please both kings,
with good meet, good drink, and good speeches. I do
often say (but not aloud,) that the Danes have again
conquered the Britons, for I see no man, or woman
either, that can command herself. I wish I was at
home :—*O rus, quando te aspiciam ?*—And I will, before
the Prince Vaudemont cometh."—*Nugæ Antiquæ. Ed.*
1804, I. 348, *et seq.*

[1] The author, in common candour, ought to have excepted Charles from a charge, which might perhaps
have been justly preferred against his father. The following account of his temperance is confirmed by all
contemporary authors :—" As he excelled in all other
virtues, so in temperance he was so strict, that he abhorred all debauchery to that degree, that, at a great
festival solemnity, where he once was, when very many
of the nobility of the English and Scots were entertain-

And it is worthy of observation to consider the carriage of the King of Denmark
and his son usually in his own. country :
for at my being there, I saw the old king
(as his custome was,) to call for the master
of his household ; when he made a voyage
or progress, wrote on a pastboard what he
should doe, and so took the waggon to go
to his boares houses, ' and eat Martlemas

ed, being told by one who withdrew from thence, what
vast draughts of wine they drank, and that there was
one earl who had drank most of the rest down, and was
not himself moved or altered, the king said, that he deserved to be hanged ; and that earl coming shortly after
into the room where his majesty was, in some gaiety,
to shew how unhurt he was from that battle, the king
sent one to bid him withdraw from his majesties presence ; nor did he in some days after appear before
him.—CLARENDON, iii. 198.

' The King of Denmark had large demesnes, which
he cultivated by means of serfs, boors, or bondsmen,
as was anciently the mode of husbandry in most countries of Europe. Colonel Munro, among other memo-
rabilia of his majesty, informs us that he was " praise-
worthy for his œconomy in keeping of storehouses to
feed oxen, and stalls for keeping of milch cows, whereof
is received yearly great income of monies for butter
and cheese, made in great quantity."—MONRO his Expedition, 1636. p. 87.

beef, powdred pork, bacon, or such like as
they had ready; and after repast, took for
a collation the handsomest daughter, kinswoman, or servant in the house (all her kindred adorning her with all sorts of wearing
ornaments) whom the king carried to one
of his guest-houses, where he had not above
three or four lodgings and a kitchen, and
solaced himself with this jewel so long as
he pleased; and after brought her home.
A fruition made her in much esteem with
her friends, after so adulterous a fact.

Likewise it was the custome of his son to
ride on a sled drawn with horses, bells fast-
ned to them, which tingled as he passed
through the townes; the noise caused the
women to run out of doors: the prince beholding one more amiable then the rest,
beckoning to her with his finger, presently
she came to the sled, and accompanied him
to some hostery, till he had satisfied fully
his lust. [*]

[*] We may hope this brutal exertion of despotic
authority is exaggerated; but that the King of Den-

Also their usual course is to prophane
the Sabbath in such sórt, as all the carpen-
ters in the kingdom that day work gratis,
to make the kings ships ; and the people

mark possessed the power of abusing his authority, even
to the extent mentioned in the text, is but too certain.
Munro, who saw the matter in a more favourable light
than one would have expected, gives the following account of the arbitrary authority of that monarch :—

" Having had the honour to have dined with his majesty at his table, then in the gorgebus and pleasant
palace of Freddesborg, taking leave of his majesty, having kissed his hand, I retired to Alzenheur, where I
began to think that this king could have said of his
kingdom, as Scipio said, " You see not a man amongst
all those but if I command him he will from a turret
throw himselfe into the sea :" even so this magnanimous
king, to my knowledge, was of absolute authority in his
kingdome, as all christian kings ought to be in theirs,
ever obeyed in the Lord, without asking the head a reason why do you command us thus ? For we read that
the favour of the Lord was in Juda, in giving them one
heart in doing and obeyiug the commandments of the
king, and of their magistrates and principalls, as I did
cleerely observe in this kingdome of Denmarke, the
goodnesse of government for the flourishing of the
kingdome, where *Totis orbis componebatur ad exemplum
regis.* He commanding, they obeyed ; both lived in
prosperity, the ruler or king heroick, wise, noble, magnanimous, and worthy. - - - - - -

go to church in their worst cloaths, making no difference 'twixt the Lords day and other daies ; who, instead of godly exercises, use much prophaneness.

Give me leave to repeat, that this king ordinarily would be drunk, [1] and, namely, one time (Sir John Pooly being his servant,

---

" Moreover this kingdome is worthy commendation for the order of justice and lawes, having their law books deciding all controversies amongst them; and if it come to any great difference, the kings majestie, as being above the law, sits in judgement as the interpreter of justice, and according to his princely dignity, mitigates as pleaseth his majestie the law, and decides the controversie."—Monro's *Expedition, ut supra,* p. 86, 87.

[1] Howel gives us a good picture of the intemperance of the court of Denmark, at an entertainment given to the Earl of Leicester, then ambassador from England to Christiern. " The king feasted my lord once, and it lasted from eleven of the clock till towards the evening; during which time the king began thirty-five healths; the first to the emperor, the second to his nephew of England; and so went over all the kings and queens of Christendom, but he never remembred the Prince Palsgrave's health, or his niece's, all the while. The king was taken away at last in his chair, but my lord of Leicester bore up stoutly all the while; so that when there came two of the king's

after an inhabiter at Wroungay in Norfolk,)
he commanded Pooly' to ask any gift to
the value of half his kindome, and he should
have it. But he finding his master so beastly out of tune, demanded a great pair of
stags hornes ; for which, after so moderate
a request, the king bestowed on him three
thousand dollars.'

guard to take him by the arms, as he was going down
the stairs, my lord shook them off, and went alone.

"The next morning I went to court for some dispatches, but the king was gone a hunting at break of
day ; but going to some other of his officers, their servants told me, without any appearance of shame, that
their masters were drunk over night, and so it would
be late before they would rise."—HOWELL's *Letters.*
London, 1726. 8. p. 236.

' There can be very little doubt that Shakespeare's
account of the carousals of the usurper of Denmark
was derived from what was the current practice of that
northern court, during the reign of Christiern.

> This heavy-headed revel, east and west,
> Makes us traduced and taxed of other nations;
> They clepe us drunkards, and with swinish phrase
> Soil our addition ; and indeed it takes
> From our achievements, though performed at height,
> The pith and marrow of our attribute.
> HAMLET.

It is not known to all Germany, that his drinking out of reason with his commanders lost marfy battels to the Emperours General Wallestine, which proved a disaster to the united protestant princes, so that he was faine to submit to the emperour, with much loss and disgrace, to the prejudice of the cause of God. ' In which war

---

' Colonel Monro, whom we have already quoted, and who served under Christiern, during his unsuccessful attempts to support the cause of the protestant princes in Germany, gives a much more favourable account of his exertions:—

" This magnanimous king, to my knowledge, deserved to have been worthily thought of, and well spoken for his noble enterprizing of the warre. And though the success was not answerable, I dare be bold to affirm, it was none of his majesties fault, for his majestie not onely bestowed much in advancing of it, but did also hazard himselfe and his crowne in maintaining of it. Neverthelesse there are always some cynicks that doe barke at his majesties proceedings without reason; where we may see that no man, no, nor kings themselves, can escape the lash of censure, and none can eschew to be traduced by the ignominious aspersions of the malevolent tongue. Therefore it is good to do well, and then we need not care what is said; except the sayer put his name to his assertion, and then he may be made to foote his boule in maintaining of it, or un-

his brother King James proved a coward
to back a religious cause ; for he would not
raise men nor money ; yet the parliament
incited and urged him thereto : to whom

worthily to refuse it."—MONRO *his Expedition with the*
worthy Scots Regiment, called Mackeye's Regiment. London, 1637, fol. p. 30.

But from the same authority we learn, that the vice
of drinking beyond measure prevailed not only in the
army of the King of Denmark, but even in the better dis-
ciplined forces of Gustavus Adolphus. Nay, if we can
judge of the worthy colonel's taste, by the unction with
which he speaks of German beer, it would seem he had
no objections to that generous liquor :—

" This regiment, in nine yeeres time under his majesty of Denmarke, and in Dutchland, had ever good lucke
to get good quarters, where they did get much good
wine and great quantity of good beere, beginning first
with Hamburgh beere in Holsten, and after that in
Denmarke, they had plenty of Rustocke beere, and now
at Barnoe, and thereafter they tasted the good Calvinists
beere at Serbest, and our march continuing out of Low
Germany towards the upper circles of the empire, as
in Franconia, Swabland, Elas, and the Paltz, they were
oft merry with the fruits and juices of the best berries
that grew in those circles; for to my knowledge they
never suffered either penury or want, I being their lead-
er, but oft times I did complaine and grieve at their
plenty, seeing they were better to be commanded when
they dranke water, then when they got too much beere
or wine. But my choice of all beeres is Serbester beere,

he made this answer, he would not give so
bad an example to support his son-in-law
against the emperour. Whereas the laws
of the empire were, if the emperour did unjustly, the seven electors might depose him :
for certainly the joyning of Bohemia with
the Count Palatine of Rhine, might have

being the wholsomest for the body, and cleerest from
all filth or barme, as their religion is best for the soule,
and cleerest from the dregs of superstition.

" Being once at dinner with the Rex Chancellor of
Sweden, having dranke good Serbester beere, he asked
me what I thought of that beere ? I answered, it pleased
me well. He replied merrily, no wonder it taste well
to your palet, being it is the good beere of your ill religion. I asked his excellence how the good wine on the
Rhine would taste at Mentz, being the good wine of a
worse religion ? He answered, he liked the wine and the
beere better than both the religions. But I said to be
his excellences neighbour neare Mentz in the Paltz, at
Crewtsenach, I would be content to keepe mine own
religion, and to drinke good Rhinish wine for my life
time."— *Ut supra*, p. 47.

Gustavus used, Monro informs us, to suffer his officers occasionally to make merry ; but his own custom
was never to drink much but upon very rare considera-
tions, when he had some plot to effectuate that concerned his advancement and the weal of his state.—*Ibid.*
p. 40.

been a chief prop to support the protestant
party; which, by Denmarks fault, and King
James his wilfulness, the emperour got the
mastery of: though after God raised Gustavus Adolphus King of Sweden, to turn
the scales to the united princes side, yet in
conclusion the Swedes have sought more
their owne interest then God's.

Behold, if we examine Queen Mary, she
cannot cleare her reputation with Harry
Jermine;[1] for if King Charles had not been
so blinded, it had been discovered long ago,
and she punished or divorced; but the king
being guilty of the same crime, winked at
it; which made him purblind, and count it
a venial sin, as the papists terms them, but
swallowed the mortal; yet urged by an earl

---

[1] Henry Jermyn, afterwards successively Lord Jermyn and Earl of St Albans, adhered to Charles I.
during all his distresses. The only foundation for the
calumny thrown out in the text, was the favour he enjoyed with Henrietta Maria after her husband's death.
This, however, was so great that it seems to have been
generally surmized at Paris, that they were privately
married.

much with him, if he would not believe the
unsutable behaviour between the queen and
Jermine, if he would go into her chamber,
he might be satisfied, and behold Jermine
sitting upon the bed with the queen; so
the king and the lord went in, and found
her and Jermine in that posture. The king
presently, more ashamed of the act then
blaming her, departed, without speaking a
word; yet for all this, the queen was very
jealous of the king; insomuch as he loving
a very great lady now alive, whom he had
for a mistress, to the intent he might have
more freedome with her, sent her lord into
the Low Countries; in the mean while, daily
courts her at Oxford in her husbands and
the queens absence: but the lord returning,
the king diverted his affectionate thoughts
to another marryed lady, of whom the
queen was jealous at her return from France;
so that on a time this lady being in Queen
Maries presence, and dressed *a la mode,* the
queen viewing her round, told the lady she
would be a better mistris for a king then a

wife for a knight. The lady replyed, Madam, I had rather be mistris to a king, then any mans wife in the world. For which answer, she was constrained to absent herself from court a long time.

Now, as all men and their affaires are subject to mulation by a heavenly providence punishing sinners for sin, the wheel turns greatness from top to bottome, of which I have given you a notable lantskip in the fraile condition of the imperiall family of the Stuarts, who, raised to a glittering glory by the succession of many kings, are now tumbled from the mount of ambition and highest authority over three kingdomes, and at last reduced not to be lord of a visible molehill; whose heat of fiery pride hath consumed into ashes of ruine their felicity. Let us mark the shipwrack of those who will not vaile the sailes of tyranny and oppression; they shall not avoid a tempest of Gods anger for precipitation.

In this revolution, God had a special

hand, who, when he determined to bring this family to destruction, accomplisheth it not only by poor and weak means, but by his mightiest thunderbolts of vengeance.

This truth manifested itself perspicuously in this tragical history, who have made the flourishing condition of these three kingdoms stumble, by advancing and giving ear to corrupt instruments of state placed at the helm; who wept not for our common calamity, but in the tears of inferiours; and therefore I demonstrate, that never shall justice be so well done, as by parliamentary proceedings, to settle this commonwealth upon a pious basis, where they proceed in justice to banish oppression, that property may fall into the right channel, and holy men advanced and rewarded, and wicked punished, to the end that the people may be lulled asleep in the cradle of ease and tranquillity; so shall love of governors be in such estimation, as body and purse may be at command; for fear poysons a nation with distrust and hatred ; the first makes firme and stable the foundation of any state ; the last brings it by insensible steps to fal and moulder away like a crazie building. Provided alwayes, until the state have a perfect cure, there may be armed chirurgeons to cut off the gangren'd part, which might putrifie the head, resembled to wise counsellors, who will preserve the whole body ; so they endeavour that taxes be moderated, as the temper of the pulse and health shall appear.

And therefore I beseech you give me leave to turn my pen out of the road, with a counsel from my heart not impertinent to my dear countrymen, to profit by the storm past, reduced by Gods providence to a calme ; to make a pious use of his great miraculous deliverance. I being a man can speak by experience, who hath been most justly worryed by the hand of the Almighty for sins ; therefore let them consider that the chidings of a friend are better than the

kiss of an enemy, a proverb of Solomon;
which, if we shall confide in, we may be
stiled children converted to good; if not,
may be accounted despisers of the road:
which maxime I illustrate the truth of, by
the Grecian Alcibiades; by how much his
banishment was more cruel by the Athenian
Ostracisme, by so much more his qualities
and worth were esteemed. The skill of the
mariner is not at all observed in a calme,
but in a tempest; the wise Ulysses had
perished, if he had not been in danger of
ruine: pleasures blunt and strangle piety;
when adversity moulds the will and humours to a byas of fearing God, inclines us
to know ourselves, and understand the end
of creation and birth to the glory of God,
and good of our country: we are not born
for ourselves: Our eyes are closed with delights, open in chastisements; in the one,
sin draws more punishment; in the other,
we see clearly our aberations, as spots in a
glass. We are here on a theatre for every

one to play his part; the tragical seems
more difficult, by hatred, envy, and jealousie, the slaves of reason ; yet in truth,
are banished in troubles, when God loves
the afflicted better, who, as a soveraigne,
resembleth the ocean, which receives that
it gives, to the end the revenging justice of
heaven turn not wrath against them; but
the divel, enemy of repose, inchants us in
luxury, when affliction imitates nature by
degrees from a little to more, and from more
proceeds to a humane perfection in piety.

I heartily desire you take this advice
above a humane, the command of God:
Be subject to the higher powers, for they
are of God. Wherefore, I beseech you,
respect those set at the helme, whom God
hath made instruments of our happiness;
for naturally we are hooded, and cannot
see that God hath done miraculous works:
Look not upon them as men, but as Gods
instruments, to execute his will; brought
out of the shop of his Almighty work-house,

to accomplish his determination; and are
not to be laid aside, till by Gods appoint-
ment they turn into the tyring-house: for
certainly we have great cause to give thanks
to God for the parliaments valourous success of army and navy; both for general,
lieutenant-general, serjeant-major generals,
colonels, officers, and souldiers; as for the
admirals and captaines at sea, whom God
hath miraculously preserved, to prevaile
over the enemies of the state; and so let
God have the glory, and we tranquillity all
our dayes.

But when I revolve in my thoughts the
opinion most are possessed with, as with a
divel, that parliament and army are a punishment for their sins, and attribute so
great victories to chance, I may justly suspect their atheisme, whose lives I never
see more amended, by Gods immediate
hand on us, to make the omnipotent Father
of spirits to have no hand in it; or if acknowledged in words, return not from ini-

quity, and are not thankful for arriving to
so safe a harbour as they are in, nor see
that God is about to mould the world in
another fashion, as he hath declared by his
prophets of old ; and so, like swine, look
down on the earth, and not to heaven, to
see a divine cause of a mighty alteration.

Now to shew that the parliament proceeded justly in this war, I will prove it by
arguments divine and humane, reason and
law.

First, if we regard the scripture, we shall
finde Rehoboam, the son of Solomon, ' justly lost the ten tribes, because he laid such

! In comparing Charles I. to Rehoboam, Sir Edward
Peyton seems not to have forgotten his father's title of
the British Solomon. When this epithet was once applied to him in the presence of Henry IV. of France,
he said he hoped it was not given to his brother monarch because he was David the Fiddler's son. The unfortunate Lord Sanquhar, afterwards hanged for assassi-
nating one Turner, a fencing-master, was said to have
been present at this unseemly allusion to the history of
David Rizzio, and.James, it is further stated, afterwards
alleged his silence on the occasion as a reason for refusing him his pardon.

heavy burdens on the Jews, who declared
they had no share in David, wishing Israel
to depart to their tents; although God had
made a covenant with David, that his posterity should sit on the throne for ever, on
condition they continued to serve the lord
as they ought; which covenant Rehoboam
broke by sins, in such sort as God punished sin with sin, suffering him to oppress
and impose more heavy taxes on the people then his father; a reason God disswa-
ded: The children of Israel refused God, and
would have kings to rule over them, to enthral them to his will; but they persisted
not to follow the counsel of the Almighty,
therefore it was just the kingdome should
be divided for their disobedience: or if king
Rehoboam did wickedly, he could not be
stiled Gods vicegerent over the twelve tribes;
for God, whom governors represent, never
oppresseth his people but for sin. When
kings cease to imitate God, they cease to
govern or be governors, and represent not

God ; when they are not Gods deputies,
they insult over the people without authority : for this is an infallible rule (not to be
gainesaid) in scripture, that if the people
sin against God, and the king do not oppose it, but yeeld to it, they are punished ;
and if the king sin, and they concur with
him, they are punished : so that if the parliament had not opposed King Charles,
God would have been revenged on them.

Now when a father wrongfully injureth
his children, his love to them is at an end,
and so is his paternal power ; for children
are bound to be obedient to parents, not
to be ruined by them : so that subjects are
bound to obey the sovereign, so long as he
keeps himself in bounds of justice and doing right ; but if the king would destroy
his people, they are no more his subjects,
nor are they bound to obey ; but he is a
tyrant.

God never punished a pious king that
used his people well, otherwise God should
be unjust.

If God were author of the conquest over King Charles in so many battels ; who is the God of Sabbaths, that is, of battels ; if he were not the cause of our victories, he were not God of battels ; in, which belief they should give a deity to the parliament forces, which is blasphemy ; for they conquered over the Cavaliers : by which it appears, God sent this as a punishment on the king, and the victory was not a punishment on the parliament, who defended the people in their rights.

Kings are ordained for the good of their subjects, not for their hurt ; nor were people brought into the world to have kings over them, but to honour and glorifie God : God is not glorified, when inferiours are oppressed by their superiours ; a sin God highly punished in the Jewes ; God were the the author of oppression, if kings had such a deputation from him.

This prince committed a great fault, in adhering too much to his unbridled will ; preferring his passion above the good of his

people : there may be excuses in youth,
for want of experience ; in stealing, for the
occasion ; in killing, for injuries offered ;
in adultery, for perswasions of love, and
heat of youth; in rebellion, for defence : but
for offences against the commonwealth,
there is not satisfaction but a block or a
gibbet.   For a shepherd to sheare the fleeces off his flock, may be tolerable ; but to
flea them, and cut their throates, is abominable before God and man.

For kings should have the care of a master, love of a father, tenderness of a protector, diligence of a shepherd, to preserve
their subjects from wrong : for without a
parliament, kings have no ears nor eyes to
see the injuries of the publicke, but by their
favorites ; who, for to encrease wealth (raised from nothing,) are like bloodsuckers,
to drain the people, and make themselves
rich.

If every member of the commonwealth
ought to preserve the state above his own
life, much more a king is chosen Gods vice-

gerent on earth, to preserve his people committed to his charge in safety.

Therefore God took from Rehoboam and
Belshazzar their kingdoms, by his instrument the people ; and Nebuchadnezzar and
Sennacherib, both for pride, and wronging
Jews ; the one was reduced to grass with
the beasts, and the other was overthrown
in battel with hundred thousands.

· The example of Attilius Regulus is commendable ; who, rather then the honour of
the Roman senate should suffer prejudice,
performed his promise, and returned to
Carthage, to undergo exquisite torments.
If subjects, much more a king God hath intrusted with his people, should have care
of his parliament and people, then much
more should he take care of the lives of the
people.

Wherefore the parliament seeing King
Charles did raise an army to defend ill counsellors, and ruine his people ; the parliament,
rather then the king should ruine the people, first they employed the army to take

away from him bad counsellors, and bring them to condigne punishment; but King Charles justified their destructive advice by a war, to ruine the authority of parliaments; and by this made himself an enemy of the commonwealth. Therefore it was just the parliament should defend themselves by a war, yea subdue the kings power, which would destroy the representative, which maintained the liberty of the subject and property of their personall and reall estates.

And though it may be objected, he had most of the gentry and nobility; yet I answer, they had the major part of the electors sided with the parliament in their purses.

Also some object, that the king had many members of parliament; but for certaine, if they would depart from the lawfully-called parliament, to ruine the people, the remainder in the house were the representative, to adjourn the parliament from day to day; for otherwise it had been *sine die*, and *ipso facto*, dissolved the parliament; then had the whole nation remained slaves

and vassals for ever, at the kings mercy.
And therefore it was most just to subdue
and put King Charles to death, as a mortal enemy, who laboured to destroy the
commonwealth with all his power; for if
a member, who hath an inclusive right,
ought to have sentence of death, much
more a king, who hath an impositive care
from God, ought to have sentence of death:
— for kings now are not the anointed of God,
as David was; but, by the Scripture, every
saint is anointed; which, by the popish
clergy, was usurped to them, and after by
their policy attributed falsely to kings to
maintaine their hierarchy.

.Wherefore, we may justly argue, that the
author of spirits had a long time continued
patient, in suffering three several families
to be superintendents over three kingdoms
five hundred years; when he raised the several houses to the throne to make an es-
say to their behaviour, to bring up the
people in the fear of God; whose time was
long spent in idolatry, and after reduced to

a prophanness, and then to a peece, and little part of a reformed way, and not to a total ; partly serving Baal, and partly God, which caused Gods errours at last to flie abroad, and shot the last prince with a mortal blow : for it is manifest, a king could not make a war with his parliament till it were ended ; and the king passed an act not to end it till all the three estates were agreed : and when it ended, all he could do, should be to indict them by a jury, to finde them guilty ; but by making a war, he leaves them at liberty to defend themselves ; so that what he did amiss, should be complained of in the next parliament after.

In the war, the kings purpose could not be to make them obedient, which is too harsh a way : for in so doing he becomes their enemy, and then they are out of his protection. Or if the subjects war with the king, and he oppose, they are not subjects. A king is not a king when he makes a war against his subjects, but he is a ty-

6

rant; and they are not rebels, no more then
when a king treateth with his subjects, are
they not subjects: by such a war, he rati-
fieth them to have a right and power to
contest with him; as the fifteen provinces
were made by the King of Spaine, in a negotiation, a free state: much more the reason holds in a war.

How many times did the parliament
court the king, yea humbly petition him,
and treated with him by commissioners, to
do divers things most necessary for the good
of the then kingdom, and he remained ob-
durate. If he were so obstinate when he
was under the power of the parliament, (as
in the Isle of Wight,) how averse would he
be, or rather domineer over and ruine them
when they were in his clutches, as if a par-
tridge (being neer to a faulcon) intangled
with his varvels, ' might peck and tach her,
yet would not she yeeld to so smal a bird;
what could the faulcon do when he had

' The straps which fasten a hawk's bells to her feet.

her trussed? surely plume on her, and at last wring off her head.

How many times have the people in this nation assumed the power to themselves, for kings over-flowing the rules of moderation! as in the times of Henry the Third, Edward the Second, Richard the Second, Henry the Sixth, and after, upon good behaviour, they resigned the keys of soveraignty to the intrusted keepers; as, namely, in choosing the supream officers, which of right belonged to the parliament; and a long time since, by intrusion, kept in the hands of the diadem, but in a parliamentary orbe; wherein, when the great officers were fixed, they kept their course from retrogradation by their aromatical influence upon the good of the people; but after they were at the devotion of the chief, by that derivation they wronged the people, and augmented the power of invassalage; as who, in name of the upper, insulted over the inferiour, that all the English world was con-

formed to an incomparable subjection and
submission, too unjustly imposed.

Therefore it was impossible that Charles,
which had his hands in the blood of hundred thousands, by his instruments, should
after that carriage be free from cruelty, indignation, and injustice; no more then a
leper can be made pure, or a blackamore
white, or a leopard clear from spots. Therefore I will justly conclude, the cup of Gods
vengeance was filled to the brim, for King
Charles his family to drink the dregs.

Now if the war of France and Germany
were just, especially the last, when the emperour transgressed the laws of the empire,
to make the united princes to raise an host
to defend themselves, and rectifie what was
amiss, by ingrafting another scion in the empire, which continued too long in one house
of Austria; much more just is that of the
parliament, which hath legislative power,
and authority to acts for the good of the
subject, to which the king is alwayes in-

joyned not to end the assembly, till he had
signed such acts, and reformed all abuses
complained of. If the king should retire
from the great counsel, and not signe bills of
right, twelve of the lords, and twenty-four
of the others were to repair to him, to
know the cause of his absence, and urge
the king to signe such bills, and remove
grievances. If he did not sign nor come
in the space of forty days, they ought to
chuse a protector ; and if he did persist in
his absence, they might justly depose him,
as appears in the book of the manner and
fashion of holding parliaments. And this
was the reason of the former kings removal.

If a master of a family, who hath wife,
children, servants, stock, and cattle, in a
madness, should go away from his house,
and bring a force to destroy his family, kill
his children, take away his cattle off his own
ground, and burn his house, he were a mad
man, and fitter for bridewell, then to be a
master of a family : As likewise a protector,

6

who ought to protect his people, if he would destroy them, because they would have a pious and vertuous government, he is to be accounted a destroyer, no protector.

But some will say, the king had a number of his subjects, and the better part.

But they were such as supported a power would take away the property of their real, personal, and vital estates, which the king might do if he conquered : if there was not parliaments, a check on the soveraigne, to protect inferiours, such kingly power would grow to such a height, as no moderation might be 'twixt mercy and tyranny.

I have often heard the cavaliers say, they meant not to take away parliaments, knowing they were for their good and benefit.

But if the king had prevailed by their means, they should never have had parliaments after : then they would have been like deer put in a toyle, and would have proved in the second degree after us slaves ; of which slavery they were principal authors.

Open your eyes, ye cavaliers, and see
what noose you had prepared for your own
necks ; when it had been too late to get
your heads out after the conquest, and parliament ruined. Look into France, when
the parliament-estates were destroyed, they
were no better then slaves. How many of
the nobility suffered! as Montmorancy,
Count of Soysons, Bouillon, and others ;
and the people generally so miserable, as
they can hardly live.

For bills of grace, I see no authority for
it ; a prerogative intended only by the
power of kings ; for people (when they
chuse one to rule over them) would justly
be dealt with, and not harshly, when obedient ; for then the soveraigne ought to be
loving to them, and a father to them.

But when the king takes his sword to
fight with his subjects, they ought to defend themselves ; especially the parliament,
which is the highest appeal for any wrong
offered by the king.

Therefore it was that our common law

allowed every one a plea upon a writ, jus-
tifying any against the crowne, for taking
away of real and personal estate. Also if
Magna Charta forbids any free man to be
imprisoned, and allows him an *habeas corpus,* much more life may be preserved and
defended by the sword; for upon an indictment of man-slaughter *in se defendendo,*
it is a good plea to save his life in his defence, although he kill the other.

If any one defend his estate against the
king, much more life may be defended, by
a parliamentary power, which is of a higher
nature: if every subject, then the parliament, which represents the whole body,
may raise an army (if the people be willing
to undergo it;) on purpose to defend their
lives.

All warrants of peace and good behaviour were made in the kings name; so
then if the king raise an army to murther
his subjects, he hath lost to be a defender
of them, and hath suspended, or rather lost
his prerogative of soveraignty; for every

subject may kill one another, when there is no power to restraine them; and the king cannot defend when he raiseth a power to kill them. The king had two capacities, one as a king, another as proprietor of lands, honors, and seigniories: when he lost his first capacity, the parliament, which is the representative in right of the people, might justly assume the supream authority to themselves, to defend those the king would murther; for the people first granted or suffered kings to have authority over them for their good; but when the king abuseth it, he ceases to be any longer their king, but becomes a cruel tyrant; and then he may be justly tryed in his second capacity as a subject, and lose his life, forfeit lands and goods, by the parliament, the supreme judges.

And therefore it was, that Richard the Third, before Henry the Seventh conquered him, was held a lawful king, and Henry the Seventh attaint as a rebell by parliament; but after the conquest, Henry the

Seventh his attainder was reversed, and Richard the Third affirmed to be a tyrant.

This declares positively, that parliaments have onely power to ratifie and annul kings, and no other. For else, by power, any one may be a soveraigne without the parliaments approbation : but never any ascended the throne that was not confirmed by parliament ; not only in way of ceremony, but essentially and really performed by an act to allow and ratifie the present king, or else he could not lawfully govern.

Besides, the king takes an oath at his coronation, to maintaine all the priviledges of the people : but when he brings them to oppression and tyranny, he is perjured, and loseth the title of a father and protector of his people, and is in the capacity of an enemy to the commonwealth.

Many examples are in the world, that kings, when they become tyrants, have been deposed and killed ; as in Muscovy, among the Turkes, Babylonians, Persians, Greeks, and Romans ; and he who is an

enemy to the commonwealth deserveth to
die by all laws, humane and divine.

Kings have augmented their prerogatives,
and so by intrusion have tyrannized over
the subject : for they have in the interim
of parliaments had prerogatives to pardon
man-slaughter, and such as are expressed
in the acts of parliament; and by their
greatness they incroached their power: for
kings could not take away the life of any
subject, but by indictment and arraignment, and that by a jury of twelve men,
who must finde the delinquent guilty or not
guilty ; not in parliaments, but in the interim of them :- wherefore King Charles his
coming with an armed power to take out
the five members was a high breach of priviledge ; and for declaring he would break
the neck of parliaments, he deserved to be
dethroned : this was to destroy the right of
his subjects, so that they should have no
property in estate, real or personal, nor life:
for while the parliament sate, he ought not
to question any ; and afterwards he could

not take away the life and estate of any without a jury, but it would be questioned the next parliament, as many presidents in the rolls of parliament sheweth.

A parliament is a free place, where every one ought to speak their mind freely for the good of their country. Now it was the fashion of King James and King Charles, when any spoke for the good of the people, to corrupt them with preferment, and make them royalists who were afore for the commonwealth; preferment drawing them opposite to the commonwealth; as Sir Henry Yelverton, Sir John Savill, Sergeant Glanvile, Sir Robert Heath, my Lord of Strafford, and Master Noye; but Master Noye shewed afore his death a great remorse for it to some of his intimate friends. It was greatness so bewitched them, and increased the kings power, to wit, by preferment and honors; insomuch, as Sir Edward Hoby, a factious gentleman, at a committee in the parliament, chosen to punish some boyes that abused old Master Jordans gloves,

certaine boyes being proved to be the authors of that roguery, the committee de-
bated what school-masters should correct
them, whether WESTMINSTER or Pauls;
Sir Edward Hoby (I say) told the committee he had found out one would lash on
both sides, meaning Master Yelverton; Sir
Henry being newly chosen Solicitor-General
for the king, to signe bils of grace, which was
only in parliament to be done, when lords
and commons had signed them afore, but
out of parliaments the kings had no such
right. It's true, kings might in interim of
parliament, upon an invasion, raise an army,
and impose monys upon many of the subjects; but this was authorised by parliament, and if he did amiss, it was questioned the next parliament. This shews plainly, that the parliament had the power, not
the royalty.

It is true, kings had a power to call parliaments; so have the beadles in the universities power of calling assemblies; stewards of courts to send out warrants to keep

courts, and yet both are subject, one to the chancellors of the universities, the other a servant upon the matter to the lords of mannors.

We need not fear darlings of the multitude in this state'; every one will labour to be a darling of the people, and none will make himself great, unless he meanes to be ruined, and be an ostracisme.

Certainly to prevent this, it were good to extinguish all the print and stamp of monarchy, not to give a provocation to raise power.

The pretorian cohorts advanced emperours at their pleasure; the Janizaries the great Turkes; but our army is so pious, there is no fear, especially being not in body, but some in Ireland, some in Scotland, and dispersed in several countries : those who pay the souldiers shall have obedience ; but, as the proverb is, no money no Swiss : no money no obedience.

While the Romane senate was rich, none durst assaile the monarchy; but, as Taci-

12

tus reports, when the greatness of the senate and riches decayed, then Cæsar inva-
ded after he had conquered Pompey.

It is to be observed, that what overthrows
monarchy, the same overthrows a senatical
government. The maiors of the palace at
Paris had power to raise and depose kings
at pleasure, till it was justly taken away:
if there be any such power in the city of
London, it is to be taken away; for they
may, by wealth, potency, and multitude,
do the like to the parliament. Yet they
deserve much to be respected; for they
have done as much for the good of the
state as any city ever did in the whole
world; and therefore are to be incouraged
to have immunities and priviledges bestowed on them by the parliament.

I deny not that there were priviledges
belonging to the kings of England, but
those are due to him so long as he is a defender of the people and a good king: but
if he proves not Gods vice-gerent, but becomes an enemy to the commonwealth, his

regency is suspended, and he is but a common person : otherwise, kings might destroy the people, and become an enemy. So that his title is annihilated, and made void ; as a shepherd, who ought to preserve his sheep, when he goes about to kill and slay them, he cannot be called a shepherd, but a destroyer of his sheep.

The example of King Henry the Eighth, who, when the House of Commons would not consent to pull down the abbeys, sent for them, and kept them in a room all night, and in the morning came to them, and perswaded them to pass the bil, who, in fear, next day did it ; this is no argument to shew the power of kings : it was their obstinacy to oppose against the will of God, who determined to destroy those wicked houses, which were erected in a blind zeal, thinking by their erection to make their souls saved.

A king is compared to a father ; if he would kill his own children, he ceaseth to have care of them, and is to be justly stiled

a murtherer and no parent to preserve the
issue of his body.

Parliaments were to be called every two
or three yeers, to reforme abuses in the nation : but King James said they were assembled to supply his wants, and raise money; and therefore he denied them any
other discourse ; whereas, indeed, parliaments were called for all the members to
complaine of their grievances, which were
always redressed there. And there were
tryers of petitions within the house, to examine whether their complaints were just:
and certainly, if there were some now appointed without the door of the parliament
to take petitions, and examine whether they
were fitly to be delivered to the house or
no, it would give great content to the people : for I am confident there have been
many petitions delivered, which ought not
to be presented to interrupt the weightier
affaires there transacted. And upon this,
the parliament have unjustly been charged
that they would not hear them, when in

reason they ought not to be preferred ; for many of them might have been redressed by law or some other way.

Now, to shew how the prerogative was advanced : and that was done by making lord-lieutenants in every county, and so deputy-lieutenants ; a device invented by the Earl of Leicester, when he returned from being deputy-protector of the Low Countreys, under Elizabeth protectress, who wished the queen (from a form he had observed in those parts, from whence he came, for a way that furthered the opposing of Spaine) to make such ; for if there should be an invasion or rebellion in England, it would be too long to send up to the councel ; but it might easily be suppressed by them ; two of the deputy-lieutenants having power to suppress them, by raising forces to oppose and subdue them.

Whereupon, I remember, there was a rising against the inclosures of commons, (so much irksome to the people,) for in some places the people rose to pull them

down, and were suppressed by the power
of the deputy-lieutenants, and divers hanged up; but the deputy-lieutenants were
after faine to get pardons, it being contrary
to law. Likewise a cut-purse being taken
in Whitehall in the then presence, King
James commanded the Lord Garret, the
Knight-marshal, presently to hang the cut-
purse, which was done instantly; but the
Knight-marshal was fain to get a pardon
under seal. This shews plainly that no king
can take away the life of any without a lawful tryal by jury; *ergo*, he cannot murther
his subjects, nor raise a war during the sitting of the parliament, for there he is to be
in person; then the king is less, and the parliament supreme.

Now when the king takes his sword into
his hand, and departs from the parliament,
he loseth his priviledge of king in parliament, and becomes an enemy to the state;
and then justly his name as king ought to
be put out in any commission, and the parliaments authority is to be used only.

I am therefore perswaded that the adoring of kings hath wrought this misprision and mistake of the power of kings, which by law of God and man they have not; so that idolizing them hath ruined the right of the people much; the lawyers also for preferment and advancement have given a greater prerogative to the soveraignty then was due.

If we examine our municipall laws, and all civil laws, they are no way justifiable, but as they are correspondent to the judicial laws of the Jews, which were set down by God, to be a patern for all to be paterned by. I finde no such power given by God.

And where it may be objected, that God forewarned the Jews not to have a king over them, and expressed what inconveniences would follow of having kings according to the custome of nations, what slavery they should be in; this was not to shew that it was just so to do, but that their power and tyranny would force them to it. .

Another thing that increased the prerogative and diminished the right of the people was, that the printed statutes were not according to the records of parliament; sometime there was added to, and sometime diminished from, what was in the roll of parliament; and somewhat put in that might be advantageous to the kings, and put out what was for the benefit of the subject; as I have observed, by my comparing the printed book with the record. And truly if there were a committee to examine the records, it should be necessary to see the right of the subject.

And in *decimo octavo Jacobi*, King James sent and took what was done by that parliament, from Master Wright, clerk of the parliament.

So likewise the king by his power, and the great lords of court, made courtiers, burgesses, and some time knight of the shire by letters; who hindred much the proceedings in parliament by their vote, it being the policy of the dukes of Cornwall

in the stannaries to have multitude of burgesses, to make themselves potent in parliament; which now the parliament will
prevent, by providing that the representative may be equally chosen from all parts.

Likewise it was usual for King James
and King Charles, if any did speak in the
behalf of the commonalty in parliament,
against the prerogative, to make them she-
riffs, or impose other burthensome offices
on them; as myself and Sir Guy Palmes
were served, after that parliament of 18 *Jacobi*; or to be revenged on them some other
way, for doing their duty in parliament, as
then was invented by projectors, as I could
recite divers examples in my time.

The courtiers also laboured to make good
patriots courtiers, as Sir Dudley Digs was
made a courtier, and master of the rolls,
who was faithful to the parliament, and
dyed before a parliament came; this was
to draw their affection from the multitude
to the soveraignty; so that by those means
tyranny was increased, and the right of the

people waved; which now will be redressed and reformed by Gods blessing and prudence of the state.

Now I will draw a short lantskip, by way
of epitome, to examine what good King
James and King Charles have done since
anno Domini 1603.

The seven yeers parliament was a sage
and wise parliament, and laboured to do
much good for the then kingdome : and, as
a new broom sweepeth clean at first, King
James granted some good laws ; but the
Court of Wards they endeavoured to pull
down, which had ruined infinite families, upon offer to give the king two hundred thousand pound *in deposito,* and annually two
hundred thousand pound ; but it was opposed by Robert, Earl of Salisbury, (otherwise a very good commonwealth man,) as
too great a thing for the king to part with.
And truly that parliament took great pains
to reform abuses in church and state ; but
not much was done for the good of the subject, but great sums granted, and a good

government hoped for, rather then in fruition. For King James spent much time in
his pleasures, much money in embassies, to
make himself great ; so that there was some
good for the merchants ; but tonnage and
poundage given by parliament was for
guarding the seas, which was imployed to
the royal purse onely ; so that, although
complained of, the merchants were at a
double charge in wafting their goods.

After, King James wronged the fisher-
men and us much, by granting to his brother Henry the Fourth, King of France, for
his moneth to fish on our coast ; who, under that colour, took away the very earth
and spawn of the fish of rotchet, gurnet,
cunger, and hadduck, to Diep ; where they
have abundance, and we want.

King James granted the Hollanders to
fish on our coasts, and for a small petty
rate ; the island of Lewis in Scotland, and
other isles of Ireland, to dry their fish ; by
which they have inriched themselves above
fourty millions sterling.

In that parliament of seven yeers they laboured to reform abuses in church and commonwealth, and that the pious ministers might not be tyed to subscribe to the unlawful ceremonies of the bishops, which was not granted; but *in nono Jacobi*, at Hampton-court, were divers pious men, as Reynolds, Kniwstubs, Clerk, and other reverend divines, to dispute about ceremonies; but that the divines had not freedome of speech, for all went on the bishops sides; a cause England in all parts after were deprived of pious men, which were silenced, imprisoned, and put out of their lectures and livings; so that want of teaching caused profaneness to get the preheminence.

The parliament of *duodecimo Jacobi* was only for undertakers to raise money for King James: some bishops were questioned, as Bilson, and others; but the parliament dissolved without doing any thing.

Then was the parliament of 18 *Jacobi*, where Heath was for the commons; Sir

Thomas Wentworth, and Christopher Wans-
ford, and others, were for the king's side;
where also Sir John Bennet, Sir Giles Mum-
pheson, and Sir John Mitchel, were condemned, and the parliament so dissolved;
in which parliament, Serjeant Grimston
called me out of the house, to the Earl of
Bedford, the Earl of Westmorland, and Sir
Francis Vane, dead, to the little room in the
lobby, where they offered me ten thousand
pound, or five hundred a-yeer, which I
would choose, not to oppose the bill of the
fens in the house. I answered, no money
nor estate would make me betray the country.

This parliament was made voide, and 32
patents called in by King James, and so
he pleased the people with a toy.

Many and divers were convented by the
council-table to pay certain sums, or to
be imprisoned; whereof I was one, being
brought before the councel, when Sir Al-
bert Morton waited.

Then came the parliament of 21 *Jacobi*,

a little afore King James his end, where
were some good laws enacted; the Lord
Keeper Bacon and the Earl of Middlesex
condemned for bribery.

A little afore this, I being Custos Rotulorum of the county of Cambridge, by Buckingham, was put out, and Sir John Cuts
put in, when I had that office under the
broad seal; which could not legally be taken away from me, unless I had committed
some fault, thereby to have forfeited the
same.

Now there remaineth no more for the
parliament to do, but faithfully to keep
what they have justly gotten by Gods divine providence, and his will, in a valourous conquest; to the end, that when they
have settled the building of the state upon
a right and firme basis, they may further
inlarge the kingdome of the Lord Jesus,
by their indeavours through Europe; which
I am fully assured God hath appointed,
and will certainly bring to pass, that all

12

the world may see Gods determination in
every climate of this part of the world.

After this new state is put into the cradle
of ease and tranquillity, to make it have a
full growth, there will be nothing to hinder
the establishment thereof; no titles upon
marriage, as in monarchy, because the power
is in the people, and they chuse a representative that shall govern, every two or
three yeers making an election of members
of parliament, that every one may govern
by vicissitude ; and therefore there would
be no need of a William the Conquerour to
interrupt the proceedings of the state, and
dissettle it by establishing of new laws;
there would be no William Rufus in a hunting voyage to be slaine; no King John to be
poysoned at Swinsted abbey by a monke ;
nor there will be no beautiful Rosamonds
to hinder a pious government; no Morti-
mers to entice to his bed and lust the wives
of princes: there will be no unnatural mothers, like that French lady, who killed her

own son Edward the Second in Pomfret
castle by the power of a French pride;
there will be no Pearce Gaviston nor Spen-
cers, to draw a mighty state into their own
hands, by ruine of the people; there will
be no Alice Pearce, who sat at the pillow
of King Edward the Third, and kept a
privy councel out, that should advise a
king for the good of his people; there will
be no wanton conrtezan to pass by the
court-chambers, and loose her garter, to be
a means to settle an order; there will be
no John of Gant to deny the inheritance
of his first children, and settle it upon his
second wives; there will be no Richard the
Second to send a number of the nobility to
be murdered at Calice, to satisfie the unsatiable desires of princes; nor striving to
ruine parliaments, though it be to his own
deposing; nor no judges to counsel the soveraigne to ruine his people; there will be
no factions betwixt the houses of Yorke
and Lancaster, to imbroyle the people in
war; nor no barons wars, to make a dis-

traction in the nations; there will be no working to have burgesses in stannaries by dukes of Cornwall; nor no imprisonment of a speaker Thorpe out of parliament, nor factions for their private interests to ruine the publike; there will be no killing of Henry the Sixth in a chamber, as Richard the Third did; no alluring of Jane Shores to princes lustful beds; no murthering of princes, and smothering them, as was in the Tower; no Empsons and Dudleys to raise an estate for kings, by the ruine of the people; no pretences to make a war to gather wealth, to peal and pole the subject, and after to compose the war, and keep the money in his own purse, as Henry the Seventh did; nor pride to put down the right title of a wife, and set up their own first, that was after it; no Perkin Warbeck to be an impostor, to put by a right title; no Henry the Eighth to make void a Katherines bed, to make way for another wife; no chopping off the heads of wives, to make way for other beauties for lust; nor terrify-

ing of parliament, if they do not give way
to pass an act to enrich his coffers, as Henry
the Eighth did in the case of abbeyes; no
Cardinal Woolseys to set up their armes
afore their masters, to make way for a pope-
dom, and too late repentance, that he had
not served God so faithfully as his master,
by which he came to a tragical end to poyson himself; no poysoning of Edward the
Sixth by great Northumberlands, to make
way for the diadem; no Leicesters to grow
so potent, as to set up a school to vitiate
ladies; nor no drawing of parliament-men
from their fidelity to their country, as hath
been used in King James and King Charles
his time; nor none so ambitious as to make
themselves darlings of the multitude, to
make way for their own interests above
the publick; nor for kings to take favourites to overthrow their principals: none
unworthy without merit shall be imployed; none shall grow lawless by vertue of
princes humors.

Surely all kingdomes have a period, as

the Babylonian, Medes, and Persians, Grecian, and Roman : look in the history of all these, and you shall understand, that ambition, oppression, tyranny, and injustice, have been the changers of government to some other way or persons.

It is probable that the determination of God is to destroy all monarchy in Christendome : for if we begin with France, we shall find they have alwayes adhered to the Romish government, except a little handful of those they call reformed protestants. How much have they wronged us in our title, which belongs truly to us ! and though they seem to be governed by a salique law, yet notwithstanding they have not kept the order thereof, which they ought to have done, but have foisted in some males, which ought to have been last, afore others that ought to have been first; and the majors of the palace at Paris have set up kings at their pleasure, and not respected the right of those that ought to have had it.

The persecuting of the holy men of Towers and the Albigenses, the true apostolick descendants who ever hated the Roman heresies ; that horrible and unheard-of massacre at Paris, in Henry the Thirds time of France, by the device of the house of Guise, and Queen Katherine, who was a witch, and made julips of young children snatched up in the night to maintain her lust, as Comines doth testify ; and Henry the Fourth turning his religion from the protestant side, after God Almighty had blessed him with one-and-twenty victories over the popish league ; Lewis the Thirteenth making a war against the protestants, to murder a number of them, though it was with the loss of five thousand of the nobility of France. The Duke of Bouillon, the Duke of Fremelly, and divers others, changing their religion ; and Cardinal Richeliu giving authority and command in armes, on purpose to destroy the Hugonots, though God blessed them to be the best commanders in France. All these, I say, and many more I could repeat, will be

a means to showre down Gods vengeance
to destroy that monarchy.

Let us therefore cease from wondering at
Gods works : for if a sparrow fals not to
the ground without his special providence,
then much less is it wanting in turning
topsy-turvy principalities and kingdomes :
Certainly if this vicissitude were not, sin
would have more abounded ; piety, or at
least morality, would be banished, and men
would forget the end of their creation, and
think there were no God to punish sin nor
reward the righteous ; but do as the great
fishes, devour one another.

This makes me affirm, that it is not probable that God can bless Charles, the now
supposed King of Scots from his predecessors, if we examine the mothers side. The
grandmother was proved by the parliament
of Paris to have made abortive her sons bed
eleven times, by help of a Spanish empe-
rick ; as by Will. Murreys ambassie appeared, who returned this answer to King
Charles ; and therefore it was not conve-

nient to yield that she should return into
France : and also his grandfather turning
his religion, and was killed like a calf by
Ravilliac ; his mother for too much familiarity with Buckingham,' Holland, and

---

' Less prejudiced historians than Sir Edward have allowed the prejudice that England sustained from the
amorous frolics of the Duke of Buckingham ; but
they make it plain that Henrietta Maria was so far from
being the object of his attachment, that she suffered
from his enmity ; and so they partly confute and partly confirm the passage in the text.

"The other particular, by which he involved himself in so many fatal intricacies, from which he could
never extricate himself, was, his running violently into
the war in France, without any kind of provocation,
and upon a particular passion very unwarrantable. In
his embassy in France, where his person and presence
was wonderfully admired and esteemed, (and in truth
it was a wonder in the eyes of all men,) and in which
he appeared with all the lustre the wealth of England
could adorn him with, and outshined all the bravery
that court could dress itself in, and overacted the whole
nation in their own most peculiar vanities : He had the
ambition to fix his eyes upon, and to dedicate his most
violent affection to a lady of a very sublime quality, [the
Queen of France] and to pursue it with the most impor-
tunate addresses; insomuch, as when the king had brought
the queen his sister as far as he meant to do, and delivered herin to the hands of the duke, to be by him con

Jermine ; for the duke, for fear the French
ladies should tell tales of George, often

ducted into England, the duke, in his journey, after the
departure from that court, took a resolution once more to
make a visit to that great lady, which he believed he
might do with much privacy. But it was so easily discovered, that provision was made for his reception ; and if
he had pursued his attempt, he had been without doubt
assassinated ; of which he had only so much notice as
served him to decline the danger. But he swore in that
instant, that he would see and speak with the lady in
spight of all the strength and power of France. And
from the time that the queen arrived in England, he
took all the ways he could to undervalue and exasperate that court and nation, by causing all those who
fled into England from the justice and displeasure of
the king, to be received and entertained here, not only with ceremony and security, but with bounty and
magnificence ; and the more extraordinary the persons
were, and the more notorious their king's displeasure
was towards them, (as in that time there were many
lords and ladys in those circumstances,) the more re-
spectfully they were received and esteemed. He omitted no opportunity to incense the king against France,
and to dispose him to assist the Hugonots, whom he
likewise encouraged to give their king some trouble.

" And which was worse than all this, he took great
pains to lessen the king's affection towards his young
queen, being exceedingly jealous lest her interest might
be of force enough to cross his other designs. And in
this stratagem he so far swerved from the instinct of
his nature, and his proper inclinations, that he who was

mounted on his steed, sent them into France
contrary to the articles of marriage; so that
the queen was shut up in the chamber alone,
not to behold their departure, and cut her
fingers with the glass windows, as Duplex
the French historiographer writes. '

compounded of all the elements of affability and cour-
tesy towards all kind of people, had brought himself
into a habit of neglect, and even of rudeness towards
the queen.

" One day, when he unjustly apprehended that she
had shewed some disrespect to his mother, in not going
to her lodging at an hour she had intended to go, and
was hindered by a meer accident, he came into her
chamber in much passion, and after some expostulations rude enough, he told her, she should repent it;
her majesty answering with some quickness, he replied
insolently to her, that there had been queens in England who had lost their heads. And it was universally
known, that, during his life, the queen never had any
credit with the king, with reference to any publick affaires, and so could not divert the resolution of making
a war with France."—CLARENDON, *ut supra*, p. 39.

' Howel confirms the circumstances of the queen's
extreme resentment, and of her cutting her fingers with
the glass, the king having locked her up in a room with
him. The French attendants had behaved with cha-
racteristic petulance, and the confessor, it is said, had
enjoined the queen the very unseemly penance of walking barefoot to Tyburn, to atone for the death of the

12

And Charles the First, afore his marriage, had for a mistress a great married lady, (it

recusant priests who had been sufferers there. That Charles was peremptorily determined upon their removal, appears from the following letters to the Duke of Buckingham. *Steenie,* it must be remembered, the Scotch diminutive of Stephen, was a nickname which James had given the duke, on account of his resemblance to the picture of St Stephen, the proto-martyr.

"Steenie,

" I writ to you by Ned Clarke, that I thought I would here cause anufe in short tyme, to put away monsers, either by attempting to steale away my wife, or by making plots amongst my owen subjects. I cannot say certainlie whether it was intended, but I am sure it is hindered. For the other, though I have got good grounds to believe it, and am still hunting after it, yet seing daylie the malitiousness of the monsers, by making and fomenting discontents in my wyfe, I could tarrie no longer from adverticing of you, that I meane to seeke for no other grounds to casier my monsers, having for this purpose sent you my other letter, that you may, if you think good, advertise the queen's mother with my intention.

So I rest

Your faithful, constant, loving frende,
Charles R."

" Steenie,

" I have received your letter by Dic Greme; this is my answer—I command you to send all the French

is probable the prince would follow the same course after marriage,) by whom she had a boy; and when he was Prince of Wales, bestowed on the christening eight thousand pound; it is supposed he being so good an husband, and wise, would not lay out so much cost for nothing; when he kept a book, like Henry the Seventh, what bribes that he shared, he set down punctually; so much received for such an office, place, or honour; and would be displeased if he had not his part agreed for with his servants. And likewise the French queen, grandmother of Charles, the supposed second King of Scots, was so familiar

away to-morrow out of the towne, if you can by fayer means, (but sticke not in disputing,) otherways force them away like so many wild beasts, untill ye have shipped them, and so the devil goe with them. Let me heare no answer, but of the performance of my command.

So I rest

Your faithfull, constant, loving frende,

CHARLES R."

Oaking, the 7 of August, 1627.
(Superscribed) " The Duke of Buckingham."

with Marques d'Ancre, whom she advanced
to so high a command, that by his actions,
and the government after in her regency,
France was almost overthrown, and the
prime nobility; and by her counsel to her
daughter here, there was procured matters
of dangerous consequence to England since
her arriving; who perswaded her daughter
to draw King Charles to the Romish part,
(as by many affaires appeared,) and got a
patent to transport leather into France,
most prejudicial, which was condemned
by this parliament.

Wherefore, on all sides, Charles the Second from them may justly expect not to
prosper, especially by his rebellious invading of England; for if he had any right,
yet his invasion, and the conquest, hath
justly extinguished his title, especially King
Charles and his mother playing fast and
loose so often, that no issue from thence can
either be legitimate or pious, from so ungodly a derivative.

So that if the quantity of battels fought,
so great a revolution of the state, the several qualities and persons interested, or the
long continuance of broyles, could render
a war memorable, this the parliament hath
undergone, and the new general finished, is
in the highest degree of Gods miraculous
deliverances; after more then twenty battels in three nations, and above 300,000
slaine, and the state changed of face and
masters; multitudes of forts taken and sur-
readered; so that the victorious are but
losers, till the state be brought to be (as the
French proverb is) *en bon point*, in perfect
health, after a war that hath continued almost nine yeers.

The subject came from King Charles
leaving his parliament in the suds, and violently raising a destructive war to ruine
three nations.   It had rather been wisdome
in the king to apply to the people lenatives
not corrosives: great wounds are to be sew-
ed, not rent, which is the part of a good
chirurgeon; restoratives are to be given,

not purges, to the patient : so kings ought
to amend what was amiss, and not oppose
them with violence ; appease their fury, not
exasperate them by a war : for this thunder-
bolt, by wicked councel was contrived, to
break forth in fiery flashes at an instant in
the three nations, about the 23d of October,
1642.

Wherefore the parliament now assembled
aimes at this end, that as in grammar there -
can be no good construction nor coherence
to make true orthography, without the sub-
stantive and adjective conjoyned, which is
resembled to the parliament, the supreme
authority, now settled by Gods assistance,
appointing the counsel of state, who will
bring mighty things to pass, and cause the
annual officers to nourish all the members
in their several callings, that there may be
a semblable endeavour of the well-being of
every good citizen and inhabitant, as well
as those in authority ; that piety may be
exalted and increased by the lamps of the
sanctuary, indued with the spirit of God ;

that the whole body may be governed apos-
tolically, whereof Christ is the head, without whom nothing can be effected : for if
Christ be not chiefest in our thoughts, no
state can be durable, but like a sandy foundation will moulder away : That the electors may love the elected, and esteeme and
obey them, who spend their spirits to advance the common good, keep and defend
the weale public in health and prosperity,
that it be not hecticall meager, nor leane ,
nor too saturnicall, nor too jovial, but in a
golden temper. These are wise physitians,
who cure the maladies, fevers, and distem-
pers, that blood may run in every viene of
the state to nourish the whole body, in justice, equity, and right, through the *cava
vena*, *cava porta*, and smaller veines ; the
great cities and townes as well as the small;
that the officers and magistrates have not a
dogs appetite, to twine judicature to a bad
chylos, but to an equall distribution of right,
that the heart, the courage of the people,
may be fostred in good actions, without re-

spect of persons, but with regard to the
right of the cause : that vice and sin may
be punished, with a parenthesis of mercy;
that the republic may have foraine and native commodities; that the land lie not
freshforth, as the lord termes it, but that
there may be importation and exportation ;
that manufacture may be maintained, to
keep from the bane of idleness and debauchedness ; that trade may dish out all things
necessary for use, seemly ornament, and
lawful pleasure; that the merchant, the
purveyors of the nation, export and import
all commodities for the good of the state;
that just impositions, impost, subsidie, and
excise may be paid, without corruption and
defrauding the state ; that artificers may be
able to maintaine their families; that laws
may be kept within the chanel of Gods rule
and direction ; that potency surrounded not
the peoples property, nor wink at the spoile
of inferiours; that those in authority regard more the publick then their private
interest; that the orphant, widdows, and

fatherless, be relieved, the innocent freed,
and the nocent escape not punishment, and
that the navy, the walls and bulworks, may
be maintained in good equippage, for the
honour and defence of the nation.

By this meanes, the wise and sage counsel of state will undermine the enemies plots,
so that their malice hurt us not, by intelli-
gencers in forraine parts, employed to prevent mischief to the commonwealth; wherein the Earl of Salisbury (dead) was vigilant,
at the annual expence of 2000 pounds.
And therefore I am confident the parliament frames the state to this fashion, if
time and repose, the midwives of all affairs,
would give them leave to bring forth to action their contrived principles, in which hitherto they have been impeded by the plots
of malecontents, and by procuring provisions for subjugating Ireland and Scotland,
the enemies of God and of this state.

Consider, therefore, O England! that they
do as wise physitians are accustomed, afore
the perfect remedy of patients consump-

tion, advise not to action, imployment, and troubles in affaires, till restored to strength and vigor.

Wherefore now I come to observe how miraculous it is that my Lord General, descended by his mother by the male-stock of the Stuarts, should be a revenger, under God and the parliament, of so many horrible murthers and adulteries, oppressions, fearfull and abominable wickedness, as I have raveled out the peeces, to winde up this bottome, in some special points; but have omitted many this enchiridion is not able to containe; which, when God shall enable me, and the state injoyne, I shall willingly undergo.

I observe likewise, by his father, that this conquerour is a male of the great Crumwell, the sole contriver of the dissolution of the abbies ' (under Cardinal Woolsey) those

' It has been repeatedly asserted, that Thomas Cromwell, Esq. Sheriff of Huntingdonshire, the undoubted ancestor of the protector, was sister's son to Thomas Cromwell, Earl of Essex, and the idea is countenanced

adulterous seminaries of lust, gluttony, and idleness, that I saw with mine own eyes when I went to school at Bury, fifty four yeeres since, from a well, brought up thousands of childrens bones, which were murthered and cast in it, that the inchastity of the nuns and fryers might not be found out.

And although Crumwell, Earl of Essex, by the malice of the popish clergy, was contrived to die, yet he was a lord of transcendent parts, and a scourge to ruine those pestilent abbies; as if God would requite and revenge his death, by giving such an honour to his name and family in after-ages, to raise up a Crumwel to be Gods instrument to destroy such a wicked stock, which nourished such irreligious houses, whose hands were imbrued so often in blood; and that amongst the three generals God raised up this last, with a mind and body sutable

by his enjoying very large grants of abbey lands. But the author of his life in the Biographia Britannica combats this with arguments of considerable weight.

to finish an absolute conquest over the royalty : a work in which the heavens (Gods
creatures) appointed him to be a principall
coadjutor, under this present parliamentary
power; God dispensing so much sufficiency
of wisdome, piety, and prowess, out of the
treasury of nature, for an accomplishment;
pointing with the finger to every one, Oliver
Crumwell as a prodigy, to perform what
the great Creator resolved to bring to pass
in this Stuarticall catastrophe ; for which
he is equal with Alexander the Great ; leaving him to shine as a star placed by God
amongst all the military forces of Europe,
under the parliament and the supreme authority of the commonwealth, to be a glorious sun and a Prometheus for to bring in a
heavenly light for all Europe to behold
more clearly Gods will and determination,
which will be more sensibly and visibly
known after the next years great eclipse, to
inlighten not only the cavaliers, but also
Europe, what Gods purpose is to act in future ages ; in which course is behoovefull

for every christian to observe, that he may
manage his affaires accordingly, to the glory
of God and his own safety. For so infallible is the will of God to take revenge of injuries done, not observing the presence of
times when they were committed, but transferring occasions from one season to another,
he calleth the sinners into reckoning, when
they have least memory of them : therefore
God hath appointed this thrice honorable
parliament the instruments to punish all
those delinquents, who have raised this
storme against the commonwealth, to bring
them on their knees to petition for a composition for their estates personall and reall,
and others to forfeit their estates for their
insupportable malignancy ; who now begin
to behold that peace is better then war,
quietness then rebellion, and subjection
then opposition : for it is not sufficient that
the supreme authority of the nation do their
duty ; but as in the nourishing of the body,
though the head be well disposed, yet it is
also necessary all the members do their

office in obeying the supream authorities.
just command with all possible diligence:
so shall they be by the states indulgence
united, who were divided, and injoy the
same priviledges with us; and we all may
sit under our vines, and glorifie the God of
heaven, who will bless and prosper us.

To conclude, I humbly beseech the su-
preame authority of England assembled in
parliament, to pardon my age, if I have not
so punctually set them down in order as I
desired, being shortned by time, and wanting a faithfull, able transcriber, to write out
this Remonstrance as I could wish: my
intentions are onely to manifest Gods determination in abasing greatness, which will
not stoop to the government of our Saviour
Jesus Christ, the second person in the Trinity; to whom God hath given all power in
this sublunary world, for the good of his
elect; to which I add a gentle admonition
to all princes of Europe to give over tyranny and submit to the power of the Re-
deemer and Saviour, who hath sacrificed

his life to save wicked sinners; and so prevent a showre of Gods vengeance impend-
ing, which is ready to dissolve and pour
downe upon their heads.

O ye princes of Europe, that persecute
inferiours by tyranny and oppression, look
on the works of God since the creation, and
you shall see plainely the great Creator will
dismount your glory and pride usurped
over others, yea a power to hinder the government of Christ, that the kingdome of
the Gentiles is stopped in the election of the
saints, by adhering to the great whore of
Babylon and her superstition; who takes
upon her the authority of the son of God,
and hinders the conversion of souls: turne
your eyes back, and see, as in a glass, what
great alteration God hath brought to pass
since he made the world.

The first great change was in Enoch's
time: when men were licentious, God turned the stream, and they began to fear him.

The second was in the floud: when Noah
had preached to the old world above an

hundred yeares, and they would not be warn-ed, God sent a generall deluge, and destroy-ed all but eight persons.

The third was an odd number, in the mi-raculous deliverance of his church the Is-raelites out of Egypt.

The fourth was in Salmanassers time, when the Jewes cryed to God in their ba-nishment, and were restored to Jerusalem from captivity.

The fifth was more worthy admiration, in sending a Saviour to save sinners.

The sixth was in Charlemain's time, when monarchy began to spread and surround the earth to a potency, by priding it over the people.

But loe this last is sabbattical, and gives a rest and quietness to all your pride and ambition.

FINIS.

APPENDIX.

INTRODUCTION.

W<small>HILE</small> the preceding Tracts were at press, the
publishers have been favoured with the perusal
of a very rare pamphlet, written by some tri-
umphant loyalist, shortly after the Restoration,
in requital of Sir Anthony Welldon's " Court
and Character of King James." It is entitled,
" The Court and Kitchin of Elizabeth, commonly called Joan Cromwel, the wife of the late
usurper ;" and is graced with a frontispiece of
that lady, a jolly dame, in a hood and tippét, having, as heralds say, an ape *passant* upon her left
shoulder. The work is in two parts. The first,
which we shall here extract at length, contains
some curious anecdotes of Oliver's domestic life
and housekeeping. The economy of the protector's lady is the object of the author's ridi-

cule, which, considering she was then displa-
ced, and out of power, is, to say the least, unnecessarily scurrilous. Yet, in that point of
view, the anecdotes it contains may form at
once a companion and a contrast to those re-
tailed of the Court of the House of Stuart;
and it may be useful to notice how much the
common people are shocked at the economy,
and delighted with the profusion of their rulers.
That Cromwell attained supreme power by
fraud and hypocrisy cannot be denied; but
if, while possessed of the unlimited command
of the public revenue, his own household set
an example of sobriety and moderation, it was
most unjust to impute to him, or his wife, a real
virtue as matter of scandalous ridicule.

The second part of the work has very little
concern with the first, being merely a collection of receipts for cookery, pretended to have
been used in the kitchen of the Protector, and
compounded under the eye of his careful house-
wife. Some particulars of curious information
may even here be gleaned by the minute antiquary. He may learn, p. 49, that Scotch col-
lops of veal was the standing dish of the Lady
Protectress; and, p. 56, that she usually had

marrow puddings to her breakfast; while her
daughter, Madam Frances, preferred a sausage
made of hog's liver, agreeably to a savoury receipt, recorded p. 116. He may also sympathise
with the author's lamentation over that " truly
royal and constant dish, the haunch of venison,"
which, it seems, was first prostituted to the vulgar upon the disparking so many forests after
the civil wars. And, lastly, he may learn the
most approved method of baking a pig, as practised by Mrs Cromwell at Huntingdon brewery.
It consisted, it seems, in casing the carcase in
clay, like one of Cromwell's iron-sided curas-
siers, and then stewing it in the stoke-hole, after the manner of the civilized natives of Ota-
heite. But when these scantlings of information have been collected, nothing more will remain than can be gleaned from any old cook-
ery-book of the same period.

It appears indeed, from the whole strain
of this very rare and curious tract, which is
half household-book, half satire, that it has
been the labour of some ex-cook, or clerk of
the kitchen of the royal household, who had
viewed with natural indignation the decay of
good housekeeping in the sober days of the

Protectorate, and was willing, not only to insult over the memory of that economical government, but to contribute a few savoury receipts towards the revival of a more liberal system.

THE

COURT AND KITCHIN

OF

ELIZABETH,

COMMONLY CALLED

JOAN CROMWEL,

THE WIFE OF THE LATE USURPER,

TRULY DESCRIBED AND REPRESENTED, AND NOW MADE
PUBLICK FOR GENERAL SATISFACTION.

LONDON, PRINTED BY THO. MILBOURN,
FOR RANDAL TAYLOR, IN ST MARTINS LE GRAND, 1664.

TO

THE READER.

THAT there may no prejudice lye against this publication, as an insultory unman-like invective, and triumph over the supposed miserable and forlorn estate of this family, and this person in particular, it will be requisite to obviate and prepare against that seeming humane (but indeed disloyal, or at least idle) sentiment, and reverence to the frail fluctuating condition of mankind, which, as a general argument, is ready at hand to oppose the design of the ensuing treatise.

Not to refer the reader to the practise of all times, which have not failed to wreak the fury of the pen upon tyrants and usurpers, (if surviving to punishment, otherwise their relations and posterity,) whose execrable tragedies have wearied the world, and blunted the instruments of death and slaughter: nor to instance the particular examples thereof, as sufficient authority for this imitation; the peculiar justice due to the monstrous enormities and unparalleled insolence of these upstarts, (besides the disproportion and incompetence of any revenge to their provoking, impudent, personation of

princes,) will interestedly vindicate and defend the author from the breach of charity, much more from the
rigid imputation and charge, as of a person divested
and void of nature, compassion, and civility.

For while they yet wanton in the abundance of their
spoyl and rapine, afflicted with nothing else but the torments of ambitious designs; taking this cloud upon
them but as an eclipse of their former greatness, and
as but a turn of sporting Fortune, whose wheel may,
with an imaginary volutation, roll their petty highnesses upwards again; how can the desperate depressed
estate of many thousand loyal subjects, who are irrecoverably lost and past all means but a miracle, to their
just, or any competent restitution, or to buoy up themselves or families from vulgar or a phanatick contempt?
How is it possible for them to comport with the serenity
(instead of disaster) of this family, by whose single ac-
cursed plots and designs all their present, and many
more grievous past miseries, are derived upon them and
their posterity?

And that this may not seem the froth and spleen of
a satyr, what meaneth that bleating in their present
stately mansions? The same ceremonious and respect-
ful observances, as if they were still the *Hogen Mo-
gens*.

None of the family must presume to speak less than
my lord and my lady, to the Squire Henry and his
spouse, and the same still is used when ever any mention is made of them in the household; to which pin
the neighbours and necessary retainers addresses are
tunably raised. What is this but to strengthen their
weake, yet vain-glorious fancy, and to preserve some
reliques of their former veneration, lest rude and inoffi-
cious time should plead a disuser in bar to their con-

ceited (but airy) reversion? And no question but the
old gentlewoman, who took so much upon her, and was
so well pleased with her last grandeur, as displeased
and afflicted with the fall of it betwixt Fleetwood, Richard, and Desborough, is also served in the same manner, and with the same grandezza's; so that such is the
inveterate itch and tetter of honour in her, that nothing
but the lees of gall and the most biting sharpest ink
will ere be able to cure or stop this protectorian evil.

And herein we do but retaliate, (if they be not unworthy of such a term, as that any attribute of justice
should be profaned by their demerit, which exacts rather
popular fury,) and repay them in some sort, those many
libels, blasphemous pamphlets, and pasquils, broached
and set on foot, chiefly by the late usurper, against the
blessed memory and honour of our two late soveraigns:
more especially those vile and impious pieces, called
The Court and Character of King James, and The
None-such Charles; a great number of which were
bought up in the juncture of the late restitution, (as
particularly informed, which in the worst of times their
bold and impudent falshood made most abominable,)
were none of the least incentives to a work of this nature, in requital of that traiterous and most petulant imposture.

Whereas the guilt of this grand-dame hath this sort
of felicity, that it cannot be made worse or more odious
by any additions of devised untruths; and he must be a
very immodest and immoderate fabulist that can represent her to greater disadvantage in this way, then her
actions have famed her to the world.

Her highness must be pleased to dispense with this
frank and libertine manner of treating her, for 'tis all
we are like to have for many millions; besides an old

saw or proverb to the bargain, *Olim hæc meminisse juvabit*; a little transitory mirth for twenty years duration of sorrow; and if she thinks she comes not very well off so, she is as unreasonable in her reduction and allowed recess, (to be envied for its plenty and amplitude, far exceeding her former privacy; so that she is even yet a darling of fortune,) as in her usurped estate and greatness.

It is well for her, if his butchery (then which the sun never saw a more flagitious execrable fact, and so comprehensive, that it reached Caligulas wish) can be slighted into her cookery, and that there were no other monument of it then in paste, *Ut tantum schombros metuentia crimina, vel Thus.* That the records of his crimes were only damned to an oven. Little satisfaction serves the English nation, (the relations of those loyal persons martyred by him excepted,) and she ought therefore to be highly thankful that the scene of his tyranny was laid here; for had it light upon the southern parts of the world, their nimble and vindictive rage upon the turn would have limbed and minced her family to atomes, and have been their own cooks and carvers.

Lambert Simnel very contentedly turned a broach in the king's kitchin, after the gaudies of his kingly imposture, in the beginning of the reign of Henry VII.; and therefore, for variety sake, let this once mighty lady do drudgery to the publique.

VALE.

[AUTHOR'S] INTRODUCTION.

—————

AMONG all the monstrous effects of Cromwell's tyranny, and the fruition of his usurped greatnesse; in the affluence of all imaginary delights to gratify his sense, and candy over the troubles of his mind, (to the rendering them lesse severe and dulling their poignant acutenesse,) it was by all men much wondred at, that he was so little guilty of any luxurious and Epicurean excesses, either in his meat or drink, except sometimes in his cups, which he purposely and liberally took off to avoid the gravel in his kidneys, with which he was continually molested, and for which large draughts were his ordinary cure.

In this he differed from the rest of his sanguinous tribe and sort of men, who making use of humane blood for their drink, do saginate and fatten themselves with the superfluous variety of meats, to whose natural satisfaction such artificial devices are added, (even retorturing the creature,) that the genuine gusto is quite changed by this adulteration, and lost in the mixt multiplicity of other relishes and palatable ingredients. Here-

in like themselves, when not content with their natural
private condition of life, and the pure results and simple
innocent delights thereof, they do corrode their minds
with the sharp sawces of ambition, and so alter and in-
vert their nature, that they degenerate to other things,
and become such a quelque-chose of villany and debauchery, that we can hardly sever and distinguish a
crime which is not intervitiated with many other. And
what prodigious infamy upon his gulose and intemperate account, and by this very apt similitude, doth this
day stick upon many, if not most of the Roman empe-
rors! as I could instance in Tiberius, Caligula, Nero,
Otho, Domitian, Commodus, Caracalla, Heliogabalus,
men not to be mentioned without horrour at their wick-
ednesse; of such savage and feral manners, as if their
food had been the flesh of panthers, tygers, and bears,
and had assimilated its nutriment in their bestial qualities: but, as was said before, Cromwell, as in some
other cases, was in this wholly discriminated from them.

Yet do I not think this abstemiousnesse and temperance was due only to his disposition either of body or
mind; for his appetite, in all other things, was very ir-
regular and inordinate: but either to the multitude of
those *mordaces et edaces curæ*, biting and eating cares
and ambitious thoughts, which made him either the
vulturs or Tantalus his feast, and were his continual sur-
fets of an evil conscience :—

> *Districtus ensis cui super impia*
> *Cervice pendet, non siculæ dapes*
> *Dulcem elaborarint saporem.*
> HORAT. OD.

though I may indulge his military labours and discipline,
and example that severer abstinence; or else, which is

principally intended here as the subject matter of this
discourse, it may be cheaplyer referred to the sordid
frugality and thrifty basenesse of his wife, Elizabeth Bowcher, the daughter of Sir James Bowcher, commonly called Protectresse Joan, and vulgarly known of latter years by no other Christian name, even in the greatest heighth of her husband's power, and that chiefly out
of derision and contemptuous indignation, that such a
person durst presume to take upon herself such a soveraign estate, when she was an hundred times fitter for
a barn then a palace; so sporting, mocking fate, to
make good that of the satyrist,

Fælix à Tergo quem nulla Ciconia pinxit.

Followed her great luck with that sarcastick and dic-
terious nickname, that she with her copemate might perceive their fortune was not so entire and of so fair an
aspect and firm structure, but that the flaws and ble-
mishes and impotence thereof, were most obvious and
ridiculous; their fine feathers had swans feet; and their
beautiful mermaid, the fiction of dominion, had the ugly
tail and fins of a fish; the train of her greatnesse and
prosperity was the most vile and scornful reproaches.
And this shall suffice to be spoken of her person by way
of preface; the next elenchus or discourse is of her
mesnagery, huswifery, or housekeeping.

COURT AND KITCHIN

OF

MRS ELIZABETH,

ALIAS

JOAN CROMWELL.

———

To confine and limit this treatise to its purpose and designment prefixed in the title, we must (though with some petty injury to the reader) pass over her economy at her private home, before Oliver's bold atchievement and attainment of the supreme power, (because part of it is already publique,) when she had brought (as we say) a noble to ninepence, by her pious negligence and ill management of the domestic affairs, and was as giddy tó see her bare walls as Oliver was mad with enthusiasmes and devinations of regal furniture and all princely pomp and greatness. Those memorials may be reduced to this present use in this short corollary.

That the former extremities of her necessitous and indigent condition, upon the bettering thereof, (by the general ruine,) raised in her such a quick sense of the

misery of want, that she became most industriously pro-
vident, and resolvedly sparing and cautious for the future, and to prefer the certainty of her own care and diligence to the extempore fond and easie delusions of
Deus providebit, with which she had been fooled before
into an almost voluntary and devoted poverty.

This her aspect and consideration of the future extended itself (with more prudence and sagacity than her
husband would descend to) in some humble thoughts of
her present rise levelled to her past depression : She took
a prophetical prospect of the times, and having seen two,
three, or four variations in the calmnesse and tranquillity
of her husband's fortunes, did wisely presage to herself,
that after those hurly burlies of war and the tempest of
rebellion, wherein he had whirled, and with so much
impatient precipitancy engaged himself, there would
another turn happen, against which she concluded to be
more discreetly armed.

The first eddy of that boysterous and unruly current
of his prosperity, which at last overran all banks and
boundaries, flowed into the receptacle of her committee-
ship in the associated counties, particularly Cambridge
and Huntingdon ; where, to recover and piece up her
ruines, she, with the same spirit of zeal and piety of her
husbands, consecrated her house to be the temple of rapine, one of the prime goddesses next the cause ; whither, for sacrifices, all manner of cattel, clean and un-
clean, were brought from all the adjacent parts ; as other
costly utensils of the best moveables to adorn and enrich this sacred place, from whence to hope for any re-
delivery, was mental sacriledge, and to endevour it was
punished with irreparable ruin ; and I am sure (like
the guilt of that crime) there are some who now feel it

to the third generation, and may, without miracle, to
perpetuity.

For not only was her corban to be satisfied with the
product of such oblations, but lands were to be set apart
and sequestred, the revenue of which past first through
her fingers, and were made impropriations of her own.

Having thus recruited her estate, and adjusted her
present seizures to her past losses, and exalted above the
dignity of Mrs Sheriff, or countesse of those shires, no
person her equal in greatnesse ; upon the successe of her
husband after Marston Moore, she abandoned the dull
country, partly not enduring the ordinary demeanor of
her acquaintance towards her, nor sufferable nor endu-
rable by her betters, for her imperious and unsociable
carriage towards all persons of quality, and partly to par-
take in the supreme fruition of the city's more elaborate
and exquisite pleasures, and to huswife early admiration :
for the ladies of the cause began to appear at thanksgiving dinners, and to reckon as many dishes to a messe as
their husbands numbred atchievemn ts.

At her arrival in town she was little lesse than saluted
by the whole juncto, though not in a body, yet severally by them all, and afterwards by the pastours, elders,
and brethren of the sects, who came not a house-warm-
ing with the breath of their mouths, in zealous gratu-
lations, but brought all silver implements for her accommodation of household stuff, and offered them according to the late pattern of reformation in Guildhall.
Nor did this humor cease here, the middle sort of the
eligiously phanatique, sent her in Westphalia hams,
neat's tongues, puncheons and tierces of French wine,
runlets, and bottles of sack ; all manner of preserves and
comfits, to save her the trouble of the town ; the most
of which gifts, they being multiplied upon her, she re-

tailed by private hands, at as good a rate as the market would afford.

But much more of these was given afterwards when Oliver was returned from the ending the war, and was lookt upon as the great motion of the parliaments proceedings : not to reckon those immoderate bribes that obtruded themselves upon her, more' welcome by far then those saint-like benevolences and civil offices of love, under which their corrupting practices were vailed to no purpose, for she very well understood the very first addresses though never so innocently remote from the main design, and would rate them (as they do post miles, for she kept her constant distant stages in all her publique brocage and transactions) duely and exactly.

And indeed her house was in this respect a political or state exchange, by which the affairs of the kingdom were governed, and the prices of all things set, whether offices, preferments, indempnity ; as all other manner of collusion and deceipts were practised, and money stirring no where else. And in the other respect of provisions, it might have passed for the temple of Bell and the Dragon, (to pursue the former sanctity of her rural mansion,) where all those offerings of diet were consumed, or as good, altered and assimulated to her nature, (the use of the nutritive faculty,) by serving her covetousnesse in their reduction to money.

Now she needed no such austere diligence in the preservation of an estate, for it was more then she and her ministers could do to receive it. It was impossible to keep any decorum or order in that house where masterlesse money, like a haunting spirit, possessed and disquieted every room. It was a kind of Midas his palace, where there was nothing but gold to eat, only instead of being confined to that indigestible food, she and her

servants were most frequently invited out of dores to
most sumptuous and magnificent treatments, whence,
because of that more sacred employment at home, (like
sabbatarians that provide themselves baked and cold
meats for the superstitious observation of the day,) they
and their progging lady brought home such reliques, as
they might mumble down in the dispatch of their businesse, and save the trouble or magic of their long graces,
which had brought a curse instead of a blessing upon
their masters and mistresses first endevours, though she
her self (so hard it is to foregoe and shake off an habi-
tual customary hypocrisie and falasy) would look as religiously upon a March pane, preserve, or comfit, as a
despairing lover upon his mistresses lips.

But the war expired, and those thanksgiving and tri-
umphal festivals over and ended, this pious family began to enter upon the years of famine after those of
plenty. Her husband was now engaged in deep designes and practices upon the king and kingdome, and,
(in order to ruin them both,) upon the army ; every one
of those mischievous and Matchiavilian consultations
and projects were ushered continually by a fast ; which
being appointed for, and observed by the host, were always intimated to the friends and relations of the officers, and kept by them with no lesse stricknesse in their
private households ; which, by the frequent shifts, and
various turns of policy, which Cromwell's fate, and the
uncertainty of the times guided him to, came so often
and thick upon the neck of one another, that her domes-
ticks had almost forgot dinner time; upstart piety,
like the modern frugality hating a meal, and as that had
limited the diet to noon, this changed it, and inverted
it to night.

So that, as in other authoritative continued fasts, there

is a political and humane reason, viz. the sparing the
creature, even to the same end, this good huswife directed her domestick abstinence ; and when on such
occasions she had cause to supect a general discontent
of her people and houshold, she would up with this
scripture expression, and lay it in their teeth for better
fare :— " The kingdome of God is not meat and drink,
but righteousnesse and peace," and some such scriptu-
ral dehortations *from* gluttony and the like luxurious
intemperance, and other zealous sentences of moderation in diet, as that the pleasure of a full diet consists
more in desire then in satiety ; that to have the stomach
twice repleated in the day, is to empty the brain, and
to render the mind unserviceable to the actions of life :
no abysse, no whirlpool, is so pernicious as gluttony,
which the more a man eats, makes him more a hungry,
and the better he dines, to sup the worse ; with such
other morals, taken out of Gusman and Lazarillo de
Tormes, and only altered a little by being made serious
in practice.

Yet I cannot passe this necessary lesson of temperance, however it proceeds from this sophistical corrupt
teacher thereof, without some reflection on some more
ancient and authentique instructions ; but because it is
a little beside my design, I will conclude them in some
fit sentences, as of the satyrist Persius :—

> *Poscis opem nervis, corpusque fidele senecta ;*
> *Esto, age : sed grandes patinæ, tucetaque crassa*
> *Annuere his superos vetuere Jovemque morantur.*

English'd thus by Dr Barten Holyday :

> Thou wishest for firm nerves, and for a sure
> Sound body that would healthfully enduro

Until old age; why, be it, that thy wish
Is granted by the gods? yet thy large dish
And full fat sausage make the gods delay
To bless thee, and do force good Jove to stay.

And that other of Epictetus, worthy to be inscribed
in all our parlours and banquetting houses:—

Σωφροςυνην λεγεθαι ως ςω̈ζωςαι την φρονησιν.
Και ανην ψυχην ϊναι ςοφολάτην.

In another place, *inter epulandum duos excipere debemus
convivas, corpus et animam ; tum quod in corpus collatum
sit repente effluxurum, quod autem in animam, perpetuo ser-
vandum,* i. e. in feasting and banquetting, we must except two guests, the body and the mind; because that
which is bestowed on the body will suddenly pass away,
and that which comes into the mind will be there laid
up for ever; adding that commendation of Plato to
a friend philosopher, *vestræ quidem cænæ non solum in
presentia, sed etiam postero die sunt jucundæ,* intimating
that there is no such lasting pleasure as in a sober diet,
which, when excesses bring surfeits, renews the feast the
next day, and gives a continual relish to the appetite.

But I must beg pardon for this (otherwise seasonable)
digression, and reduce the discourse in pursuit of her
ladyships errantry from one abode to another, in the
suburbs of London, more or lesse like a sojourner, (however she inhabited whole houses,) and a great person
incognito, then as a woman of that state and degree, to
which her husbands condition and command, and great
probabilities of succeeding titles did forespeak her. If
any thing could be observable by her for state and
charge, it was the keeping of a coach, the driver of

which served her for caterer, as much occasion as she had for him, for butler, for serving man, for gentleman usher, when she was to appear in any publique place. And this coach was bought at the second-hand, out of a great number, which then lay by the walls, while their honourable owners went on foot, and ambled in the dirt to Goldsmiths and Haberdashers-halls,[1] if so fairly come by. She might, and she did ('twas thought) save that very inconsiderable charge; but the sense she had, how obvious and odious her carriage in a sequestred caroach would be to every body, made her jealous of such scorn and derision; as for horses, she had them out of the army, and their stabling and livery in her husbands allotment out of the mews, at the charge of the state; so that it was the most thrifty and unexpensive pleasure and divertisement (besides the finery and honour of it) that could be imagined; for it saved many a meal at home, when, upon pretence of businesse, her ladyship went abroad, and carrying some dainty provant for her own and her daughters own repast, she spent whole days in short visits and long walks in the ayre; so that she seemed to affect the Scythian fashion, who dwell in carts and wagons, and have no other habitations.

Her publique retinue was also very slender, and as slenderly accoutred, no more commonly then one of her husbands houseboys running by her, sometimes one, and sometimes another, with or without livery, all was one; on purpose (it may be well supposed, beside the saving the cost) to prevent her being discryed and discovered, so much suspicion and hatred had her husband

[1] The places where the committees of sequestration, with whom the cavaliers were forced to compound for their estates, held their meetings.

4

drawn upon himself, even from the vulgar, which she feared, might, by some such badge of notice, light upon herself in the streets as she passed.

She was the same recluse likewise in her habit, rather harnessing herself in the defence of her cloaths, then allowing herself the loose and open bravery thereof, as not having been used to such light armour; and her hood, till her face was seen in her highnesses glasse, was clapt on like a head-piece, without the art of ensconcing and entrenching it double and single in redoubts and horn-works. In fine, she was cape-a-pe like a baggage lady, and was out of her element in her vicinity to the court and city.

But her daughters were otherwise vested and robed, and a constant expense allowed in tire-women, perfumers, and the like arts of gallantry, with each their maid and servant to attend them; and by their array and deportment, their quality might have been guessed at; they were all (those that were unmarried) very young: but Mrs Elizabeth, who about this time was married to one Mr Cleypole's son, of Northamptonshire, (the old man having had a hand in the same disloyal service with Oliver in that county,) but with a very private wedding, no way suitable to that port and grandeur which Oliver kept in the army, where he was looked upon with the same reverence and respect as the general himself; all that was Hymen-like in the celebration of it, was some freaks and pranks without the aid and company of a fidler, (which, in those days, was thought by their precise parents, to be altogether unlawful and savouring of carnality, as the ring and form of marriage were thought superstitious and antichristian,) in Noll's military and rude way of spoyling of custhetard, and like Jack Pudding throwing it upon one another, which was ended in the more manly game of buffetting with cushions, and flinging them up and down the room.

Neither appeared there the splendor and ornament of jewells and pearls, and the like lusture of gems, whose invidious refractions like poysonous effluxes, might invenome the world with spleen and malice, at their plundered and stollen radiancy; for by the manifold surrenders and stormings of houses and castles, Cromwell had amassed good store of rarities, besides meddals, and gold and silver vessels, (the spoyls of our captivity) which it was not as yet safe to produce in such an unsettlement of his conquest, till all propriety should be hudled up in the general ruine, out of whose mixt and confused rubbish, in his new polished government, they might exert their brightnesse underivable and clear from all former title and claim, as the masse of things shall be meland calcined together, at the last universal dissolution.

And I have heard it reported for a truth, that most of the precious moveables, and other things of value, at the storming of Basing-house by Cromwell, fell into his hands either immediately or directly, the soldiers either by command, or for some smal price, returning several precious pieces of the spoyle, whose worth they understood not, to his agents, who gave an exact account thereof to the lady receiver at home, who was about that time seen to be very pleasant and prajeant at the enjoyment of those pretty things (as she expressed herself) being the best for substance and ornament that belonged to the noble marquis of Winchester and his family, which this she-usurper now listed and catalogued for her own.

And if the whole inventory of her rapinous hoard were now produceable, what a voracious monster would she appear to be! Not a corner in the kingdome which is not sensible of her ravage, and which had not a share in the lombard of her uncountable and numberless chattels.

How many rare pieces of antique gold and silver are again damned to the earth from whence they were brought, and are, by her mischievous covetousnesse, irrecoverably lost, which have been the glories and monumental pride of many families, and the only remains and evidences of their noble hospitality, now buried by this wretch in hugger mugger.

Those advantages, together with the vails of the army which she had upon every commission, and other incident occasions, for her husbands interests and authority, together with his extraordinary pay, and the appurtenances to it, and lands and hereditaments bestowed on him, besides rewards and gratuities in ready money, amounted to an incredible sum, which almost glutted her eyes to satiety, but so, that they were yet lesser then her belly, which could stow as much more with convenience enough, and conserve and secure it by a very parcimonious use, and narrow strict disbursement; for, having now quitted all fears of returning to a private condition by the insolence of her husbands fortunes, which drove at the soveraignty, the abhominable design being communicated to her; this great bank was still kept supplied by her, for the support and maintenance of that dignity and supremacy to which Oliver aspired; and to facilitate his way to it, having rightly perceived, that nothing but mony had carried on the war, and brought things to that passe, whatever was pretended of zeal, and to the cause; and therefore there was no difference in her manner of housekeeping: only Cromwell being now in town for the most part, conspiring that execrable parricide against the king, she dispensed with her niggerly regulation, and having taken a house neer

Charing-Crosse, kept it in a manner open for all comers, which were none but the sectary party and officers, who resorted thither as to their head-quarters, with all their will projections, and were entertained with small beer and bread and butter, which, to the animation of the approaching villany, was as bad as aqua fortis and horse flesh : for, as was said of Cæsar, *Nemo tam sobrius ad rempublicam evertendam accessit*, no man came more sober to the destruction of the commonwealth, so I may aptly and more justly say, that no men of more abstemiousnesse ever effected so vile and flagitious an enterprise upon so just a government.

That being in perpetration, Mrs Cromwell ran out of purse some score of pounds, (for it is to be remembred that she stewarded it all along, Oliver's head being busy with greater and worser matters) very much to her regret and vexation ; but that villany over, and some two or three private treatments given his most sure and addicted complices, in exaltation of their monstrous successe, the dores of the house were again barred, and all persons hindered, and of difficult admittance, upon what score or businesse soever ; and now she was returned to her former privacy and ordinary diet as before.

During the rest of the time while Cromwell staid in England, she kept the same tenour, having received (besides a confirmation of the Marquiss of Worcester's estate, to the value of five thousand pounds a year) upon the account of the defeat given the levellers by her husbands treachery at a thanksgiving dinner (whereto he was invited by the city,) a piece of gold plate of very good value, which discharged the former expence.

I must omit many other passages during his absence in Ireland and in Scotland, and, after this liminary, but prolix account, sum up all in her menage of her domes-

tique affairs at Whitehall, for which she had so long
prepared and furnisht herself with rules of government
and œconomy fitted for her usurpation and the times.

For her husband brought not so great and haughty,
as she base and low-spirited thoughts and resolutions to
the grandeur of that place, the habitation and residence
of the greatest and most famous monarchs of the world,
and famed throughout it for truly royal and princely
pomp and immense munificence and entertainment.

She had flesh enough indeed to become any room in
that spacious mansion, but so little of a brave spirit, that
the least hole of it would have made her a banquetting
house; but like a spirit she came only to haunt, not to
enjoy any part of it; the penates and genii of the place
abhominating this prophane and sacrilegious intrusion,
neither giving him one hours quiet or rest in it, from his
troubled, mistrustful, and ill-boding thoughts, nor her
any content and satisfaction, but what she found in re-
pining and vexing herself at the cost and charge, the
maintenance of that beggerly court did every day put
her to.

It was in the year 1653, that Cromwell first possessed
and seated himself there, as in his own right and in chief,
and brought his worshipful family thither to their several appartiments, she having appointed one Mr Maid-
stone to be steward of his house, and one Mr Starkey to
be his master cook, who afterwards was betrayed and
taken drunk in his cellar, designing the like upon my
lord maiors sword-bearer, while my lord was in conference with the protector, so that he could not conceal it
from the houshold, who (out of spight to him, as being
a spie over their actions and behaviours) first acquainted
their lady, and she Oliver with the fault, aggravated by
the scandal and wastful excesse, insomuch that Starkey

was commanded to come before him, where, instead of
a complement and excuse, he delivered himself by vomit in the very face of his master, and was thereupon
dismissed the house.

It will not be too distant a review to observe and re-
marque her introduction to and seizin of this royal mansion, (which we have only mentioned) before any other
procedure in the œconomy thereof.

The first preparatory as to publique notice, was an order from the new council of state, after the dissolution
of the parliament, commanding all persons to depart out
of White-hall, which was then the den of a hundred
several families and persons of power and office in the
anarchy; which being difficultly and grumblingly executed, she herself employed a surveyor to make her some
convenient accommodations, and little labyrinths, and
trap stairs, by which she might at all times unseen passe
to and fro and come unawares upon her servants, and
keep them vigilant in their places and honest in the discharge thereof.

Several repaires were likewise made in her own appartiments, and many small partitions up and down, as well
above stairs as in the cellars and kitchins, so that it looked like the picture of Bartholomew faire; her high-
nesseship not being yet accustomed to that roomy and
august dwelling, and perhaps afraid of the vastnesse and
silentnesse thereof, which presented to her thoughts the
desolation her husband had caused, and the dreadful ap-
parations of those princes, whose incensed ghosts wan-
dred up and down, and did attend some avenging opportunity ;ᵗ and this was the more believable, because she

---

ᵗ This reminds us strongly of a splendid passage in Burke's Speech
on Œconomical Reform: "Palaces," said this orator " are vast inhos-
pitable halls. There the bleak winds, there Boreas and Eurus and

(not to name her husbands mis-giving suspicions and frights,) could never endure any whispering or to be alone by her self in any of the chambers.

And it is further here fit to be instanced, that upon her first coming, when her harbingers had appointed her lodgings the same with the queens, which yet retained their royal names and distinctions, she would by no means hear of them, but changed them into other appellations, that there might remain no manner of disgust and discontent to her ambitious and usurping greatnesse: and therefore they were adapted now into the like significations, by the name of the protectors and protectresses lodgings, as more proper and fitter terms to their propriety and indisputed possession.

Much adoe she had at first to raise her mind and deportment to this soveraign grandeur; and very difficult it was for her to lay aside those impertinent meannesses of her private fortune; like the bride-cat by Venus's favour metamorphosed into a comly virgin, that could not forbear catching at mice, she could not comport with her present condition, nor forget the common converse and affaires of life; but like some kitchin maid preferred by the lust of some rich and noble dotard, was ashamed of her sudden and gawdy bravery, and for a while skulkt up and down the house, till the fawning observances and reverences of her slaves had raised her to a confidence, not long after sublimed into an impudence.

Caurus and Argestes loud, howling through the vacant lobbies, and clattering the doors of deserted guard-rooms, appal the imagination, and conjure up the grim spirits of departed tyrants,——the Saxon, the Norman, and the Dane, the stern Edwards and fierce Henries—who stalk from desolation to desolation through the dreary vacuity and melancholy succession of chill and comfortless chambers."

And this was helped on by Madam Pride, and my Ladies Hewson, and Berkstead, Goff, Whalley, &c. who all came to complement her highnesse upon the felicity of Cromwell's assumption to the government, and to congratulate her fortune, and so accompany her to her palace of Whitehall, where, like the devil cast out, she entred by fasting and prayer, after the usual manner, and like devout Jezabel, took possession of Naboth's vineyard.

And thus we have waited on her to this Basilicon, now swept and cleansed for her fiendly entertainment; and the chymneys smoked and heated again, which had suffered so long a damp; and after so long a vacation, especially her highnesse took care and gave strict charge to have all the rooms aired, for fear of those ill sents the Rump had left behind them, and was willing to be at the charge of perfumes to expel the noysomnesse thereof, the account of which hath been seen by divers, allowed by her own hand; but foul odour was so equally natural to all the grandees, that Oliver when he died left it in a worse condition then when he found it, as is publique in several treatises.

Cromwell was now his own steward and carver, not limited to any expences of housekeeping, no more then to the charges of the government; but was absolute both at dinner and at council board, neither of which were yet well setled; and therefore, besides the nearness of his wife, it was necessary he should appear extraordinary frugal of the peoples purse, (who wished every bit he eat might choke him, for all his temperance) in his private and publique disbursements. Only that he might not appear so much a military governour, but have something of the prince in him, about noon time, a man might hear a huge clattering of dishes, and noise of servitors, in rank and file marching to his table, (though

neither sumptuously nor extraordinarily furnished) in
some imitation of Paulus Æmilius in his answer to the
Grecians, after his triumph and conquest of Perseus, the
last Macedon king; *Ejusdem esse animi et aciem et con-*
vivium instruere, illam quidem ut formidolosus hostibus, hoc
ut amicis gratus appareat; in English thus, 'Tis of the
same spirit to order a battle, as to furnish a feast, by the
one a man appears terrible to his enemies, and by the
other pleasing to his friends.

But at his private table, very rarely, or never, were
our French *quelque-choses* suffered by him, or any such
modern Gusto's, whether with the fright he was prejudiced of poyson, by such devices, (at an invitation made
him and his general the Lord Fairfax, with the other of
the supreme commanders of the army, by a small officer
therein, who was formerly a cook, at a ladies in Ham-
mersmith, where with one leg of mutton, drest all sorts
of ways, he entertained them all, but upon their discovery of the fellowes audaciousnesse in bidding them,
which prompted them to believe it was a design against
their lives, and put most of them to the vomit, was like
to have been drest himself by the hangman) or by some
stronger or more masculine appetite, which partaked with
his other robust faculties is uncertain; sure it is, that
when in treatments given his familiars such things were
set upon the table, 'twas more for shew and sport then
for belly timber, and about which the good huswife
never troubled her head.

She, to return to her government, very providentially
kept two or three cowes in St James's park, and erected
a new office of a dairy in Whitehall, with dairy maids
to intend that businesse solely, (as most of the employment for servants was managed by females, for there
were no sergeants but such as waited with halbeirds on
the guard) and fel to the old trade of churning butter,

and making buttermilk, nor were. Oxford Kates [1] fine
things half so famous among the cavalier ladies, as my
lady protectors butter among the mushrome zealous ladies of the court, most whereof, being apple, or oyster-
women, or-stocking-heelers, and the-like, did much wonder at and magnifie the invention and rarity.

Next to this covy of milk maids she had another of
spinsters-and sowers, to the number of six, who sat the
most part of the day after she was ready, in her privy
chamber, sowing and stitching; they were all of them
ministers daughters, such as were inveterate noncon-
formists to the church, for which cause and the pretence
of piety (the main ingredient to things of the least moment,) they were added to the family.; nor did the Turk-
ish ministers take more care to furnish the seraglio, and
gratifie their master with choice virginities, then some
of these pious pimps did lay out for indigent. godly
maidens to pleasure this prostitute charity of hers, that
the world might take notice of her exemplary humility
and compassion. But indeed all persons of breeding
and quality abhorred the indignity of her service, and
so, rather then be served with common drudges, she erected this new order, and continued it to the term of her
usurpation; herein following the steps of her husband,
who made a new daring militia of zealous persons, since
he could not be served with generous spirits.

She was once resolved, by the assistance and advice of
her mother, to have made a small brewing place, with
vessels, and other accommodation for her own, and Oliver's drink, as not liking the city brewing, nor trusting

---

[1] She appears to have been a confectioner in Covent-Garden. In a
lampoon, entitled " The Ladies Parliament," mention is made of Kate's
as a resort of the *malignant* ladies. The republican dames frequented
Spring-Garden.

to the artifices of the town; but about the same time, a drink was then grown famous in London, being a very small ale of 7s. 6d. a barrel, well boyled, and well tasted and conditioned, called and known by the name of Morning Dew (from the brewers name, as I have heard) which was thence brought into request at court, and was the diet drink of this temperate couple, and the cool refreshing entertainment of those bouncing ladies that came weltring and wallowing in their coaches instead of drayes to visit her.

And for the kitchin and pantry a great reformation was intended, but the multitude of comers and goers upon her first setling there, and number of mouths which came gaping for preferment, being to be stopt with victuals, put her besides her proposed regulation; yet was there not a joynt of meat for which the cook was not to give an account, which she overlooked, as it came from them to the steward, whose accounts likewise were punctually cast up by her, and firmed by her hand, as well as afterwards by the protectors.

Nay, so severe and strict she was in this thrifty way of house-keeping, that she descended to the smallest and meanest matters, the very chaffer and price of the market; and, that the reader may not think he is imposed on and deceived by a general imputation of her niggardlynesse, I will give him two notable and apposite instances.

The first was the very next summer after his coming to the protectorate in 1654, in June, at the very first season of green pease, where a poor country woman living somewhere about London, having a very early but small quantity in her garden, was advised to gather them, and carry them to the Lady Protectresse, her counsellors conceiving she would be very liberal in her reward, they being the first of that year; accordingly the poor woman came to the Strand, and having her pease, amounting to a peck and a half, in a basket, a cook, by the Savoy as she passed, either seeing or guessing at them, demanded the price, and upon her silence, offered her an angel for them, but the woman expecting some greater matter, went on in her way to Whitehall, where, after much adoe, she was directed to her chamber, and one of her maids came out, and understanding it was a present and rarity, carried it in to the protectresse, who, out of her princely munificence, sent her a crown, which the maid told into her hand; the woman seeing this basenesse, and the frustration of her hopes, and remembring withal what the cook had proffered her, threw back the money into the maids hands, and desired her to fetch her back her pease, for that she was offered five shillings more for them before she brought them thither, and could go fetch it presently; and so, half slightingly and half ashamedly, this great lady returned her present, putting it off with a censure upon the unsatisfactory daintinesse of luxurious and prodigal epicurisme: the very same pease were afterwards sold by the woman to the said cook, who is yet alive to justifie the truth of this relation.

The other is of a later date. Upon Oliver's rupture with the Spanyard, the commodities of that country grew very scarce, and the prizes of them raised by such as could procure them underhand: among the rest of those goods, the fruits of the growth of that place were very rare and dear, especially oranges and lemmons.

One day, as the protector was private at dinner, he called for an orange to a loyne of veal, to which he used no other sauce, and urging the same command, was answered by his wife, that oranges were oranges now, that crab oranges would cost a groat, and for her part, she never intended to give it; and it was presently whispered, that sure her highness was never the adviser of the Spanish war, and that his highness should have done well to have consulted his digestion, before his hasty and inordinate appetite of dominion and riches in the West Indies.

I might confirm this by other retrenchments of expence, whensoever she could confine his table to her own privacy; particularly it was a great mode, and taken up by his court party, to roast half capons, pretending a more exquisite taste and nutriment in it, then when dressed whole and entire; where I cannot but smile to think how it puzzled her ladyships carver, to hold him to the knife, and to apportion half and quarter limbs according to art.

Much more do I wonder what those fellows at Rome did, or what they would have done here, who kept carving schools *ludi structorii,* and had all manner of fowl and fish, and such other grand festival meat carved in wood, which they marked out with wooden knives with very great curiosity, and instructed their scholars, who learned it as a worshipful employment and way to preferment, as the satyrist very elegantly.

> *Sumine cum magno, lepus atque aper et Pygargus,*
> *Et Scythicæ volucres, et Phænicopterus ingens,*
> *Et Getulus Oryx hebeti lautissima ferro*
> *Cæditur, et tota sonat ulmea cæna suburra.*

Englished thus:

> The sow's large teat, the hare and bore and deer,
> Scythian, and Africks fowl and bearded beast,
> The gawdies of the town, in wood appear,
> So with dull Iron carv'd sounds elmy feast.

And if it were not made almost incredible by the superfluity and excesse of her fortune, which cannot be supposed to have no way advanced her thoughts from

her former industry, and frugal care and intendency,
I might insert a story of her enquiry into the profit of
the kitchin-stuff, and the exchanging of it for candles,
which those that knew her humour had purposely put
into her head; till she was told to whom it belonged,
and the customes of the court, to most of which she answered, they should not think to have them take place
as in the other womans dayes, for she would look better
to it: like Vespasian, she had learnt, that *Dulcis odor
lucri ex re qualibet,* gain was sweet from whatever thing.

And the reason she used to give for this her frugal in-
spection and parcimony, was the small allowance and
mean pittance she had to defray the household expences,
which, at her first coming to court-keeping, was barely
sixty four thousand pounds per annum, until Collonel
Philip Jones came to be comptroller of the houshold,
when the weekly charge was nineteen hundred twenty
three pounds odd money, the defalcation of the rest,
from the just sum of two thousand pounds, at the rate
of a 100,000l. yearly, making up the four thousand pound
for the two weeks above the 50, so exactly was this
charge computed, and method punctually observed, that
there might be no place for excesse, and by means thereof, for deceit or any colluding practises.

Her order of eating and meal times was not lesse regulated, and though inverted, yet designed well to the
decency as well as conveniency of her service; for, first
of all, at the ringing of a bell, dined the halberdiers, or
men of the guard, with the inferiour officers; then the
bell rung again, and the stewards table was set (in the
same hall neer the water stairs,) for the better-sort of
those that waited on their highnesses; ten of whom were
apportioned to a table or messe, one of which was chosen by themselves every week for steward, and he gave
the clerk of the kitchin the bill of fare, as was agreed

upon generally every morning: to these ten men, and
what friends should casually come to visit them, the value of ten shillings in what flesh or fish soever they would
have, with a bottle of sack, and two of claret, was appointed; but, to prevent after comers from expecting
any thing in the kitchin, there was a general rule, that
if any man thought his businesse would detain him beyond dinner time, he was to give notice to the steward
of his messe, who would set aside for him as much as
his share came to, and leave it in the buttery.

Suppers likewise they had none, eggs or some slaps.
contenting Cromwell and her ladyship; and to his ex-
emplar all was conformed; in lieu thereof, for the family
there was constantly boyled eight stone of beef early in
the morning, to keep her retainers in heart and in earnest of a dinner, the broth whereof, and all the scraps and
reliques of dinner, (to give her her due) were alternately
given to the poor of Saint Margarets, Westminster, and
Saint Martins in the Fields, according to the churchwar-
dens roll of each parish, and that very orderly, without
any brabble or noise; so that, amidst so many curses
and imprecations, which were uttered against him, he
had some prayers and blessings from those hungry jack-
dawes, that frequented and attended this dole. But those
lame, decrepit, and starved precepts never reached half
way, and, like impotent suspended meteors, hoysed half
region high, fell distinctly at last upon himself and family.

His feasts was none of the liberallest, and far from
magnificence, even those two he gave the French embassador and the parliament in 1656, upon their gra-
tulation of his Syndercombe deliverance, which last
amounted not to above 1000l. and she saved 200l. of it
in the banquet: for a big-bellied woman, a spectator,

neer Cromwell's table, upon the serving thereof with sweatmeats, desiring a few dry candies of apricocks ; Colonel Pride sitting at the same, instantly threw into her apron a conserve of wet with both his hands, and stained it all over; when, as if that had been the sign, Oliver catches up his napkin, and throwes it at Pride, he at him again, while all of that table were engaged in the scuffle ; the noise whereof made the members rise before the sweat-meats were set down, and believing dinner was done, goe to this pastime of gambols, and be spectators of his highnesses frolicks. Were it worth a description, I could give the reader a just and particular account of that Ahab festival, as it was solemnized in the banquetting house of Whitehall.

But I must passe it, and those other nuptial entertainments at the marriage of his daughters, and the treats he gave to Duke De Crequi and Monsieur Mancin, the cardinal's great counsellors, and familiar nephew, as things beyond her sphere, and out of her charge and my purpose, and instance the common ordinary diet of this family, whereby the reader will better perceive, and be perhaps advantaged also by the intention and nature of this discourse.

[*Here the Author proceeds to his second part, or catalogue of receipts, which we omit for the reasons given in the Introduction.*]

END OF VOLUME SECOND.

EDINBURGH:
Printed by James Ballantyne & Co.

CPSIA information can be obtained
at www.ICGtesting.com
Printed in the USA
LVHW081627210819
628447LV00011B/297/P